A Spirit of Dominance

Viv Richards speaking at the inaugural lecture series in his honour celebrating the 21st anniversary of his Test début. The Centre for Cricket Research organized the lecture series at the University of the West Indies, Barbados, in 1995.

A Spirit of Dominance

Cricket and Nationalism
in the West Indies

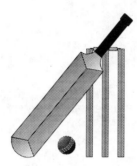

Essays in Honour of
Viv Richards
on the 21st Anniversary
of his Test Début

Edited by
Hilary McD. Beckles

Canoe Press
University of the West Indies
●Barbados ●Jamaica ●Trinidad and Tobago

Canoe Press University of the West Indies
1A Aqueduct Flats   Mona
Kingston 7 Jamaica

Printed in Jamaica
ISBN 976-8125-37-3

02 01 00 99 98   5 4 3 2 1

CATALOGUING IN PUBLICATION DATA

A spirit of dominance : cricket and nationalism in the West Indies :
essays in honour of Viv Richards on the 21st anniversary of his test
debut / edited by Hilary McD. Beckles

  p. cm.

  Includes bibliographical references.

ISBN 976-8125-037-3

1. Richards, Viv. 2. Cricket – West Indies – History.
I. Richards, Viv. II. Beckles, Hilary McD.

GV915.R5S64 1998   796.358092 dc-20

Set in 9.5/13pt Palatino
Book design by Prodesign Publishing Services, Red Gal Ring

Photographs: Courtesy of the Public Relations Office,
University of the West Indies, Mona.

The six revised texts of public lectures which appear in this
volume were presented as part of the Viv Richards 21st
Anniversary Lecture Series on West Indies cricket history and
culture sponsored in 1994 by CLICO International Life Assurance
Company and the University of the West Indies. We acknowledge
the permission of the contributors (Hilary Beckles, Keith Sandiford,
K.H.L. Marshall, Rex Nettleford, Alan Cobley and Gordon
Rohlehr) and the sponsors to reproduce these lectures.

Contents

Abbreviations

ACA	Antigua Cricket Association
ANC	African National Congress
AWU	Antigua Workers' Union
BBC	British Broadcasting Corporation
BCA	Barbados Cricket Association
BCL	Barbados Cricket League
BEGF	British Empire Games Federation
BET	Barbados External Telecommunications
CANA	Caribbean News Agency
Caricom	Caribbean Community
CCR	Centre for Cricket Research
ICC	Imperial (later International) Cricket Conference
MCC	Marylebone Cricket Club
NCA	National Cricket Association
NRC	Native Recruiting Corporation
NZCC	New Zealand Cricket Council
PNM	People's National Movement
SACB	South African Cricket Board
SACBOC	South African Cricket Board of Control
SACOS	South African Council on Sport
SACU	South African Cricket Union
TCCB	Test County and Cricket Board
UWI	University of the West Indies
WICBC	West Indies Cricket Board of Control

Contributors

Hilary McD. Beckles is professor of Social and Economic History at the University of the West Indies, Cave Hill, Barbados. He is also the founder-director of the Centre for Cricket Research on that campus.

Vaneisa Baksh is a professional journalist in Trinidad. A former features editor at the *Guardian* newspaper, she is also a co-founder of the *Independent* newspaper in Trinidad.

Alan Cobley is head of the History Department at the University of the West Indies, Cave Hill, Barbados. He is an authority on Southern African studies, and has published widely on the subject.

Tim Hector is a well-known Caribbean journalist, political activist and lecturer. He is currently a senator in the Antiguan government. He has served as a member of the West Indies Cricket Board of Control, and is an occasional radio commentator on cricket.

K. H. L. 'Tony' Marshall is senior assistant director of Barclays Caribbean operations. He is also president of the Barbados Cricket Association. He has served as manager of the West Indies cricket team in 1996, and is a member of the West Indies Cricket Board.

Rex Nettleford is a distinguished Caribbean intellectual and artist. He is deputy vice chancellor of the University of the West Indies and professor of Continuing Studies. A prolific writer, he is also artistic director of the National Dance Theatre Company of Jamaica.

Gordon Rohlehr is professor of West Indian Literature at the University of the West Indies, St Augustine, Trinidad and Tobago. He is acknowledged as a leading authority on the history of West Indian popular culture, particularly the calypso and steel pan movements.

Keith A. Sandiford is professor of History at the University of Manitoba. He has established a reputation as a leading researcher and writer on nineteenth century cricket culture, and has published widely on the subject.

Chris Searle is a poet, journalist, educator and social worker in Sheffield, England. He has worked with the immigrant community in Yorkshire, and was an active supporter of and participator in the Grenada Revolution.

Introduction

In 1994, I was asked by agents representing Viv Richards to assist in the Barbados promotion of his just published autobiography, *Hitting Across the Line*. They had no structured programme in mind and hoped that a dialogue would produce something workable. It was not clear to me then why they had contacted me. My perceptions and assessment of Viv the cricketer had not been publicly aired, yet his agents seemed surprised that I had never met the great man. I immediately conveyed considerable enthusiasm for the project and indicated that I would make a proposal within 48 hours.

I responded within one hour. It was an invitation I could not refuse, and the time frame given for the purpose immediately seemed excessive. I proposed that we organize a three-hour symposium on the text. This was agreed upon, and the suggestion that we convene at the Cave Hill campus of the University of the West Indies (UWI) was greeted with much interest. Tim Hector was invited to participate as a speaker and he agreed. The two of us would share the platform, and the Caribbean News Agency (CANA) would hook up the exercise for regional broadcast. I suggested that the symposium be called "Struggle within the Boundary". Tim liked it, and we proceeded.

Viv could not attend. At that time he was representing Glamorgan County Cricket Club and the English competition was running hot. Glamorgan was doing well; Viv was scoring hundreds as was expected. He took time out to phone in his comments on the occasion, and set the tone for a fascinating discussion. The Caricom Secretariat heard of the debate and expressed an interest in publishing an edited version of my presentation in *Caricom Perspectives*, its in-house magazine, which is prepared for Heads of Government Meetings. I agreed and they did.

(Right to left) Former captain of the West Indies Team, Viv Richards; Cave Hill Principal, Sir Keith Hunte; Dean of the Faculty of Humanities, Professor Hilary Beckles; and an executive of CLICO, enjoying the inaugural lecture in the 1994 series hosted by the Department of History, Cave Hill, in honour of the 21st anniversary of Richards' entry into Test Cricket.

On reflection, it appears as if the ground was being prepared for a series of related events. It was an intellectually exciting Saturday morning, and a major step for the UWI community. We have not looked back. We were offering a semester course entitled "West Indies Cricket History since 1820" to History majors in their final year. Students in other faculties, Law and Social Sciences especially, were demanding equal access to the programme with colleagues in Arts. I found its popularity encouraging, and decided to develop the Faculty's interest in cricket culture as far as resources would allow.

Within this context, the symposium was opened and presented as an integral part of our academic programme. I took the opportunity to announce that my colleagues in the History Department were supportive of my intention to establish within its academic structure a facility to be named the Centre for Cricket Research (CCR). The CCR would engage in teaching, research and publishing, as well as facilitate exercises in the public service by UWI. It would require an injection of resources by UWI. Such an investment I considered the best indicator of our commitment to the sustainable development of West Indies cricket culture.

Two years later the CCR was out in the middle, and looking the part. The end of its first year at the crease coincided with the twenty-first anniversary of

Viv's test debut. Something had to be done to celebrate and claim Viv's historical moment. We took the decision that the CCR would organize an eight-part public lecture series on West Indies cricket history and culture. The series was sponsored by Clico Holdings (Barbados) Ltd and called the Clico-UWI Viv Richards 21st Anniversary Lecture Series. The programme was delivered in communities throughout the West Indies; to date Barbados, Antigua, Nevis, St Kitts, St Vincent and Dominica have received these lectures by distinguished university academics and one cricket administrator.

This book, then, constitutes the revised texts of well received public lectures. Some additions are made by way of two commentaries, an interview with Viv and an introductory essay by the editor. Together they represent a tribute to Viv, as well as a substantial contribution to the historiography of West Indies cricket. While this material will serve students in the classroom well, we are sure that the public who participated in and enjoyed these lectures will wish to have this text in their possession for further engagement. It is therefore offered in this spirit of continuing dialogue.

Viv

Hilary McD. Beckles

C. L. R. James knew, in a way that few people did, how to cut away the tissue and expose the raw nerve. For some, his analytical and oftentimes acerbic forthrightness paid no attention to individual sensitivities and sent shivers down many spines. One effect of his argued opinions was that individuals were often left to ponder the discursive usefulness, or inadequacy, of their passionately held general views. He published no extensive essays, nor did he offer any detailed commentary, on Viv Richards in the way he had examined Learie Constantine, George Headley, Frank Worrell, Gary Sobers, and Rohan Kanhai. This is not phenomenal. By the early 1980s, when Viv was at the height of his productivity, James was well advanced in years. His cricket writings had virtually ceased. The few comments he offered with respect to Viv, however, said a great deal, and were conceptually consistent with the methodology he had used in earlier analytical assessments of the game's greats.

The specific context within which James made a final categorization of Viv was one he knew only too well: a West Indies tour of England in which a clash of Old and New Atlantic cricket cultures and sensibilities would rendezvous in aesthetic celebration of performance excellence. It was the long summer of 1984. Five tests were played, starting at Edgbaston in mid June, climaxing in a fifth test at Kennington Oval in mid August. The West Indies, under Clive Lloyd's leadership, won at Edgbaston by an innings and 180 runs, with Richards scoring 117. The second test at Lords was won by the West Indies by 9 wickets with Richards top scoring in the fifth innings with 72; the third test at Headingley they won by 8 wickets. The West Indies won the fourth test at Old Trafford by an innings and 64 runs, and the fifth test by 172 runs. H.A. Gomes had a marvellous tour, scoring 143 in the first test, 92 not out in the second, and 104 in the third. Gordon Greenidge was similarly productive, with innings of 214 in the second test and 223 in the fourth.

At the end of the 5–0 'blackwash' (another clean 'washing' was inflicted on England by the West Indies under Richards' leadership in the 1985/86 tour to the Caribbean), James examined the West Indies team that had swept England, and all other opposition, as no team had done in the history of the game. He did it in his usual detached and clinical style, locating Richards within the specific circumstances of the series and the wider traditions of methodological excellence. First, his views on the team:

> It is necessary to get down to principles. A winning team must be well established in certain departments. The team should have a good pair of openers. It should have three good batsmen, and it would do no harm if one of these is a great super batsman. By super batsman I mean one who is not disturbed by any bowling or any crisis. Super batsmen are rare, and a team can be a good team without having a man of that style.

With respect to the composition of the batting department, James continues:

> I look to their batting, and I think that there is one super batsman – that is Richards. Richards is undoubtedly a batsman who can be ranked with great batsmen of any time. Apart from Richards, frankly I do not see any outstandingly great batsmen on that West Indian side.

Lloyd, Gomes and Greenidge he described as good players, competent and distinguished, but not 'great' in the sense of belonging to a category of rare players over which Sobers presided.

Few who have studied the game would disagree with this judgement. A player's capacity for scoring hundreds, James argued, is an insufficient feature in such a determination. Great players, on balance, should dominate all kinds of attacks under diverse circumstances. There is no structural weakness, no fatal flaw. Perfect adaptability is expected. The ability to answer all challenges and to place one's team in a position of authority are the hallmarks of the great player. Opposing teams have always felt the psychological power of such players, a kind of charisma at the crease that enhances a spirit of defeatism in their ranks. James saw all these distinctive features in Richards, and was brief in summation.

Viv, in addition, was not just great, he was the world's greatest batsman of his generation. He also held a reputation within Caribbean society that extended beyond the boundary and connected to political and philosophical discourses that continue to engage students and academics seeking an understanding of the project of West Indian nation building and the post-colonial dispensation. Subjective judgements often underpin much of what academics say about the relationships of individuals to society. It is always difficult to escape the line of reasoning that seeks to ascertain whether individuals did the best they could for their time. Each generation, says Frantz Fanon, has its mission which it can fulfil or betray. Viv knew and fulfilled what was expected of him by West Indian society. It is a story of a turbulent but rewarding journey to excellence that has its place within the classrooms of academics. It contains important principles of political and moral philosophy and speaks metaphorically to the tensions, paradoxes and contradictions of postcolonial social consciousness.

When I encountered Richards for the first time in 1976, a number of circumstances had positioned themselves at the centre of my being. The West Indies cricket team had not long departed from Australia, where they received the kind of whipping that only old headmasters know how to administer. They arrived in England, still bruised and sore, to face those whose colonizing yoke our foreparents had recently thrown off in a firm but silent revolutionary fashion. I had just completed an undergraduate programme in historical studies at Hull University in Yorkshire. There, those like myself whom God had blessed with an adequate quantum of melanin were disenfranchised with respect to the local cricket culture. As a student of history I knew only too well that it was not very long ago that a similar brand of ethnic prejudice and discrimination had applied to people of my ilk in the West Indies. When Lloyd's men arrived in England, then, the moment for me was charged with concerns about past injustices, current anxieties and future expectations. It was a time when my mind was still trying to evaluate references to the loss of Martin Luther King and Malcolm X on the one hand, and observations of the carnage that was taking place in Vietnam, Angola, Mozambique, North Ireland and Zimbabwe – not to mention the brutality of the English police towards West Indian people in the inner cities.

It was a familiar West Indian type of summer in England in 1976. There was a drought and water rations in some places. Richards was thirsty for runs and before he fully unpacked started scoring hundreds. I watched him closely. I remembered my grandfather, who was forced to make a living cutting the white man's cane on the white man's plantations on the white man's island of Barbados (home!). There was something in Richards' manner that reminded me of my grandfather; perhaps it was my grandfather's slow, graceful walk to the canefield, the rolling of the sleeve, and the precise but unpredictable swinging of the cutlass. But there was nothing agricultural about Richards, except that he was reaping that which those who went before him had sown. That is how the struggle for justice evolves everywhere. I understood the meaning of many things that summer.

From the beginning, Richards was businesslike in his demolition of English cricket. His powers of concentration and above all his haste made me wonder if he possessed a hidden agenda. It did not matter in the least; his was a level of mastery I had never seen before, and wished to see in all of our people's endeavours. I believed that he understood the seriousness of our condition and was prepared to act with all means necessary. We, the wretched of the inner cities, had never seen the likes of it. Frank Worrell had signalled that an emissary would come from the Leewards; we waited as only believers know how. I examined him with all the skills available to me at that time. There had been many false prophets in the past, and many pretenders. Time was running out on us; we were about to be packaged as volatile, calypso sunshine boys who entertained on a good day but packed up and went home disgraced when the clouds came over. I therefore examined his method, his concepts and his sense of purpose. I concluded that the survival struggle for West Indians with respect to postcolonial Englishness was being placed at a higher level.

Sir Gary Sobers, it seemed to me, had gloriously entertained the in-crowds at Lords with his genius; Richards, however, intimidated, mocked and perhaps humiliated such gatherings. It was political; he said so, and I knew it. The score had to be settled. He wore the colours of the Rastas, who said that he was sent by the Conquering Lion of the Tribe of Judah – Ras Tafari Makennon (Haile Selassie), the Redeemer from Ethiopia. With us, there is always religion and mythology within the politics. I felt that we were seeing what some said was the beginning of the glory. Bob Willis, Chris Old, Mike Hendricks, Tony Greig, Derek Underwood and others who bowled for England knew not what had befallen them. Richards broke all the rules, and tore up the Lords Treaty which said that 'hitting across the line' was an offence punishable by the withdrawal of approving adjectives. By the end of the summer, John Arlott of the British Broadcasting Corporation (BBC) was describing him as the 'Lord of Lords'. For us he was the 'king' of the Oval, Lords, and all venues where cricket was played that summer. How can anyone forget Arlott's coining of the term 'intimidatory batting'? You had to see it to believe it; fast bowlers afraid to follow through in fear of losing their ears; infielders preferring outfielding; umpires standing well back; and the unending click of the electronic scoreboards.

It is rare indeed that great men locate their genius within the social circumstances of their humble origins. It is also rare for great men to humble themselves before movements that surround them and which they could ignore to much profit. We felt then, that Richards was doing something for us. Each century, each double-century, peeled away the optic scales accumulated over four hundred years of inhuman subjection. The English were thrown into panic, not because of the aggregates – they had seen them before – but because they sensed that with Richards it was more than sport; it was the business of history and politics – the struggle against injustice and inequality. We assisted them to understand these things by our unfettered spectator responses. This worsened their condition, and I understood then the potence and social importance of strategic solidarity at the frontier.

In the course of that summer, we thanked our Antiguan brothers and sisters for sending Richards and we begged their forgiveness for not having allowed them to send more of his kind in the past. For me, it was a moment of new beginning. Many young West Indians felt compelled to do for their generation in diverse endeavours what Richards was doing on the cricket field. The articulation was clear, and the need was pressing. We were taken through a steep learning curve, and I decided to return to university for graduate research. I could not separate these things in my mind. Richards, you see, was an icon for those in my condition, and we were inspired by his self-confidence, ideological firmness and determination. He delivered the goods, and this made us recognize the meaning of productivity in new and different ways.

Undoubtedly, Viv was a rare but not phenomenal type of West Indian cricketer. C. L. R. James would have said that his coming was anticipated, and would have been surprised had he not arrived. It has to do with a certain kind of reading of Caribbean history, its logic, internal dialectics, and ideological trajectory. It is not a question of mechanical determinism in an understanding of history. Rather it has to do with how possible futures are perceived as a result of careful scrutiny of historical evidence. It is not the art of the speculator. There is nothing random about it. It is the science of those who can feel and sense the evidence of things not seen.

Viv did not walk onto the cricket field in search of himself. Neither did he discover his consciousness within the context of sporting contests. He was sent in to do battle by villagers, not only those in Antigua, but all those from little places in this diaspora; people who have been hurling missiles at the Columbus project since it crashed into their history five hundred years and ten million lives ago. His strut was not designed as part of a sterile social discourse that speaks of conceit and arrogance, but was an expression of a mind made up, hardened by a discarded plantation landscape that carries the marks of injustice and denial. He was determined to tilt the scales, even if marginally and temporarily, in favour of those whose view of the world is from the bottom up.

Preparation for such a task is never consciously done. There is no formal organization of ideas, and no exposure to texts that detail the visions of those who went before. Neither is there an awareness of the forces that conspire to fashion the consciousness from day to day. Ideas are encountered along the way, in a normal way in regular places, among people who see themselves as going nowhere, but who at the same time are always looking about themselves for emissaries. Villagers, from both town and country, have the vision of

5

dentists; they smile in recognition of the perfect form, but possess keen eyes that easily spot the rot that indicates a painful flaw. It is a process of deep-seated collective responsibility, shaped by a culture of relentless criticism that is designed to assure high standards.

The geometry of these relations is now well known. The domestic and neighbourhood worlds that produced Viv's mentality, and the wider history of black people's survival, represent the base for his departure into the orbit of an empowering pan-Africanist vista. The behaviour of 'natural rebels', we have been told, is not learnt by trial and error; it is a kind of carriage, bred by generations of social expectation and uncritical acceptance of social responsibility. For sure, three hundred years of colonial demand on the Antiguan land planted the ideology within Richards' being that 'arrival' and 'conquest' at Lords – the centre of civilization held in high esteem by those responsible for him – had everything to do with the collective West Indian midsummer dream. There is no contradiction in any of this. The lines were drawn before his time. His mission was to produce and secure a legitimate nationalist cartography that gave his people new undisputed boundaries and a land of their own.

Hitting Across the Line, Viv's autobiography, is precisely this – a mission statement, as well as an ideological account, the beginning and the end of a journey. It is a text that shows where the new boundaries are drawn, and where the land beyond the imperial line can be identified. At the same time it is more, much more. It belongs to an old tradition, but breaks new ground and can therefore stand on its own. Few autobiographies from the Caribbean have had the intellectual content to rise above the specific circumstances of their appearance to generate a life of their own. This statement by Richards therefore needs careful scrutiny. But we must begin with the idea.

It is a fact that in the West Indies the cricketer's autobiography represents the principal literary form of working class male expression. Men from the labouring class have had little reason to prepare texts detailing the evolution of their lives. The cricketer's memoirs, then, are a unique literary form in which the voice of the villager is heard on its own terms and, more importantly, in its own tone. In recent years there have been many such publications, but none of them details a narrative that flows through the hardened veins of West Indian history. There are reasons for this, and here there are no surprises. It is a text that reflects the rugged journey from the game's colonial periphery to its imperial centre and demonstrates how and why polarities had to be exchanged. It documents a mentality committed to subversion and revolution; it speaks of self-assertion and liberation. It is the treatise of the villager who rejects other people's notion of his space, and who always knew that he was global and in possession of the information to prove it as well as the technology to demonstrate it.

Viv's journey in search of ideological ancestry would rendezvous somewhere in 1933 with the publication of Learie Constantine's autobiography, *Cricket and I*. The lineage is clear, the resemblances are obvious, and we have no reason to doubt ideological paternity. Constantine's struggle was to break free West Indies cricket from its colonial scaffold, establish the foundations of a 'nationalist' culture against the grain of divisive social racism. His political mission was to promote the concept of merit as the organizing principle of the selection process. He had no time for the 'cousin cricket' played between white West Indians and English teams. For him it smacked of colonial subservience and promoted a self-denial of West Indian legitimacy. *Cricket and I* served as the voice from within the boundary of the progressive movement, and represented the clearest condemnation of the social forces that had denied George Headley his rightful place as captain of the West Indies test team during the 1930s.

Since then the cricket autobiography has proliferated, but within a different genre. Most are generally accounts of selected encounters, important moments, and performances within the general evolution of a career. At best they offer insights into publicly reported issues, but rarely touch the nerve as they are oftentimes written by ghost-writers contracted from the British media. While their principal contribution lies in offering entry to individual mentalities, they are limited in contextual sensitivity and sociological meaning. *Hitting Across the Line* breaks radically with this literary form and connects to Constantine's *Cricket and I*, bridging a time span of some three generations.

The title itself is a declaration of a new sense of sovereignty and independence – a rupture with an imperial tradition and a legitimization of an indigenous methodological approach. The tradition of batsmanship established by English technical experts disapproves violently of an approach that includes hitting across the line of the ball. Batting is understood as a side-on technology that loses its aesthetics and soundness when the ball is struck to the side-on if the line and trajectory is to the offside, and vice versa. Such transgressions are tabooed, and offending batsmen are described as lacking technique and correctness. It is within this nineteenth century English tradition that twentieth century West Indian batsmanship grew up and matured.

Viv's legitimization of 'hitting across the line' was in fact revolutionary, a unilateral declaration of cultural freedom. There are two issues here that require scrutiny. First, English opponents, more so than others, sought to contain Richards by setting defensive offside fields to which they would bowl. Indeed, setting an offside field is standard strategy in English first-class cricket, and bowling an off-line the norm for most types of bowlers. Two forms of counterattack are possible under such circumstances. The batsman could either try to penetrate a densely populated offside, or strike the ball across the line to the onside wilderness. The latter is considered a high risk and low interest response, the former is approved, particularly as it requires precision of placement and the patience of Job.

Viv's cricket nature was to counter and discredit the integrity of such strategies. He would hit the ball across the line at will, invariably using a straight bat on contact, leaving opposing captains to deny the efficacy of their field placing. The destruction of bowlers' self-confidence and the extraordinary rate at which he accumulated runs, speak to his innovative brilliance and conceptual brilliance. It was, of course, his remarkable hand-eye coordination that allowed for the effectiveness of this methodological departure. Tradition, he seems to be saying, is a safe haven for those of average ability; the way of the genius is to redraw the boundaries and discover new space.

This spirit of independence and departure was part of the West Indian social environment that shaped Viv's consciousness as a youth. The ideological discourse of black liberation as a pan-African imperative emerged from the region during the 1960s and early 1970s. In some places debates evolved into intense political mobilization and revolutionary politics. But everywhere, the youth began to speak a different language, ritualized their conduct in new directions, and searched for solutions to the culture of marginalization and exclusion that typified their condition. Theirs was a spirit of protest that filled the streets; communities, in town and country, began to march to the sound of ancestral drums.

It is evident, then, that Viv was as much a part of this discovery as Walter Rodney, who provided its leadership with historical context and clear ideological articulation. This is why *Hitting Across the Line* has to be 'read' as a manifesto of the progressive movement in much the same way that Rodney's *Groundings with my Brothers* is understood. They both evolved from the same set of anxieties and expectations that excited the faces of Caribbean youth in the morning of their new day. Both men infused their immediate worlds with visions and philosophies and transformed much of what they touched. Africans everywhere embraced them and sought to sustain the moral integrity and historical coherence of their interventions. The shape of Rodney's words and the echoes from Richards' bat connected to the rhythms and vibes of Bob Marley's music. For a moment – a lifting and painful decade – West Indians sniffed the future with all its epic possibilities. Rastafari came to the centre and provided the leadership. Viv was sympathetic to this arrival. He displayed the colours of the 'brethren' in new places and gave them enlarged dimensions and significance.

At the centre of this celebration of self-discovery was a constellation of ideas – some fully matured, others in the making. The uprooting of racism from the soils of an island civilization built upon it would not be easy, but it was necessary on principle to take a stand. "The racists", Viv says, "are people with a perverse kind of pride, who think we have no right to be competing on the same stage as them." "My pride, for the record," he concludes, "is as big as that of any other man!" The pride of which he speaks has to do with the right to be different, to be respected and not to be denied without just cause. Constantine used the same language in 1933, and was determined, as the owners of the Imperial Hotel in London discovered in 1944 when he took them to court for refusing him normal service on the basis of his race. But true pride for Viv had more to do with achieving results from the correct use of the collective intelligence of players in the pursuit of clearly understood and important objectives. "Success", he says, "does not have a lot to do with how much talent you have; what matters is how you manage to collect and nurture that talent." The binding of a West Indian character that speaks with a single voice and rallies behind a single flag has proven illusive in most areas of interaction, and is still troublesome in cricket. "When we are separate, we are nothing", says Viv, a fact that seems to stand without contest, yet the nature of daily discourse within the region remains divisive and at times acrimonious.

For sure, Viv's location of his world views within the pan-African movement, at home and abroad, meant that his social experiences would be characterized by considerable political turbulence and extreme social reactions. Caribbean societies remain deeply divided, torn and tortured in fact, by positive representations of the African ontology. The economic domination of these societies by elites of European ancestry, whose historic imposition of their value system remains hegemonic, cannot readily accommodate ideological and political challenges that speak on behalf of black redemption. The considerable corporate power of these groups continues to define and guide public discourse with respect to the authority and capacity of the state to devise and apply national policy in favour of the psychologically fractured people of African descent. Ironically, non-West Indian white elites have had less difficulty in accepting the validity and necessity of a pan-Africanist epistemology. One result has been that Viv was able to establish positive and lasting relations with business elites around the world, while considerable tension and unease continue to surround his interactions with elite Caribbean society.

An important aspect of this ambivalence is found in the attitudes of Afro-West Indians themselves. Despite the formal projection of a political dialogue that rests upon the aspirations of black society with respect to social and economic inclusion, many blacks have had considerable difficulty with the articulation of an agenda that directs attention to their structural disenfranchisement. An overwhelming number of people in society seemed divided on what was described during the 1970s as the 'Black Power Movement'. The established media had no difficulty in convincing many blacks that the movement was constituted and led by 'racists', 'ethnic cleansers', and anarchists. To speak on behalf of a democratic political programme of black empowerment in these societies, where colonial legacies continue to be supportive of white supremacy ideologies and values, is to encounter the wrath of elite society, particularly the cruder version expressed by its non-white elements.

Richards, then, was undoubtedly a highly developed product of the second paradigm in West Indies cricket. The first paradigm was that of the nineteenth century in which cricket was the instrument of colonial exclusion, used by white elite society to distance itself from the black majority. By the 1930s, this model was under attack, and the rise of the three Ws (Weekes, Worrell and Walcott) against the background of Learie Constantine and George Headley signalled the rise of the second paradigm. During the 1950s and 1960s cricket became hinged to the process of anticolonial reforms and the movement to independence and nation building. The political projects – rise of nation states and cricket as a symbol of West Indian liberation – grew hand in hand and together account for the ideological positions taken by Viv on a number of issues. There is nothing surprising, then, about this summary of his philosophy:

> The whole issue is quite central for me, coming as I do from the West Indies at the very end of colonialism. I believe very strongly in the black man asserting himself in this world and over the years I have leaned towards many movements that follow this basic cause. It was perfectly natural for me to identify, for example, with the Black Power movement in America and, to a certain extent with the Rastafarians. I cannot say that I have ever reconciled myself totally to Rastafarianism. However I have many Rastafarian friends and I have always despised the way they have been discriminated against. Even in Antigua I have been put down in the past for simply having Rastafarian friends. It was hinted once that my career might not progress as far as it might simply because I was friendly with Rastafarians. Now that is certainly a case of prejudice and it goes back a long way in the Caribbean, back to when the Rastaman was initially regarded as nothing more than a subversive influence. Many people in the Caribbean have treated them in a bad way.

The question, then, for Viv is one of supporting just causes within the political morality of the immediate postcolonial culture which insists, correctly, from an ideological standpoint on social inclusion and collective empowerment.

The social manifestations of ideological disapproval with Viv, however, are propagated everywhere; these have never been subtle nor discreet. It has to do with power, and its reproduction – the very essence of decolonization in the ideological sphere – and is therefore for many a matter of life and death. Decolonization, says Fanon, "is always a violent phenomenon", even if only in the language of ideological discourse. It is violent because it "is quite simply the replacing of a certain 'species' of men by another 'species' of men". Richards narrowly escaped being nailed to the cross on this matter of replacing one type of man with another. Lloyd was established and had to be replaced; the West Indies Cricket Board of Control (WICBC) waxed and waned on the question of Richards' succession.

Trevor Macdonald, in assessing Richards' career, makes references to the persistent tensions between Richards and the WICBC, and makes comparisons with an earlier stage when difficulties existed between the establishment and Frank Worrell. He suggested that Richards paid, and continues to pay, a price for his defiant position in promoting the radical tradition within West Indies cricket culture. Two generations earlier the young and ideologically aggressive Frank Worrell was severely criticized in Barbados and by WICBC officials, who felt that he was an arrogant, radical 'upstart'. Worrell eventually chose to depart from Barbados, and took up residence in Jamaica and Trinidad where the social culture seemed more liberal and accommodating of progressive mentalities.

The ideological tension, then, between the conservative and radical traditions within West Indian cricket would surface from time to time and find expression in the political postures of individuals. These forces are very well understood by the English, largely because as an imperial nation they are experienced in the matter of seeking out dissidents and putting down insurgents. As colonizers, they understand all too well the responses of the colonized, and have developed a powerful ideological machinery to discredit, defeat and eliminate challengers.

Robin Marlar, writing for the *Sunday Times*, 4 July 1993, against the background of the changeover from the Richards to the Richardson captaincy, says:

> It is clear that the West Indies Board thought that when Vivian Richards retired it was time that the leadership of West Indies cricket shifted its centre of gravity away from black activism and back towards the mainstream of the international game. Haynes was too close to his predecessor to achieve this objective and the mantle passed to the younger less confrontational Richie Richardson.

This shifting of the centre of gravity in West Indies cricket, therefore, is as much part of the making of the modern nation as the ideological metamorphosis of

Viv Richards (left) at reception given by UWI Chancellor Sir Shridath Ramphal (centre) to mark the first Vice Chancellor's XI match, 1996.

political parties and trade unions. The 1990s witness a similar preference for conservative leadership in public invitations throughout the Caribbean, and constitute, for example, the cemetery within which the Grenada Revolution now rests.

Lloyd stayed as captain longer than he intended. His extended term came as the result of a request from the WICBC. He had named Richards, his vice captain of five years, as his successor and received a reprimand from the WICBC for doing so. Richards was hurt, wounded to the core, by the politics of succession. He felt rejected by the hands he had supported and fought for. He belonged to one species of man, while his employers belonged to another. There was nothing extraordinary about this relationship. It constituted a metaphor for the discourse of political decolonization. In the West Indies, many champions of popular movements lie broken, dejected and hidden from history, defeated at the greased hands of emergent middlemen who stepped forward to broker 'a peace' and took the largest 'piece' for themselves. Viv wrote:

> I believed that at one time there was a conspiracy, of sorts, to prevent me from taking over the leadership of the squad. After we had lost the World Cup to India, Clive announced that he would be giving up the captaincy and that I would be his immediate successor. I had been his vice captain for five years and I felt, at that particular time, that I had paid my dues. I had actually captained the West Indies, in Clive's absence, as far back as 1980 in England. Nobody knew the West Indies game more than me. I thought I

had done my job as deputy very well throughout that period and, I am not trying to be big-headed, but the captaincy rightfully belonged to me. Clive knew this, which is why he stated it, on a couple of occasions. But Clyde Walcott, the touring manager of the side, told Lloyd that he should not have made those statements, that the WICBC had not at that point, decided that I was to be captain. But I knew that was wrong. Clive had decided to quit and there was no way that they should have persuaded him otherwise.

But they did, and although I know that Clive tried to ring me to tell me of his decision to carry on, he could not reach me. I heard the news on the radio when I was in Somerset. Of course, it was immensely frustrating for me, not because of Clive's decision to carry on, but because I knew why he had been persuaded to do so. I knew that there were people who did not want me to take over.

When the ballot for the captaincy was finally held by the West Indies Board, Viv had won by a margin of one vote. Malcolm Marshall, young in years and tenure on the side, but aged as a professional, almost upstaged his mentor.

Despite being an outstanding motivator of players, and having successfully rebuilt the team after the departure of Lloyd, Croft, Garner, Holding, Gomes and other stalwarts, and never losing a test series in the process, cricket officialdom withheld its praise for Richards' leadership. With a statistical record superior to that of Lloyd, the establishment continued to identify Viv as the sort of 'rebel' not to be encouraged. This further denial of just reward intensified the pressure on Richards, forcing him at times to appear injudicious in his off-field assessments and action. In his autobiography, *Lion of Barbados*, Desmond Haynes expressed sympathy and a rare understanding of the pressure applied by the English press in particular to Viv. Circumstances, Haynes said, were sometimes planned to upset Viv. "People wanted to get him", said Haynes, "because he was the symbol of our dominance." He was a man under siege by an array of ideological forces that were never comfortable with persons of his ilk. He had friends, and sympathizers, but they were insufficient to keep off the pressure and allow him to go into retirement as a contented and graceful old warrior.

Michael Holding, in his autobiography, *Whispering Death*, offers insights into what he considered the predicament of Viv, and the paradox his leadership posed for players and administrators. It had nothing to do with his supreme ability as a player or his right to be captain. Holding stated:

Viv certainly had no challengers as Lloyd's successor. No one in the team stood out as potentially a better skipper. He was a strong character who set high standards of performance for his players, precisely because he was so fiercely conscious of what success meant for the West Indies and West Indian people. The upshot was that he came down hard on those who fell short of his expectations. His players didn't seem to warm to him and I detected in his later years that individuals were playing more for themselves than for the captain. Man-management calls for tact, patience and understanding but these did not come easily for such a passionate man as Viv Richards.

The view has subsequently been expressed that this divide (between Richards' lack of social tact and his abundance of cricket tactics) caused the premature retirement of Michael Holding and Joel Garner, and signalled the final restructuring of the Lloyd regime. On assuming the captaincy, Richards made clear to all his determination to continue with the 'winning ways' achieved by Lloyd, but by doing things his way. He was a captain of strong views and an iron will, not always the best combination in circumstances, says Holding, that required a light hand and gentle touches.

The turbulence and ambivalence that had surrounded his entry to the captaincy intensified during the period of his retirement. Richards had outlined to the WICBC and the public his wish for a phased departure from first-class cricket. First, he wanted to give up the captaincy of the test side, and openly proclaimed Desmond Haynes, his vice captain, as his successor. Secondly, he declared his desire to play in the Australia-New Zealand World Cup which was just weeks away. Neither desire was honoured by the WICBC. Richie Richardson was appointed captain and supported the decision of selectors to exclude Richards from the World Cup squad. Richards was bitterly hurt. Richardson had been the beneficiary of his training, advice and special favours. His compliance with the decision of selectors was received by Richards as an act of cowardice, betrayal and capitulation. In Antigua, the home of both men, the word on the streets is that Richard(son) bit the hand that fed him, and cannot be forgiven.

Thrown into unexpected retirement from West Indies cricket, officialdom moved to make light weather of the fact that Richards had not only been the world's greatest batsman, but also statistically the most successful of West Indies captains. He considers himself banished by the establishment, with no one speaking publicly on his behalf as a candidate for a post as manager or coach. He returned to the English county and league circuit where he had first come to global prominence. His class and form were shown everywhere he played, and these opportunities and experiences provided the kind of soft landing that West Indies cricket had unreasonably denied him. He is currently employed by the Sultan of Brunei as a coach and cricket consultant. It is a long way from home, but for Viv it is another stop in his sojourn in exile.

All of this constitutes another paradox in the journey of the 'Enterprise of the Indies'. Toussaint L'Overture died in Napoleon's jail in France, and Marcus Garvey, another truly great revolutionary hero, was driven out of the islands to die in the hands of the colonial oppressor that had opposed his every initiative. The return of Richards to the West Indies, however, will be more than a physical one – but a step further in the process of self-discovery and recognition of identity by people who at this time remain fractured in terms of historical consciousness. There is no doubt that the exile of Richards has had a dampening effect on the 'soul' of West Indies cricket. The masses of cricket spectators know it. This is why West Indians turned out to fill Sabina Park on 23 March 1996, to pay a final and respectful farewell to the 'Conquering Lion' during the UWI Vice Chancellor's XI game against the touring New Zealand side. As always the masses of people have ways of knowing and feeling the unjust use of power by the elite, and more often than not do what they can to mitigate the effects of the injustice.

Richards, then, walks in a tradition we know well from the records of Caribbean oral historiography. His trajectory is that of the uncompromising spirit that gave no space to the reactionary forces that encircle efforts to mend broken minds. Elevated by the positive dreams of a people, he now exists in the margins of their nightmare, a place where heroes are buried in fast succession. Viv, however, has always been quick on his feet, and possessed of an extraordinary eye for 'reading' the moving ball and responding with precision and timing. For these reasons, if no others, history is on his side, if not behind him, and he may strike back sooner rather than later.

Cricket in the West Indies
The Rocky Road to Test Status

Keith A. P. Sandiford

When, in 1928, the West Indies were accorded full test match status, they were only the fourth to achieve this distinction. The very first official test was played between England and Australia at Melbourne in mid March 1877. South Africa became the third country to play test cricket when it opposed England at Port Elizabeth in March 1889. It is tempting for social historians to argue that, as so-called white colonies, Australia and South Africa were admitted to the first-class ranks at once, while the non-white settlements were excluded for longer periods because of considerations of race. What this chapter aims to do is examine the background of international cricket more closely to see what role, if any, racism played in the decisions reached by the Marylebone Cricket Club (MCC) which acted for many years as the supreme court in the cricketing world.

Cricket as an Instrument of Social Control and its Role in Cultural Imperialism

Cricket was freely and unabashedly used as an instrument of social control by Anglo-Saxon imperialists from the eighteenth century onwards. The sport was seen as an important tool in both the civilizing and administering process. It was very fervently held that devotion to cricket could produce law-abiding citizens at home and draw the subjects in the far-flung colonies much closer to the metropolis. British traders, soldiers, statesmen, priests and educators thus took cricket with them wherever they went in search of markets and colonies. By the middle of the nineteenth century the sport had consequently spread to many parts of the world.[1]

While cricket made relatively pedestrian progress in other sections of the colossal British empire during the Victorian age, it quickly flourished in Australia, Canada, India and the West Indies. In each of these territories, the colonists agreed with the colonizers that cricket was the greatest panacea for a multiplicity of ills and they therefore played it with a considerable degree of enthusiasm and intensity. For largely demographic reasons, cricket fared less well in such colonies as New Zealand and South Africa. It also failed to take deep root in most parts of Africa and was played with only mild enthusiasm by British colonists in Europe. While the sport prospered greatly in Canada for about 100 years after 1775, it gradually languished thereafter in that country, which became far more interested in curling, lacrosse and ice hockey.[2]

Australia

By the third quarter of the nineteenth century, Australian cricket had advanced to the point where a composite Australian team could compete on relatively even terms with the best cricketers England had to offer. In fact, on the first Australian tour to England in 1878, the visitors created a great sensation when they defeated a powerful MCC team at Lords. An even greater sensation was provided by an Australian test victory at the Oval in 1882, which led to the everlasting legend of the 'Ashes'. By 1885, Australia had already made four tours of England, winning no fewer than 48 of their 90 first-class matches, drawing 25 and losing only 17.[3] Up to this point, the two countries had participated in 21 test matches of which the Australians had won 9, lost 8, and drawn 4, partly due to the fact that no fewer than 16 of these contests had taken place on their home grounds.[4]

England had no qualms about according first-class status to games against Australian teams from the very beginning and the equivalent of test match status was conceded to all those games contested between the elevens of England and Australia, going back to 1877. No one can deny that the Australians deserved this honour. The bulk of the tests have always been keenly contested. But the major point to note here is that while the Anglo-Saxons dismissed Aboriginals and Maoris in Australasia as innately incapable of playing a sophisticated game like cricket, they clearly understood that gentlemen of their own stock could be expected to offer very keen competition.

It is often forgotten that the first Australian cricketers to tour England did so in 1868. It was in that year that a team of Australian Aboriginals, led by Charles Lawrence, an English coach and former professional, played a series of cricket matches in England. Their standard of play was most creditable indeed, but the spectators went more to see their post-game displays of athletic skill than to watch their cricket. Everyone agreed that Cuzens and Mullagh were potentially first-class players, but they were considered aberrations and the matches themselves were not accorded first-class status. The Aboriginals, after all, could not possibly represent Australia. They undertook a very strenuous itinerary that required them to play 47 cricket matches in 126 days on unfamiliar terrain and in hostile conditions. They won 14, drew 19, and lost on only 14 occasions, despite the fact that their opponents were much more experienced. The results made little difference to a Victorian public that had already convinced itself that non-whites were congenitally incapable of playing cricket with any intelligence or skill.[5]

The first Australian tour of England in 1878 by transplanted, but full-fledged, Anglo-Saxons was an entirely different matter. The schedule was equally hectic and it was perhaps foolhardy to expect 12 men to play 37 matches in a matter of a few months. But the Australians acquitted themselves remarkably well, winning 18 and losing only 12 of the total matches played. Of their 15 first-class games, they won 7 and lost only 4. Mindful of the misfortunes that had befallen James Lillywhite's England side in Australia during the tour of 1876–1877 nobody ever considered the possibility of regarding the Australian whites as second-class cricketers when they undertook their first English campaign.[6]

South Africa

The same courtesy was extended to the South Africans in the winter of 1888–1889 when an English team travelled there under the captaincy of C. Aubrey Smith. It did not matter that the standard of cricket was low in that country. In fact, all of the matches, with the exception of the two against composite South African XIs were played against odds, and the tests were most one-sided. England won the first by 8 wickets and the second by an innings and 202 runs. This was the case, despite the fact that the tourists had to acclimatize themselves to the hard grassless pitches which were much livelier and faster than those in England.[7]

South Africa did not really present a serious challenge until the first decade of the twentieth century, when they emerged with a trio of quality spinners experimenting with the dreaded 'googlie' which B. J. T. Bosanquet (of Oxford University and Middlesex) had recently invented. Between 1888 and 1905, no English team ever lost a first-class match in South Africa. Altogether, in four tours, they played 75 matches, including several against odds (and therefore not counted as first class) and won no fewer than 49.[8] Obviously the standard of play was lower in this country than in England or Australia. But all regional matches there were accorded first-class status from the inception of the Currie Cup competition in 1889–1890 and all the matches between England and South Africa have achieved test status from the very beginning. England consequently won the first 8 matches in this series with ridiculous ease.[9]

The main difficulty in South Africa was that too little effort was made to communicate with the vast majority of the population which was black. The blacks were routinely segregated from the whites who were themselves divided on Afrikaner and Anglo-Saxon lines. As the Afrikaners did not often play cricket, this meant that the game made progress only in those urban centres where there was a sizable minority of British expatriates. The turning point for South Africa came during the winter of 1905–1906 when an English team, led by P. F. (later Sir Pelham) Warner, failed to cope with the leg-break bowling of Aubrey Faulkner, Reggie Schwartz and Bert Vogler. The team never adjusted to the hard and bouncy South African matting wicket and lost the test series by a convincing margin of 4–1.[10] It was impossible for South African cricket to be belittled thereafter, and its continued improvement was most evident during the tour of England in 1907 when the visitors won no fewer than 21 of the 31 matches they played. That was the summer dominated by the great Aubrey Faulkner, whose all-round skills produced 73 first-class wickets and more than 1,000 runs.[11]

While it is manifestly evident that the white Australians and South Africans were initially granted test and first-class status largely on the basis of race, it must therefore also be said that they amply confirmed their status by improving their cricket technique and competing extremely well with England's finest players. When the famous triangular tests were arranged in 1912, Australia, England and South Africa were opposing each other, quite rightly, as equals.

New Zealand

Yet the same was true for New Zealand, another so-called white colony. It took much longer for cricket to establish itself in this country and there was no official structure or organization in place until the formation in Christchurch on 27 December 1894 of the New Zealand Cricket Council (NZCC). This led in due course to the introduction of the Plunket Shield in 1906–1907, which facilitated the growth of first-class cricket in New Zealand.[12] While the first full tour of English cricketers was to Canada and the United States in 1859, New Zealand did not attract such a visit until 1902–1903. It was in that winter that Lord Hawke, the famous cricket evangelist, was requested by the NZCC to lead a team to that country. Owing to his mother's illness, Lord Hawke had to decline and it was Pelham Warner who led a squad of 13 players, including 2 professionals, from Liverpool on 12 November. The majority of the matches were played against huge odds, and the seven first-class games, against Auckland, Canterbury, Otago, South Island, Wellington and New Zealand (twice) all ended in defeat for the local teams. In the unofficial tests, the New Zealand batsmen failed miserably to cope with the bowling of George Thompson and C. J. Burnup, who were by no means the best bowlers that England had to offer.[13]

In the winter of 1906–1907, when the MCC sent an all-amateur side to New Zealand, the local teams performed much better. Auckland and Wellington achieved honourable draws while Canterbury achieved a notable and surprising triumph, thanks to the excellent bowling of J. H. Bennett and S. T. Callaway. But despite the establishment of first-class cricket in New Zealand and a number of contests between English and New Zealand XIs during the first quarter of the twentieth century, New Zealand had to wait until 1929 before achieving official test match status. Cricket failed to progress as rapidly here as elsewhere mainly because the Anglo-Saxons tended, so to speak, to occupy scattered pockets of civilization and too few public schools were established in nineteenth century New Zealand after the Eton-Harrow model. Cricket in this country made huge strides only after World War I and this was most evident when, in a full tour of England in 1927, New Zealand won 7, lost 5, and drew 14 of its 26 first-class matches. By this time, some of its stars, such as Roger Blunt, C. C. R. Dacre, C. S. Dempster, Thomas Lowry, W. E. Merritt, and John Mills had emerged among the world's leading cricketers.[14] Even so, New Zealand did not achieve its first test victory until March 1956, when it finally defeated the West Indies at home. Their triumph at Auckland in the fourth test of that series meant that they had won their maiden victory after 45 tests in 26 years.[15] New Zealand also had to wait until 1978 for its first test victory against England.[16] One of its major disadvantages was its geographical isolation. Because of its location in the far southeastern corner of the globe, few countries attempted to visit it prior to the 1950s and Australia, a somewhat arrogant and unfriendly neighbour, unfortunately ignored cricket in New Zealand for an unconscionably long time.[17]

India, Pakistan and Sri Lanka

The four countries that are now regarded separately as Bangladesh, India, Pakistan and Sri Lanka were all lumped together as one prior to the great partition of 1947. India, as it was then called, was by no means a 'white colony'. But its indigenous population very soon became attracted to cricket and the game made steady progress in that vast subcontinent throughout the eighteenth century. By the Victorian age, cricket was well established in the major urban centres. Indian cricket, however, suffered from racial and religious segregation which proved a major handicap for many years. Hindu, Muslim, Parsi and European teams tended to play in isolation and it was not before 1926, for instance, that a team of Anglo-Indians condescended to play on the grounds of the Hindu Gymkhana at Poona. Racism therefore hindered the growth of Indian cricket and this was reflected in the tendency to select mainly Europeans to represent 'All India' as late as 1926–1927 when the Calcutta Cricket Club, an Anglo-Saxon organization, arranged the visit of Arthur Gilligan's MCC team.[18]

Considering that such cricketers as Lord Harris (1890–1895) and Lord Willingdon (1913–1918) had served as Governors of Bombay and had also been presidents of the MCC, it is astonishing to discover that Gilligan's tour of the subcontinent was the first ever attempted by the MCC. While several amateurs were anxious to tour South Africa and the West Indies in the winter, few apparently relished the food or the climate in India. Travelling long distances on dusty and difficult roads also added to the discomfort. Indian cricket therefore had to develop without the stimulus provided by frequent English (or other) invasions. In the summer of 1889, a team of amateurs, led by George F. Vernon, a Middlesex amateur, played 13 matches in India. It was hardly representative of England's true strength and in fact contained only three regular county cricketers (Lord Hawke, J. G. Walker and the captain himself). The competition was interesting, albeit uneven, and the one significant result was the defeat that the Parsis of Bombay inflicted on the tourists, thanks to the all-round excellence of Dr Melhasa E. Pavri, who was regarded by his compatriots as India's answer to England's great 'champion' Dr W. G. Grace. The match against the Parsis was the only one that Vernon's team lost.[19]

Three years later, Lord Hawke led a slightly stronger squad of amateurs to Ceylon and India but again lost to the Parsis of Bombay when his men found Pavri still in magnificent form with the ball. The European teams in Calcutta, Bombay and Madras showed some improvement but the best cricketer on the subcontinent was still Pavri. Nevertheless, when Lord Hawke met 'All India' on this occasion, he was opposed by Anglo-Saxon expatriates. This same pattern prevailed when the third England team, the Oxford University Authentics, visited India in 1902–1903. The tourists again achieved very favourable results against European competition but lost, as was now the custom, to the Parsis of Bombay.[20]

What these tours proved, if nothing else, was that native Indians were capable of playing very good cricket indeed and that the country, with its vast resources of manpower, could become a cricketing force once the racial, cultural and religious barriers were demolished. This much had already been suggested by the career of the greatest Hindu batsman of them all. The famous Kumar Shri Ranjitsinhji, later to become the Maharaja Jam Sahib of Nawanagar, had demonstrated almost magical skills as a stroke player at the turn of the century. In 307 first-class matches for Cambridge University, London County, MCC, Sussex and England, he had amassed almost 25,000 runs at no more than 56 runs per innings.[21] 'Ranji' ought to have shown the Anglo-Saxons that native Indians were not as effete and as effeminate as they had previously believed. But, as in the case of Cuzens and Mullagh, they simply regarded him as an exceptional freak of nature.

Even before Ranji had burst upon the late Victorian scene, the Parsis had become so devoted to cricket that they felt impelled to organize their own tours to England. This provided English spectators with an opportunity to see the great Pavri in action. He was one of the finest fast bowlers in the world during the 1880s and had much to do with the success of the 1888 tour when the Parsis won 8 and lost 11 of the 31 matches they played. Pavri claimed 170 wickets at less than 14 runs apiece. He created a great impression even though the majority of the games were against clubs and not counties. But the Parsis performed well enough to encourage Vernon to take a team to England in the winter immediately following.[22]

The two events which ultimately hastened the decision to grant India test match status were the All-India tour of England in 1911 and the MCC tour of India in 1926–1927. The initiative in 1911 was taken by Bhupinder Singh, the Maharaja of Patiala, who personally financed the trip. In cricketing terms the tour was not successful but it provided enough evidence that native Indians were potentially fine players. So keen was the competition during the tour of 1926–1927 that it was difficult to deny India test match status indefinitely. One of the immediate problems here, however, was the lack of a centralized body to coordinate Indian cricket over so many disparate areas. It was not before 1928 that the Board of Control for Cricket in India came into being. Interestingly, it was an Englishman, M. E. Grant Govan, who served as its first president. Four years later, India participated in its very first test match when it met England at Lords.[23] Pakistan, of course, joined the test lists shortly after achieving its own independence and Sri Lanka showed sufficient improvement over the years to merit similar promotion during the 1980s. Bangladesh, however, has not achieved test match status.

The West Indian Experience

This, then, was the global context in which the game of cricket developed in the Caribbean basin. First-class cricket was first played here in 1865. That was the year in which Demerara (later known as British Guiana) paid its first visit to Barbados. Trinidad shortly after joined the intercolonial competition and Jamaica did so in the 1890s. By 1895, the sport had developed sufficiently in the territory to attract a team from England, led by Robert Slade Lucas, another Middlesex amateur. So successful was that first tour (in both a social and a cricketing sense) that no fewer than four English teams came back to the Caribbean within the next ten years.[24] It was clear, in fact, by 1900, that cricket in the West Indies was of a very high standard.

This prompted an invitation to England and 15 West Indians made the proverbial pilgrimage to Mecca in that year. Despite the evidence provided by the Slade Lucas, Lord Hawke and Arthur Priestly tours to the Caribbean in the 1890s, and the fact that the majority of those earlier matches had been considered first class, the MCC refused to grant the tourists first-class status in 1900. This inconsistency has never been satisfactorily explained. Significantly, however, the late Victorian press took the view that the 'men of colour' were incapable of playing such a sophisticated game as cricket with the same patience and intelligence as Anglo-Saxons.[25] The fact that there were only five blacks among the 15 tourists in 1900 seemed to have escaped the notice of the journalists.

It is clear, then, that status in cricket at the turn of the century depended upon much more than the simple ability to play. The colonies at that time were governed in varying ways by a metropolis that discerned essential differences in their make-up. In an age of blatant racism, sexism and snobbery, it was improper to treat all races, sexes and classes on an equal basis. English professionals, coming mainly from the lower classes, could not be treated as social equals by the patrician amateurs.[26] Colonies also had to be classified and governed accordingly. Some were designated white and others non-white. Australia, Canada, New Zealand and South Africa formed a cluster of so-called white colonies despite the multiracial nature of their populations and they were allowed a considerable degree of local autonomy. The fact that the white population comprised only a minute percentage in South Africa did not prevent Britain from viewing that colony as essentially a white one by the simple expedient of allowing the whites to monopolize all of its economic and political resources.

Until the middle of the twentieth century, non-white colonies were generally considered incapable of handling their own economic and political affairs. They therefore had to endure such illiberal systems as Crown Colony governments and protectorates which displayed none of the democratic spirit on which the Anglo-Saxons had so long prided themselves. This was the political backdrop providing the context in which cricket was played in those days. Liberalism and democracy in cricket had to await the coming of liberalism and democracy in the wider sociopolitical framework.

Some cricket historians, in fact, would argue that it was the other way around. It was the politicians who followed the lead of the cricketers. The Australians and the South Africans achieved test status in the nineteenth century several decades before they were accorded dominion status. India had to wait until 1932 before becoming a test-playing country. Indian politicians then regarded that as a significant step towards Indian self-government which finally came after World War II. If the West Indians achieved test status in 1928, this was a significant improvement over their political fortunes. The territories did not achieve their political independence until more than 30 years later.

These are some of the considerations that the historian must first reflect upon when analysing the decisions reached by the MCC and other administrative bodies. But status in cricket must also depend, to an even larger extent, on the quality of cricket played. There are several former colonies, particularly in central, eastern, northern and western Africa, where cricket never prospered at all and in such countries as Sri Lanka and Zimbabwe, the sport has only recently attained first-class standards. That these countries have been admitted to the test ranks in the last few years tells us perhaps more about their cricket than their politics.

In the West Indies, too, there were huge handicaps in the beginning which did not depend entirely on politics. All the earlier cricket clubs in the various Caribbean territories were strictly amateur organizations, playing the game largely for fun and doing so mainly on Saturday afternoons. For many years, the development of West Indian cricket was hindered also by the lack of administrative infrastructures. Organized cricket, for example, was not played in Barbados until the establishment of the Challenge Cup Committee in 1892.[27] Other territories started even later and this was one of the significant reasons why cricketers in such islands as Antigua, Dominica, Nevis and St Vincent were generally overlooked by West Indian selectors until relatively recently. For the most part, during the late Victorian age, the organization of cricket in the Caribbean was haphazard in the extreme.

This makes it all the more remarkable that teams could be assembled to represent Barbados and Demerara in the 1860s and that the colonies could provide such stiff opposition to English touring teams in the 1890s. When Slade Lucas undertook his famous tour in the winter of 1894–1895, his side lost to Barbados by 5 wickets in the first match and won the return by 25 runs mainly because of inexperience on the part of the home side and the inflexibility of the current laws which automatically enforced the follow-on when the Barbadians might have done better to make the tourists bat last on a wicket that would not have favoured them.[28] The Englishmen defeated Demerara and Jamaica with some ease but fell to Trinidad by 8 wickets largely due to the excellent fast bowling of J. Woods, who was then regarded as a 'professional'. It is true that the Slade Lucas XI, all amateurs, can never be considered a representative England team. But at least they all had first-class experience and were accustomed to playing three-day matches on consecutive days, while the local players were merely Saturday afternoon cricketers.

If Slade Lucas's team was a mediocre one below the level of a first-class English county team, the same could not be said for the team that Lord Hawke led to the Caribbean in 1896–1897. It included such fine players as G. R. Bardswell, H. R. Bromley-Davenport (who had accompanied Slade Lucas two years before), J. M. Dawson, Christopher Heseltine, H. D. G. Leveson-Gower, Pelham Warner and R. W. Wickham.[29] They won matches in Barbados and British Guiana but fared very badly in Trinidad, where they lost twice.

That same winter, as a result of a misunderstanding with Lord Hawke, Arthur Priestley also brought a side to the West Indies. It included C. A. Beldam, R. C. N. Palairet, A. E. Stoddart and S. M. J. Woods, and would have been quite competitive in county cricket. But while it easily defeated Jamaica twice, it encountered all kinds of difficulties in Barbados and Trinidad where it lost five of its six first-class matches, including one against a composite West Indies XI at Queen's Park. That unofficial test was a triumph for B. Cumberbatch and Clifford Goodman, who demonstrated the kind of pace bowling skills that would have made them successful at any level and in any country.[30]

By the end of the nineteenth century, therefore, it was clear that the West Indies team was capable of playing very good cricket. Lord Hawke certainly thought so and encouraged them to undertake a tour of England as soon as it was convenient. Pelham Warner also made that suggestion but was careful to add that it was pointless to go to England without a 'few professionals', like Cumberbatch and Woods, without whose fast bowling the West Indies would be unable to cope with the powerful batting of the stronger counties.[31]

These suggestions led to the very first West Indies tour of England in 1900. All kinds of problems surfaced from the very beginning. There was no central administration to orchestrate the enterprise; there was no acknowledged selection committee to choose the side; and no sponsors were forthcoming to finance the tour. In other words, West Indies cricket faced more serious obstacles than those that obtained elsewhere. In the first place the territories were separated from one another by natural boundaries provided by the sea. Communication was therefore slow and cumbersome. When Slade Lucas's men, for instance, tried to get to Jamaica from Barbados in 1895 the journey took four days. As late as 1913, the MCC captain, A. W. F. Somerset, was lamenting that the nine additional days of travel that a visit to Jamaica would have entailed made it impossible for that English team to play against the Jamaicans.[32] This natural geographical isolation had bred a good deal of insularity and each colony was anxious to gain as much representation on the team as it could. To overcome that difficulty, the leaders of the region agreed to a quota system, which inevitably meant that the strongest combination could not be chosen.

In the upshot, the squad departed for England without a recognized wicketkeeper and without its fast bowler (Cumberbatch), but all things considered it was a good enough side, capable of holding its own in county cricket, if only its members could become quickly acclimatized and accustomed to the regimen of constant cricket, six days each week, throughout an English summer. Of the 15 players who made the trip, there were 4 from Barbados, 4 from Trinidad, 3 from British Guiana, 2 from Jamaica and 2 from the so-called small islands. Led by Aucher Warner (Pelham's elder brother), the team was composed of William Bowring, W. T. Burton, Lebrun Constantine, P. I. Cox, D. S. D'Ade, Percy Goodman, Delmont Hinds, M. M. Kerr, George Learmond, G. L. Livingston, W. H. Mignon, C. A. Ollivierre, Stanley Sproston and J. Woods.[33]

Second-Class Status in England, 1900

Considering the performance of the West Indian XI against Priestley's team in 1897, the tourists ought promptly to have been accorded first-class status. But they were not, and the MCC seemed to think that its curious decision was amply justified by the results of the initial matches. The team of 1900 faced a most arduous itinerary, which began with a match against a most powerful London County XI, then led by the legendary but ageing Dr W. G. Grace. It took the West Indians several weeks to become accustomed to the travel and the weather. Losing the toss consistently in the opening matches did not help. The first half of the tour was simply disastrous.[34]

When, towards the end of the summer, the tourists had become more familiar with the daily grind, they accomplished victories over the Minor Counties, Leicestershire, Hampshire, and Surrey. Altogether, in their 17 matches, they won 5, drew 4 and lost 8. It was a great learning experience and some observers felt that, notwithstanding all the obstacles, they would have done much better had they taken Cumberbatch with them. The English batsmen made light of the majority of the West Indian bowlers, but showed great respect for Burton and Woods, who between them took 150 wickets at less than 22 runs each. Another fast bowler would certainly have tilted the balance in their favour. But the main weaknesses were in their fielding and their batting. The tourists had not yet learnt how to adapt to the pace of three-day games and only Ollivierre, Constantine and Cox averaged more than 30 runs per innings. Considering the number of times that individual batsmen reached the target of 25 runs, their failure to achieve higher scores would suggest a defect in temperament rather than technique, notwithstanding those negative comments in the *Sun* about the crudity of their batsmanship.[35]

It took the West Indies a very long time to profit from the lessons of 1900. From the cricket perspective, they improved their technique largely by organizing the game more effectively at the local level and abandoning the practice of one-day club games in their first divisions. In Barbados, for instance, the Cup Committee extended the first division matches from one to two and eventually to three Saturdays. It also introduced a second division in 1903.[36] Throughout the Caribbean, there occurred a steady escalation of clubs as the game increased in popularity. Visits by England teams, under R. A. Bennett in 1901–1902 and Lord Brackley in 1904–1905, gave the game a real fillip, while intercolonial matches were now being arranged with increasing frequency.

First-Class Status in 1906

The results of the second West Indies team to tour England in 1906, nevertheless, showed little improvement on the first, even though some of its matches were now considered first-class. The MCC decision here made no more sense than its first, since the West Indies touring team in 1900 had appeared to justify its second-class ranking. Apparently, however, the MCC felt that the local lads had performed creditably enough against Lord Brackley's touring team which had lost three keenly contested matches in Barbados and Trinidad.[37]

The West Indies again started the tour with a series of embarrassments before finding their feet in the summer of 1906, and then losing only one of their games after the middle of July. On the field, there was some improvement in all aspects of the game, notably in batting, where the West Indies were now more adept at constructing a long innings. Several fine performances in this department came from Percy Goodman, S. G. Smith and the 18-year-old George Challenor. Their wicketkeeping was immeasurably better in 1906 as they had avoided the costly error of 1900. On this occasion, they took a specialist, C. K. Bancroft, one of the finest wicketkeepers ever produced by Barbados, to undertake that task. In the final analysis, however, the tourists won only three of their first-class games while losing eight. That was not a good enough record to suggest that they deserved to be granted test match status.[38]

To their credit, it must be admitted, the West Indies continued to profit from their experiences in England and from the intercolonial tournaments that were being arranged with increasing frequency in the Caribbean. Their progress was reflected in the kind of opposition they were able to present to English touring teams in the decade before the outbreak of the Great War. An MCC squad, led by A. W. F. Somerset in 1910–1911, was not particularly strong and achieved only limited success against the improving islanders. It ran into immediate difficulties in Bridgetown, losing twice to Barbados by more than an innings, before moving on to the unfamiliar matting pitch at Port of Spain and losing two matches also to Trinidad. Even in Jamaica, which was not yet as strong as the other West Indian colonies, Somerset's men were held to a draw and a tie, the first such result in Caribbean first-class cricket. In the end, the MCC won four and lost four of its eleven first-class matches. It is significant, however, that the islanders failed to win either of the two 'unofficial' tests that were played and in fact lost the first at Bridgetown by 4 wickets in a low scoring game.[39]

Another MCC team, in 1912–1913, was much stronger than its predecessor but still succumbed twice by more than an innings to a powerful Barbados eleven, led by C. A. 'Johnnie' Brown, George Challenor, Will Gibbs, Harry Ince and Tim Tarilton. Again significantly, three matches were arranged against composite West Indian teams and the tourists won that unofficial series 2–1.[40] Even in Bridgetown, where Barbadian XIs were accustomed to winning by huge margins, the test team could not hold its own. The message here, obviously, is that the West Indies were not yet equal to the sum of the component parts. It was for a long time very difficult for them to develop the necessary *esprit de corps* so vital at the highest level. While eleven Barbadians could perform wonders at the Kensington Oval, and eleven Trinidadians could do equally well at Queen's Park, a team of eleven West Indians, rather arbitrarily and haphazardly assembled, could seldom do very much.

West Indies Cricket during the 1920s

This same disturbing pattern was to continue after World War I, when Barbados could defeat a powerful MCC touring team in the winter of 1925–1926, but the West Indies XI could not. While Barbados won its game at Bridgetown by an innings and 73 runs, the West Indies lost theirs at Port of Spain by 5 wickets. This English tour was one of the serious turning points in West Indian cricket history. It was the first time that the MCC sent out a team that was almost representative of England's true strength. Led by F. S. Gough-Calthorpe, it included such fine professionals as Ewart Astill, George Collins, Walter Hammond, Percy Holmes, Roy Kilner, Fred Root, E. J. 'Tiger' Smith and F. B. Watson. But Collins was its only fast bowler and its attack was not sufficiently penetrative to dismiss the local batsmen twice within the allotted three days. As the islanders themselves lacked bowlers of quality, apart from George Francis and Herman Griffith, no fewer than nine of the twelve first-class matches were left drawn.[41] It was the first time that an MCC squad would return to England with but two paltry victories to show for its pains.

The decision to send such a strong team to the Caribbean in 1925–1926 was really the result of the performance of the composite West Indian team in England during the summer of 1923. H. B. G. (later Sir Harold) Austin captained a very good side on that occasion. It included George Challenor, George Francis, Harry Ince and Tim Tarilton from Barbados; Learie Constantine, George Dewhurst, George John, Victor Pascall and Joe Small from Trinidad; Snuffie Browne, Maurice Fernandes and C. V. Hunter from British Guiana; and J. K. Holt, R. K. Nunes and R. L. Phillips from Jamaica.[42]

Certain observations on the structure of this side spring promptly to mind. First is the total absence of representatives from the Leeward and Windward Islands. By this time, the failure of the smaller islands to develop their own infrastructure meant that they could be excluded altogether from enterprises of this sort.[43] This was rather a pity, as history has subsequently shown that islands such as Antigua, Dominica, Grenada, Nevis and St Vincent are capable of producing very good cricketers indeed. Secondly, the West Indies had not yet abandoned the old fashioned 'quota' system and were thus compelled to select at least three players each from British Guiana and Jamaica, although these colonies were admittedly weaker in those days than Barbados and Trinidad. This meant that places could not be found for such deserving cricketers as Johnnie Browne, Herman Griffith and Wilton St Hill. Had Hunter, Holt and Phillips been left behind, the tourists would have been very much stronger. As it was, Hunter and Phillips took little part in the proceedings as they were injured for most of the summer and the squad was never really more than 14 strong. The quota system also meant that Nunes had to assume the role of the reserve wicketkeeper, while Piggott, an excellent wicketkeeper from Trinidad, was left behind. Such a shrewd judge of talent as C. L. R. James was convinced that 'Piggie' was superior to Dewhurst, the team's leading wicketkeeper, whose claims were bolstered more by his social status than his cricketing skills.[44]

In spite of these obstacles, the West Indies enjoyed a very fruitful summer, winning 12 of the 26 matches they played and losing only 7. Although George John was by this time well beyond his peak, he still captured 49 wickets in the 10 matches he was allowed. With Francis, who took 82 first-class wickets that summer, he formed one of the most fearsome opening partnerships of the day. But the real star was George Challenor, then at his peak. He scored 1,556 delightful runs at an average of more than 51 runs per innings and left a profound impression on all those who watched him. He struck no fewer than 8 first-class centuries and finished third in the English averages, ahead of such great batsmen as Jack Hobbs, Herbert Sutcliffe and Frank Woolley.[45] He was selected one of *Wisden's* "Five Cricketers of the Year", offered an honorary MCC membership, and lionized as one of the leading batsmen of his generation.[46]

It was Challenor's majestic batting, more than any other single factor, that accelerated the pace towards test match status. By 1927, West Indian friends in Britain, including Pelham Warner, himself a native of Trinidad and an alumnus of Harrison College of Barbados, were encouraging the islanders to prepare themselves for test cricket by establishing more formal administrative structures in the region. Similar suggestions were made by Lord Hawke and the Hampshire captain, Hon. L. H. Tennyson, who was so impressed with Jamaica that he visited it twice in consecutive winters during 1926–1928.[47]

The Establishment of the West Indian Cricket Board of Control

Caribbean cricketers had long felt a need for an establishment of this kind. There was no central organization to coordinate the regular intercolonial tournaments, to select composite West Indian XIs and to arrange West Indian tours to England and elsewhere. In fact, apart from a West Indian tour of Canada and the United States in 1886, no team had ever been selected to tour any country apart from England. But the geography and culture of the Caribbean territories militated against the foundation of a centralized framework. It took all the diplomatic skills of an influential MCC member, R. H. Mallett, to bring the territories together immediately after Calthorpe's tour. Mallett was a great friend of West Indian cricket. It was he who had managed their tours of 1906 and 1923 and was destined to manage their first ever tour of Australia in 1930–1931. Representatives of the 'Big Four' finally got together, under Mallett's direction, to create the WICBC in 1927.[48]

Social historians still know too little about the formation and early workings of the WICBC. It is known that a small group of wealthy individuals held a preliminary meeting in Bridgetown in 1926 out of which an informal structure (the West Indies Cricket Conference) emerged, holding its first official meeting at the Bridgetown Club in Barbados on 22 January 1927. This meeting was attended by George Challenor (Barbados), W. E. Dolly (Windward Islands), Fred Grant (Trinidad), R. H. Mallett (England), A. C. O'Dowd (Demerara), Joseph Schoult (Trinidad), Tim Tarilton (Barbados) and C. V. White (Demerara). The duties of secretary were performed by H. A. Cuke (later Sir

Archibald) of Barbados. In H. B. G. Austin's absence, L. T. Yearwood, vice chairman of the Barbados Cricket Committee, presided. Delegates had been invited from Jamaica and the Leeward Islands but unfortunately were unable to attend.

It was this group of ten, of whom four were Barbadians, who resolved to create the WICBC, which would include a president, a secretary, two delegates each from Barbados, Demerara, Jamaica and Trinidad, and one representative each from the Leeward and Windward Islands. The WICBC's first meeting was held at Port of Spain, Trinidad, on 17 and 18 June 1927, under the presidency of Harold Austin, the Barbadian cricketer who had captained the West Indian teams to England in 1906 and 1923. Also present on that historic occasion were H. N. Leacock and L. T. Yearwood (Barbados), A. C. O'Dowd and O. Webber (Demerara), F. G. Grant (representing Jamaica), A. Cory-Davies and J. G. Kelshall (Trinidad) and C. A. Child (representing the Windward Islands in W. E. Dolly's absence). Unable to send a delegate to the meeting, the Leeward Islands were represented by Yearwood. Jack Kidney of Barbados was appointed first honorary secretary/treasurer. Thus, as in the January meeting of the short-lived West Indies Cricket Conference, the WICBC was dominated by the Barbadians and Trinidadians who comprised no fewer than seven of the ten executive members.[49]

Apart from Mallett and Austin, the guiding forces behind the establishment of the WICBC appear to have been the Hon. Laurie T. Yearwood, Fred Grant and Alty O'Dowd. Lacking the financial resources, the WICBC was little more than a small, almost unofficial body, comprised entirely of members of the white elite in the territories. Problems of distance and money often meant that representatives of Jamaica and the smaller islands could not attend meetings that invariably were held in Bridgetown and Port of Spain. The Barbadians and Trinidadians tended consequently to dominate the majority of the early meetings. The WICBC naturally adopted very conservative attitudes from the very beginning and was, in any case, much too weak to impose its will on local clubs or associations. Its main concern in 1927 was preparation for the tour of 1928 which the West Indies were invited to make. It discussed the problem of quotas and attempted to embark on a more progressive policy by arranging a series of trial matches in Barbados between teams from the 'Big Four'.[50]

The WICBC was determined that the West Indies, having now been promoted to full test match status, should make a good showing in England in 1928. It discussed the important matter of professional fees and agreed to offer £3 per test match in addition to the weekly allowance of 30 shillings to each member to cover out-of-pocket expenses. It also devised a scheme providing for talent money to be paid to individuals for outstanding feats in first-class games. These decisions marked an obvious advance in West Indies cricket, but they could not bridge the huge gap between hardened county players, accustomed to cricket six days every week, and Saturday amateurs who were afforded too few opportunities for first-class play.

Test Match Status and its Immediate Results

Such enormous handicaps could not be overcome by three trial matches played in Bridgetown during December and January 1927–1928. Despite all attempts to avoid the quota system, the structure of the West Indies team that toured England in 1928 was not much different from its predecessors. Among the 17 players finally chosen were 5 Barbadians, 4 Trinidadians, 4 Guyanese, and 4 Jamaicans. This distribution was as even as one could manage, and once again there was no specialist wicketkeeper among the group. No provision having been made for the Leewards and Windwards to participate in the Bridgetown trials, the squad did not include a single player from the smaller islands. The captain had, of course, to be a wealthy white cricketer, whatever his other qualifications, and the lack of funds militated against the selection of more than a few so-called professionals.

The team which set out under Karl Nunes of Jamaica in 1928 included Lawson Bartlett, George Challenor, George Francis, Herman Griffith, E. L. G. Hoad (Barbados); Snuffie Brown, M. P. Fernandes, J. M. Neblett, C. V. Wight (British Guiana); F. R. Martin, Karl Nunes, E. A. Rae, O. C. Scott (Jamaica); and Learie Constantine, Clifford Roach, Wilton St Hill and Joe Small (Trinidad). On paper, it looked competitive enough, but on the field it fared very ill, due in large part to its atrocious catching. The three fast bowlers, who would ordinarily have held the county batsmen in check, suffered from a surfeit of dropped catches throughout the summer. With the ageing Challenor now well past his prime, the batting generally lacked the necessary determination and discipline, and the wicketkeeping deficiencies were painfully glaring. The West Indies won only 5 of their 30 first-class matches, and lost no fewer than 12, including all of the three tests.

A glance at the test results of 1928 would seem to indicate that the West Indies were not yet ready for the promotion that the MCC had accorded them. The first match at Lords in June ended in disaster. England won the toss, scored 401 and dismissed the West Indies in two separate heaps for 177 and 166. The visitors failed to offer much resistance to the bowling of A. P. 'Tich' Freeman, V. W. C. Jupp, and Maurice Tate. The great Harold Larwood captured Challenor's wicket in the first innings but retired from the game after bowling only

15 overs. The West Indies failed to take advantage of England's misfortune. Apart from Constantine in the second innings, no West Indian was able to record a half-century. England won by an innings and 58 runs.[51]

At Old Trafford in July, Nunes won the toss, saw his team reach 100 before losing its second wicket, and watched the rest of the batting fold for a meagre total of 206 runs. It would have been even worse had it not been for some spirited hitting by Snuffie and Scout at the bottom of the order. Freeman's leg-breaks completely bamboozled the West Indies, who could manage only 115 in their second attempt. Steady bowling by Browne, Constantine, Francis and Griffith, in the face of very bad out-cricket on the part of their colleagues, restricted England to 351 from 107 overs but it was all for naught. England won by an innings and 30 runs.[52]

At the Kensington Oval in August, Challenor (46) and Roach (53) opened with a defiant stand of 91, Constantine and Scott scored 72 between them, and Wight chipped in with 23, but still the visitors could not get beyond 238. The only pleasure they squeezed out of this bitter experience came from the opportunity to witness a fine century by the celebrated Jack Hobbs. England won by an innings and 71 runs.[53]

On the surface, these results seem to show that the West Indies were no more competitive in 1928 than the South Africans had been 40 years earlier. But it has to be noted that England fielded one of its very strongest combinations in 1928, whereas Aubrey Smith's squad in 1888–1889 excluded such stalwarts as William Barnes, W. G. Grace, William Gunn, George Lohmann, Bobby Peel, Richard Pilling, Walter Read, A. G. Steel and Frank Sugg (who had all played in the tests against Australia the previous summer). The West Indies were unfortunate to find England at one of its peaks. For the first test, they had to face the following batting order: Herbert Sutcliffe, Charles Hallows, Ernest Tydesley, Walter Hammond, Douglas Jardine, A. P. F. Chapman (captain), Vallance Jupp, Maurice Tate, Harry Smith (wicketkeeper), Harold Larwood and 'Tich' Freeman. At Old Trafford, the mighty Hobbs replaced Hallows, while Jack 'Farmer' White and Harry Elliott came in for Larwood and Smith. At the Oval, Larwood reappeared, having recovered from his injury, and Elliott gave way to a healthy George Duckworth, universally acknowledged as one of the finest wicketkeepers ever produced by Lancashire. Maurice Leyland and Patsy Hendren also replaced Jardine and Jupp. It is difficult to find a stronger England XI than the one that overwhelmed the West Indies at the Oval. This same combination, led by Chapman, proceeded in the following winter to defeat the Australians in Australia by a margin of four tests to one. England thus won seven consecutive tests before yielding to Australia at Melbourne in March 1929.[54]

Australia shortly rebounded from its four straight defeats and so too did the West Indies, who regrouped to square the series against England in the West Indies in 1929–1930. They lost the second test at Port of Spain but won the third at Georgetown and drew the first and fourth. By this time, they had discovered an exceptional talent in George Alphonso Headley, who announced his arrival on the international scene by scoring four test centuries in a single series before reaching the age of 21. It was Headley who saved the West Indies from certain defeat in the last match at Kingston by scoring 223. He established a longstanding West Indian record with an aggregate of 703 runs in a test series. Headley was ably supported by Karl Nunes and Clifford Roach. The former helped to achieve an honourable draw in the fourth test, while the latter covered himself in glory by registering the first century by a West Indian in test cricket and topping that by scoring the first test double century by a West Indian two matches later.[55]

It is interesting to reflect that, while it took South Africa nine chances to win their first test against England, the West Indies succeeded in their sixth attempt. The South Africans won their first series against England after 17 years, while it took the West Indies only 7 as they won the 1934–1935 series by two tests to one. The South Africans did not win their first series against England *in* England until 1935, almost 50 years after having been granted test match status. The West Indies, however, required only 22 years to do so. They easily won the 1950 series in England by three tests to one. These are all positive signs.

On the debit side, the West Indies did not fare as well abroad as most other teams after having been accorded first-class status. Even New Zealand out-performed the West Indians in its first full tour of England and was not humiliated to the same extent in its early encounters with England in test cricket. England managed to defeat New Zealand only three times in their first 18 tests between 1929 and 1949. The New Zealanders succeeded in drawing the other 15.[56] While the West Indies could win only 24, while losing 34 of the 101 first-class matches they played in England between 1923 and 1939,[57] the New Zealanders won 22 and lost only 17 of the 90 first-class matches they played in three tours to England between 1927 and 1937.[58]

Some Conclusions

These results point to the conclusion that the West Indies were not at all superior to New Zealand as a *team* in the 1920s and 1930s. It is highly probable, in fact, that the great New Zealand sides of 1927, 1931 and 1937 would have beaten the West Indies in a test series at that point. While West Indian teams struggled in England in 1923, 1928 and 1933, New Zealand made three successful tours of that country between 1927 and 1937. Apart from Challenor and Headley, the West Indies could not have matched the batting of Blunt, Dempster, Donnelly, Lowry, Mills and Wallace. The New Zealanders also received excellent bowling performances from Blunt, J. A. Cowrie, Dacre and W. E. Merritt.[59] Their attack was much better balanced and their fielding was more reliable, even though they had no individual to compare to the exceptionally gifted Constantine. It is also highly unlikely that the West Indies could have done well against South Africa in those days. When they challenged Australia in 1930–1931, they were easily defeated by four tests to one. They did not, in fact, defeat Australia in any series until 1965. These results make it hard to justify the claim that the West Indies deserved any promotion to test match status any earlier than 1928.

It is impossible to deny that racism and snobbery were at work. But the West Indies confronted the MCC with an intriguing dilemma. While the majority of the West Indian population was black and brown, for many years the majority of the West Indian cricketers were manifestly white. This was the case because of the racist policy adopted by cricket authorities, especially in Barbados and British Guiana. Their laws against the inclusion of 'professionals' allowed them to ignore the claims of all groundsmen and manual labourers. Hence a player like George Francis, for instance, could never participate in first division cricket in Barbados. He was a totally unknown quantity when Austin personally selected him to accompany the West Indians on their tour of England in 1923. Such fine bowlers as Alick Benn, W. T. Burton, C. P. Cumberbatch, George Francis, 'Fitz Lily' Hinds, Oliver Layne and William Shepherd thus represented their native Barbados on a total of 18 occasions all told. Every one of them in the end left Barbados for greener pastures.[60]

These policies and attitudes prevented the West Indies from fielding their strongest teams until at least the 1940s. They were much hamstrung, too, by the practice of choosing only wealthy white cricketers to lead the team. This meant that the West Indies were not always in receipt of the best possible leadership. By all accounts, Austin was a capable captain, and there are many who still sing the praises of the Grant brothers who led the West Indies during the 1930s (although it is doubtful that they performed any better than Constantine or Headley would have done). But such choices as Nelson Betancourt, Maurice Fernandes, Mervyn Grell, E. L. G. Hoad and R. K. Nunes were dubious to say the least. The leadership qualities of Snuffie Browne, Learie Constantine, Herman Griffith and George Headley were deliberately overlooked and the West Indies consequently suffered from the wilful, absurd and persistent underutilization of their most precious cricket resources.

It can be argued, therefore, that, unlike New Zealand, the West Indies created additional and unnecessary difficulties for themselves. But they were not alone in this kind of behaviour. The Australians were constantly beset by interstate rivalries and vicious conflicts between players and administrators.[61] Relics of the caste system have often made a mockery of selections to represent India and Pakistan. England's treatment of professionals was no whit more humane or enlightened than the West Indian treatment of blacks. If the West Indies had to make compromises between the 'Big Four', England also had to deal with the expectations and demands of 17 first-class counties. If the smaller islands were consistently neglected until the 1960s, smaller counties suffered a similar fate in England. If Caribbean cricket had to cope with serious travel and transportation problems, these paled in comparison with similar difficulties operating in such vast countries as Australia and India.

But there were other basic problems over which the West Indies had little control and it is almost a miracle that they were able to surmount these obstacles in their steady advance to the proverbial 'top of the greasy pole'. If the West Indies were fortunate to have been granted test match status in 1928, they used their good fortune much better than most to become acknowledged champions of the cricket world by 1965. When all of their circumstances are carefully weighed, it is an achievement of epic proportions. Leaving aside any difficulties emanating from the multiracial character of the West Indian population, the leading drawback is still the paucity of men. The total West Indian population is still less than 6 million and is very much smaller than that of all the other test-playing countries, with the exception of New Zealand's (which stands at approximately 3.5 million). It cannot at all compare with the 18 million Australians, the 897 million Indians, 128 million in Pakistan, 41 million in South Africa (of whom 5.5 million are white), 17 million in Sri Lanka, the 58 million in the United Kingdom and the 11 million in Zimbabwe.[62]

Added to this natural shortage of manpower is the equally crippling disadvantage of the absence of mineral and natural resources. The West Indian territories are blessed with fertile soil but are too small to compete on even terms with the great agricultural giants in the western hemisphere such as Brazil, Canada, Mexico and the United States. Apart from a dwindling supply of oil in Trinidad, a small amount of gold in Guyana and a dwindling supply of bauxite in Jamaica, the economic pickings are embarrassingly slim. This has meant a chronic shortage of funds over the years. Caribbean sponsors are not as wealthy as those elsewhere and Caribbean cricket has suffered accordingly. The WICBC has traditionally been hamstrung by lack of money, and this explains a number of curious decisions that it has been compelled to make from time to time. Test teams could not easily be supported even at home and local players had often to be coopted, whatever the level of their skill.

This debilitating state of penury was much in evidence when England toured the West Indies in 1929–1930. The WICBC had no money to select and play the very best cricketers in that test series. It was therefore at the mercy of local organizations which were left with the responsibility of selecting, accommodating and managing the various test teams. Some of the players themselves could not take time off from work to participate in the campaign. The result was that no fewer than 28 players represented the West Indies in the four tests, and a local captain led them on each occasion. While Teddy Hoad, a Barbadian, captained the team at Bridgetown, Nelson Betancourt, a Trinidadian, did so at Port of Spain, Maurice Fernandes, a Guyanese, took charge in Georgetown, and Karl Nunes, a Jamaican, then led the side in Kingston. Such stars as Snuffie Brown, Learie Constantine, George Francis, Herman Griffith, Frank Martin and O. C. 'Tommy' Scott had to miss games either because they could not secure leave from work or because the WICBC had no money to compensate them, or both. Thus, no fewer than six changes had to be made after the West Indies had done reasonably well in the first test and it is not therefore surprising that they lost the second. Seven further changes had to be made to the team for the third test, when the West Indies finally got it right and secured their first test victory. Incredibly, for the vital fourth test at Kingston, only two members of the triumphant Georgetown combination, Headley and Roach, were asked to participate. The Jamaican contingent for this test consisted of Ivan Barrow, Oscar DaCosta, George Gladstone, George Headley, Freddie Martin, Karl Nunes, Clarence Passailague and Tommy Scott. Conspicuously absent were Browne, Constantine, Francis and Derek Sealey, who had all done reasonably well against England when given the chance.[63]

It is more than likely that had the West Indies been able to take their strongest team to England in 1928 and to select their best players at home in 1929–1930, they would have fared immeasurably better than they did. This constant chopping and changing was destined to continue for many years. Even after World War II, when the WICBC had become slightly more stable and authoritative, the West Indies still found it necessary to choose three captains in the test series against England in 1947–1949 and to select 19 players for the four tests although they were outplaying the visitors by a wide margin. Without either of them failing with the ball, five fast bowlers (Hines Johnson, Prior Jones, Esmond Kentish, Lance Pierre and John Trim) appeared in one test each. This was also the unhappy fate of Andrew Ganteaume, the dapper little Trinidadian opening batsman, who scored 112 in his solitary test innings.[64]

If the policy of constant tinkering had its roots in chronic penury, it was also related to the absence of regular, annual, intercolonial competition on a structured basis. England's players had long become accustomed to a surfeit of county cricket; Australians had been involved in their Sheffield Shield competition since 1892; the South Africans had competed for the Currie Cup since 1889; New Zealanders all knew, since 1921, what it took to win the Plunket Shield; the Indians had been competing for the Ranji Trophy since 1934; and Pakistan began its Quaid-E-Azam Trophy competition in 1953. Whatever the standard of play, these competitions taught cricketers how to play at the first-class level for several days on end and the situation was thus very much different from club matches played casually on weekends. The West Indies did not establish an annual territorial competition until 1965.

Before the introduction of the Shell Shield during the age of Independence, West Indians did not generally know their players. There was simply not enough first-class cricket in the region. Even a relatively modern test player like Tony White, an automatic choice for Barbados between 1958 and 1966, played only 18 matches for the island in those eight years.[65] As a result, White was not well known in the rest of the Caribbean. The same was true of another test cricketer, Easton McMorris of Jamaica. When he was selected to represent the West Indies against England in the Bridgetown test in January 1960, it was the first time that he was being seen by many Barbadians. Already upset by the omission of their own Cammie Smith from the team, they never understood how anyone could be so stupid as to be run out off a no-ball for nought in an important test match. So they booed McMorris relentlessly and dismissed him contemptuously as the 'Strokeless Wonder'. This was the same batsman who had for years delighted Jamaican crowds with attractive strokes and ended up with almost 6,000 first-class runs at more than 42 per innings.[66] Nor had Jamaican crowds seen enough of Denis Atkinson, the Barbadian all-rounder, to appreciate his enormous skills. They regarded him as a highly overrated cricketer, owing his place on the team to the simple fact that he was white. They never understood how it was possible for such a bad player to perform so brilliantly against the Australians at Bridgetown in 1955.

When Jack Holt the Younger was representing the West Indies at Bridgetown against England in 1954, the Barbadians had never really seen him in action. They doubted very much whether he could bat as well as some of their local openers, like Conrad Hunte, Noel 'Brickie' Lucas and Cammie Smith. His fielding was so sloppy that some of the spectators booed him mercilessly. Their jeers were transformed into mighty cheers when, in the second innings, Holt suddenly unleashed a dazzling array of sparkling strokes in one of the finest pieces of batsmanship ever witnessed at Kensington.[67] It took one remarkable performance for Holt to vindicate himself in the eyes of a critical (and sceptical) Barbadian public.

The lack of regular first-class cricket in the region therefore meant that local jealousies were more common than they are now. The better players did not have the experience of the constant grind that is first-class cricket and consequently lost their focus and their concentration at vital times. The lack of first-class practice let them down in their catching and fielding and for many years, Constantine and Headley apart, the West Indies were notorious for giving too little support to their bowlers. The bowling generally was good, with the West Indies producing a healthy succession of fast bowlers, though failing to spawn any outstanding spinners of exceptional merit before the advent of Lance Gibbs, Sonny Ramadhin and Alfred Valentine in the 1950s. The constant preparation of hard, easy-paced strips in the Caribbean apparently militated against the production of first-class spin bowlers and it was, in fact, this paucity of spin bowlers that often let their own batsmen down when they eventually had to face slow bowlers of Tich Freeman's class. It is not accidental that Freeman never performed so well in test cricket as he did against the West Indies in 1928. In three tests against them that year, he took 22 wickets at less than 13 runs apiece. Against South Africa in 1929, he captured 22 wickets in two tests, but was then put to the sword in the third. In 12 tests altogether, he claimed 66 wickets at an average of almost 26 runs each. Against the Australians, who were much more patient and experienced, the great Freeman accomplished precious little.[68]

It was not only against the spinners that West Indian batsmanship faltered prior to the 1960s. As it was based entirely on the requirement of club cricket, with an emphasis on quick scoring, Caribbean batsmanship developed the quality to which the epithet 'calypso' came to be applied. While this approach was occasionally effective in county matches, as Snuffie and Constantine so frequently demonstrated, it was inappropriate for test cricket, at which both Snuffie and Constantine so signally failed. When Headley was being regarded as the 'Atlas' of the Caribbean, the essential difference between him and most of his teammates lay in desire and approach. Headley had a healthy hunger for runs and did not like to surrender his wicket cheaply, whatever the circumstances. He understood the basic truth, in first-class cricket, that effective occupation is almost as important as violent conquest. Others wanted to get on with the game and gave up far too easily when they were pinned down by steady and persistent bowling. Thus, in several test matches, Headley's partners scored 20–30 runs, lost their concentration, and succumbed. Players accustomed to the rigour of first-class cricket would never have done so.

This important point is demonstrated with crystal clarity by the experience of Learie Constantine. Here was one of the most skilled and flamboyant players of his, or any generation. This was recognized by many club managers in the Lancashire Cricket League, who were willing to offer Learie a more lucrative contract than to anyone else, even including the celebrated Don Bradman of

Australia.[69] He had the capacity to win any club match on his own and to defeat many a county without the assistance of any of his colleagues. But his approach to test cricket was fundamentally wrong. The sad result is that, in his 18 tests for the West Indies, he scored a paltry 635 runs at an average of 29.24 runs per innings. Statistically, the record shows that Constantine was an inferior performer at the test match level to much less gifted batsmen such as Denis Atkinson, Keith Boyce, David Holford and Collis King. As this oddity cannot be explained simply in terms of technique and temperament, one has to conclude that the answer lies in *approach* and *experience.*

There is another consideration, to which Constantine has drawn attention. He himself wanted to play attractive cricket, throughout the summer of 1928, to ensure that the gate receipts were not disappointing. He was aware that Alty O'Dowd, a wealthy Guyanese cricket fan, had undertaken to finance the West Indian tour and he did not wish that benefactor to lose his shirt because of dull play on the part of the tourists. Hence his own determination to 'hit against the clock [and to] skittle wickets down'. The irony here, of course, is that suicidal cricket to save O'Dowd from financial loss almost ruined the entire tour.[70]

As late as the 1950s, still lacking the experience and the practice that regular first-class cricket would have provided, many of the best West Indian batsmen came to grief in important test matches. When, for instance, the world championship was at stake during the unhappy tour of Australia in 1951–1952, all of the four losses could have been avoided had the West Indians adopted a test match, rather than a Saturday afternoon, approach to batting and fielding. It cannot be denied that such crucial factors as a disastrous itinerary, internal discord and incompetent leadership contributed to the negative results. But even these handicaps would not have prevented the West Indies from winning that series had their batsmen done justice to their obvious potential.

At Brisbane, in the first test, it is significant that six of the tourists exceeded 20 runs in their first innings, but none stayed long enough to complete a half-century and the West Indies were all bowled out for 216 with only Alan Rae and Clyde Walcott having failed on what everyone agreed was a batsman's wicket. Not a single partnership yielded 50 runs, although John Goddard scored 45, Frank Worrell 37, Everton Weekes 35, Roy Marshall 28 and Gerry Gomez 22. If any one of these batsmen had shown a determination to occupy the crease, the West Indies would easily have accomplished a first innings lead. In their second attempt, five batsmen achieved at least 20 runs; Weekes struck a brilliant 70, Gomez a defiant 55 and Marshall a promising 30, but the West Indies could only manage 245 altogether. Had Weekes been patient enough to complete his century, or had Marshall been less anxious to score at breakneck speed, the visitors would have placed the match beyond Australia's reach. They lost that low-scoring contest by 3 wickets and still could have won it had they accepted the many chances provided by the wizardry of Sonny Ramadhin and Alfred Valentine.[71]

When the West Indies lost the second test of that series at Sydney, the pattern was distressingly similar. Rae (170), Jeffrey Stollmeyer (36), Worrell (64), Walcott (60), Robert Christiani (76), Gomez (54) and Goddard (33) all settled down and looked very comfortable. Yet each of them suddenly and inexplicably lost his way and fell for 362 on a wicket that was a batsman's paradise. In the second innings, six players scored 20 runs or better; Weekes (56) and Goddard (57) collared the bowling but the final tally still fell ten short of 300 and the West Indies lost again, this time by 7 wickets, having suffered from impatient batting, incompetent fielding and deplorable catching.[72]

These scores and results should never be dismissed as mere details or cricket trivia. They are, in fact, enormously instructive. They tell us very little about so-called calypso cricket, even though the Caribbean batsmen had all demonstrated an abundance of beautiful strokes. They speak eloquently to the matter of *approach* and *experience*. It is highly unlikely that that same team, opposing the same Australians in 1990 would have lost any of those matches at all. It is not enough simply to say that batsmen the stamp of Christiani, Goddard, Gomez, Marshall, Rae, Stollmeyer, Walcott, Weekes and Worrell were all defective in either temperament or technique, or both. The more telling consideration is that their background, their training and their instincts were not in keeping with the demands of a five-day test match.

When, with the help of such sponsors as Benson & Hedges, Shell Oil and the Barbados American Tobacco (BAT) group of companies, the West Indies were finally able to escape from total pennilessness, cricket in the region became less and less dependent on the generosity of such private patrons as Alty O'Dowd. This allowed the players to focus more and more on results rather than style and to match all other cricketers in the area of clinical proficiency. Within 15 years of the introduction of the Shell Shield in 1965–1966, the West Indies had become the dominant force in international cricket. They have remained so to this day. Regular competition has drawn all of the islands into the WICBC fold and the talent pool from which to draw is thus much greater than it once was. There is no longer a need for the quota system, as the players are well enough known throughout the region. It was impossible for Brian Lara in 1990 to spring suddenly out of nowhere into superstardom as Sonny Ramadhin had so spectacularly done in 1950. Had Atkinson been playing for Barbados now, or McMorris for Jamaica, it is highly unlikely that they would be regarded as unknown quantities beyond the islands of their birth. The Caribbean press and electronic media are all involved in the coverage of Red Stripe matches, one-day regionals, and even youth cricket. By the time a good player reaches the age of 20, he is already a regional star. By that time, too, he is well enough known outside of the Caribbean to attract the attention of English counties and South African provinces.

What the West Indies lacked, then, was the opportunity to play first-class cricket in the region on an annual basis. They lacked the resources to put their strongest combinations on the field either at home or abroad. They lacked the will and the wisdom to abandon the policy of white captaincy before 1960. When these defects were eliminated, the intensity and enthusiasm with which the West Indians played their cricket allowed them to do much more than merely justify their elevation to test match status.

Notes

1 Keith A. P. Sandiford, *Cricket and the Victorians* (Aldershot, 1994).

2 Alan Metcalfe, *Canada Learns to Play: The Emergence of Organized Sport,1807–1914* (Toronto, 1987), 47–98.

3 Roy Webber, *The Australians in England* (London, 1953), 11, 19, 25, 32.

4 James Gibbs, *Test Records from 1877* (London, 1979), 9–10. Arthur Wrigley, *The Book of Test Cricket* (London, 1965), 11–31.

5 "Aboriginals at cricket", *Australian Cricket Journal* (April 1987). Pat Mullins and Philip Derriman, *Bat and Pad: Writings on Australian Cricket 1804–1984* (Oxford, 1984), 206–11.

6 Webber, 15.

7 Peter Wynne-Thomas, *England on Tour* (London, 1982), 29–30.

8 Wynne-Thomas, 33–34, 38–39, 45–46.

9 Wrigley, 204–11.

10 Wrigley, 212–16.

11 Louis Duffus, Michael Owen-Smith and André Ordenal, "South Africa", in E. W. Swanton, ed, *Barclays World of Cricket* (London, 1986), 114.

12 T. P. McLean, "New Zealand", in Swanton, ed, *Barclays World of Cricket*, 99.

13 Wynne-Thomas, 50.

14 T. P. McLean, 100.

15 *Wisden 1957*, 829–30.

16 *Wisden 1994*, 195.

17 McLean, 101.

18 Richard Cashman, Patrons, Players and the Crowd: The Phenomenon of Indian Cricket (New Delhi, 1980), 1–2.

19 Wynne-Thomas, 30–31.

20 Wynne-Thomas, 34–35, 51.

21 Philip Bailey, Philip Thorn and Peter Wynne-Thomas, *Who's Who of Cricketers* (London, 1984), 837.

22 R. A. Roberts and D. J. Rutnager, "India", in Swanton, ed, *Barclays World of Cricket*, 87–88. Saradindu Sanyal, *40 Years of Test Cricket: India vs England* (Delhi, 1974), 2–3.

23 Sanyal, 6–9. Roberts and Rutnager, 88.

24 Wynne-Thomas, 37–38, 39–42 , 53–54.

25 *Athletic News*, 25 June 1900, 1.

26 Keith A. P. Sandiford, "Amateurs and professionals in Victorian county cricket", *Albion* (Spring, 1983), 15: 32–61.

27 Bruce Hamilton, *Cricket in Barbados* (Bridgetown, 1947), 43–44.

28 Gerry Cotter, *England versus West Indies* (London, 1991), 9.

29 Christopher Nicole, *West Indian Cricket* (London, 1957), 28. See also Wynne-Thomas, 40.

30 Cotter, 12–14; Wynne-Thomas, 41–42.

31 *Barbados Advocate*, 1 February 1898, 6–7. Hamilton, 56.

32 Wynne-Thomas, 37, 66.

33 Nicole, 34.

34 Nicole, 34–39.

35 Cotter, 17; Michael Manley, *A History of West Indies Cricket* (London, 1988), 22.

36 Hamilton, 74.

37 Wynne-Thomas, 53–54.

38 Nicole, 51.

39 Cotter, 24–26; Hamilton, 92; Nicole, 53–54; Wynne-Thomas, 61–62.

40 Cotter, 26–28; Hamilton, 93–94; Nicole, 54–55; Wynne-Thomas, 65–66.

41 Wynne-Thomas, 76–77.

42 Nicole, 58.

43 It is true that the Antiguans had established their Cricket Association as early as 1897, but for many years to come the game was not as efficiently organized in that island as it was in the so-called Big Four Caribbean colonies. Even more important perhaps was the absence of a powerful sugar plantocracy in the smaller islands. The white elite in the larger territories did not generally regard the social leaders in the 'small islands' as their equals.

44 C. L. R. James, *Beyond a Boundary* (London, 1964), 73–74.

45 Manley, 24.

46 Benny Green, ed, *The Wisden Book of Obituaries* (London, 1986), 152–53.

47 Nicole, 71–72; Wynne-Thomas, 80–81.

48 Cotter, 35; Manley, 24.

49 Peter D. B. Short, "A brief history of the foundation of the West Indies Cricket Board of Control" (unpublished paper, Bridgetown, 1972).

50 Tony Cozier, *The West Indies: Fifty Years of Test Cricket* (London, 1978), 4. See also *West Indies Cricket Annual 1980* (Bridgetown, 1980), 20.

51 Wrigley, 298.

52 Wrigley, 299.

53 Wrigley, 300.

54 Gibbs, 24–25.

55 Cotter, 48–50.

56 Wrigley, 343–60.

57 Hamilton, 107, 125, 133, 146; Nicole, 62, 80, 105, 127.

58 *Playfair Cricket Annual 1949*, 24.

59 McLean, 100–101.

60 Philip Thorn, *Barbados Cricketers 1865–1900* (Nottingham, 1991), 21–29.

61 Chris Harte, *A History of Australian Cricket* (London, 1993), passim.

62 Approximate statistics gleaned from "The nations of the world", in the 1994 Britannica Book of the Year, 546–755.

63 Cozier, 8–10; Wrigley, 302–4.
64 Wrigley, 315–18.
65 Thorn, 30.
66 Bailey, Thorn and Wynne-Thomas, 657.
67 Cozier, 32.
68 David Lemmon, *'Tich' Freeman and the Decline of the Leg-break Bowler* (London, 1982), 81–82, 104, 138; Wrigley, 250–52.
69 Learie Constantine, *Cricket in the Sun* (London, n.d.), 65.
70 Constantine, 32.
71 Harold Dale, *Cricket Crusaders* (London, 1953), 34–73. See also *Wisden 1953*, 821–22.
72 Dale, 81–117; *Wisden 1953*, 824–25.

Pan–Africanism, West Indies Cricket, and Viv Richards

Tim Hector

To speak of pan-Africanism and West Indies cricket is to speak of a historical movement which is nearly a century old and of the vast history of cricket in the West Indies, that cultural medium through which West Indian people sought national expression. These two titanic currents produced the great Isaac Vivian Richards, acknowledged the world over as one of the greatest batsmen to grace this great game. To treat these two important forces in the brief amount of time available is nearly an impossible task. But for a West Indian who had to recreate himself or herself out of the African past, and the European crucible of sub-jugation in which we were forged, the impossible has become commonplace.

Indeed, I would want to suggest to you that the two forces have been decisive in the making of the English speaking Caribbean people: pan-Africanism and cricket.

The poet often compresses for us, in language unique and profound, the most complex historical situation, making the most complex readily comprehensible, using both an economy of time and space. It is best, therefore, for me to begin with the poet laureate of the region and the world, the Nobel prize-winning Derek Walcott. Writing in his not so well-known poem "Air", Walcott penned these lines:

> but only the rusting cries
> of a rainbird, like a hoarse
> warrior summoning his race
> from vaporous air,

> between this mountain ridge
> and the vague sea,
> where the lost exodus
> of corials sunk without trace,
> there is too much nothing here.

The last line "there is too much nothing here", powerful as ever, is not negative, nor is it a trenchant observation like that of, say, Vidia Naipaul, a great Caribbean writer of world stature, who often forces us to see the negative in our historical situation, requiring us to deal with it. Derek Walcott's great line, "there is too much nothing here" speaks to the peculiar and particular condition of the West Indian or Caribbean people, whichever one you prefer. We alone, of all people in human history, had to invent ourselves as a people, as a nation. We had to put our own stamp on their language, their economic and political structures, their literature, their fashions, their cricket, and make them our own and distinctly so. The distinction is the thing.

Produced by slavery and the racism which sprang from it, made and kept inferior, with that inferiority enforced by law and the power of internal and international force, we in the Caribbean had to, as a matter of necessity, in the words of the poet, summon a race between the mountain ridge and the vague sea, to rise, rise, rise in politics and culture, to overcome this long dark night of suppression and subordination. In particular, to overcome the self-contempt which indoctrination as to our own inferiority had left in us.

In politics then we had first of all to overcome the notion that Africa was without history and therefore without civilization. And that as sons and daughters of Africa we were somehow subhuman, forever doomed to be the world's carriers of water and hewers of wood, controlling nothing and administering less. The emancipation of Africa was a prerequisite to our own emancipation in the Caribbean, therefore, pan-Africanism.

Pan-Africanism was the politics, cricket was the vehicle of culture that we in these parts used to propel us, upward and forward. It is one of the great epics of world history, in an age without epics.

It is meet and just that I should call one of the great leaders of pan-Africanism, perhaps the greatest, W. E. B. DuBois, to define pan-Africanism succinctly, as he does in one of the great historical works of all time, *Black Reconstruction*:

> The Black man knows his fight here is a fight to the finish. Either he dies or he wins. If he wins, it will be by no subterfuge or evasion or amalgamation. He will enter modern civilization . . . as a black man on terms of *perfect and unlimited equality* or he will enter not at all. Either extermination, root and branch, or absolute equality. There can be no compromise.

Sir Shridath Ramphal and Sir Alister McIntyre meeting the Vice Chancellor's XI at Sabina Park, Jamaica, 1996.

Not by guile, subterfuge or evasion, but by clear and uncompromising effort and struggle, the black person would enter modern civilization on terms of absolute equality, or *world civilization itself* in its effort at domination, subordination and extermination, would bring about its own downfall in absolute ruin. Either absolute ruin or absolute equality. That is what pan-Africanism is all about. What else could explain the great Marcus Garvey, the first and foremost pan-African who sired sons and heirs such as Malcolm X and Martin Luther King, Kwame Nkrumah and Nelson Mandela, to name a few, who have had such decisive and definitive effect on the history of the world, in the ongoing struggle for human equality, economic and social, racial and political equality.

How else can we explain the great George Padmore, a West Indian, hailed and acclaimed as the father of African Emancipation, who from the first freed colony in Africa, Ghana, in 1957, organized the freedom fighters in the whole of Africa, including Nelson Mandela, with arms and ideas, and mobilized an entire continent against the imperial powers who boasted that the sun would never set on their empires. Padmore therefore altered human history for the supreme good of human freedom and the beginning of a truly human history, in the end free from race, gender and class domination. Padmore has few equals or rivals in the history of the twentieth century.

How else can we explain the great Frantz Fanon and C. L. R. James, both West Indians. One from the French-speaking Caribbean, contributing to freedom in Africa, the other a man in whom pan-Africanism, world revolution and cricket meet in an indivisible unity, or trinity, if you prefer.

But let us turn to cricket as part of the West Indian struggle for equality and, therefore, humanity.

If anyone had told Dr W. G. Grace, England's supreme gift to cricket, that the great grandson of a slave on a West Indian plantation would one day be the president of what he knew to be the Imperial Cricket Conference, Dr Grace would have responded with "was the hope drunk in which it dressed itself". But everywhere imperialism is collapsing and a new order painfully being born, Imperial Cricket Conference inclusive.

If anyone had told me in 1985, a mere ten years ago, that a West Indian cricketer from a tiny island would become the president of the International Cricket Conference (ICC), and that he would be dubbed Sir Clyde Walcott, I might have said not yet, and the wish was the father of that thought. Yet it is today a fact. Sir Clyde Walcott heads the ICC, succeeding a man, Sir Colin Cowdrey, born to the purple of privilege and power: Eton, Cambridge and the corporate halls of world financial power. Needless to say, Sir Clyde's elevation is due as much to his own gifts, as to the relentless struggle for equality waged on the cricket fields of the West Indies, and by the West Indies team wherever cricket is played. The pre-eminence of the West Indian team today – unbeaten for so long – a record not likely to be equalled by any other cricketing nation and resulting in Sir Clyde Walcott's elevation, is most significant.

It means that we have not only mastered cricket and made it our own means of national expression, but off the field in the international administration of cricket, we are pivotal. This is most striking. For we are people who for centuries were denied administering anything, and who had control over nothing, there being 'too much nothing here'. We have now gone from the bottom to the very top in the administration of cricket, internationally. Clyde Walcott's own deep-seated sense of equality, forged on the cricket field, mark you, will carry the struggle for human equality to higher heights.

Let us look for a moment at our cricket beginnings. Evidence shows that it was British officers stationed in the West Indies, in the sea-faring battles over empire and between empires in the nineteenth century, who played a role in the introduction of cricket in the West Indies, more so after the battle of Waterloo. No doubt the planters' sons batted with their slaves or ex-slaves as bowlers, in another peculiar division of sporting labour. The secondary schools came later, reinforcing Thomas Arnold's conception of games, following Plato's dictum that cricket instilled virtue without it being taught.

In 1842, the first known cricket club in the West Indies was formed, in of all places, my own West Indian parish of Antigua, which parish was for a long time excluded from the playing fields of West Indian cricket. Andy Roberts and Vivian Richards would right history, in the quest for equality through cricket.

We know too, that an English cricket team toured the Caribbean in 1895, playing at Antigua where eight of eleven who represented Antigua were black. The sons of planters in Antigua did not stay to be educated there, but were sent to England. This probably accounts for limited white representation, and perhaps accounts for why Antigua, the Leewards and indeed the Windwards were for so long kept out of white administered West Indian cricket. The planter class was for a long time now unable to represent itself on the playing fields of the Leewards and Windwards, and since they could not be looked upon as providing white cricketers for West Indies teams, little or no heed was paid to them.

But we will not tarry here now. The first intercolonial cricket match in the West Indies took place in 1846, eight years after the abolition of slavery. Up from slavery less than a decade, we were travelling very fast and far – in cricket.

The first cricket team from the West Indies to tour abroad did so in 1864. It was not, as you would expect, to England, but to the USA, in a response to the growing commerce between the USA and the West Indies. This West Indian side, made up of players from Barbados and Guyana, played in Philadelphia, where they were beaten, winning only one of the five games played in the series. The USA thus has a most distinguished cricket record.

Cricket and pan-Africanism met overtly in the 1895 English tour of the West Indies under Slade Lucas, giving a stimulus to Marcus Garvey, who followed cricket throughout his life, and more importantly to the author of *Froudacity*, J. J. Thomas who challenged the racism of Froude, one of the pinnacles of English civilization. Thomas thought that the 1895 cricket victories of the West Indies were proof positive "that we were as good as they, the more privileged, and we proved as good in all facets of the game". Cricket was proof of our equality when all else determined by power, economics and politics showed otherwise. At any rate, it was so to J. J. Thomas, the earliest of the pan-African writers and thinkers from the West Indies.

After that, the West Indies toured England in 1923, under the famed George Challenor, a white Barbadian, who made eight centuries on the tour, with an aggregate of 1,556 runs at an average of 57.86. Incidentally, Challenor placed ahead of the great (Sir) Jack Hobbs in the 1923 averages, as well as above the famous Herbert Sutcliffe and Frank Woolley. G. N. Francis, a Barbadian fast bowler, headed the West Indies bowling averages with 82 wickets at 15.58 each.

He was the first of the great West Indian fast bowlers. The pace bowling and fielding of the 22-year-old Learie Constantine was notable on the 1923 tour, as was his father's batting on the 1900 tour, scoring the first century on English soil against Middlesex.

At the end of the 1923 tour, the English authorities of cricket in MCC declared the West Indies not just ready for full internal self-government in cricket, but for full independence in a regional body, as an independent test playing country.

This must have had no small effect on C. L. R. James, then 22, who was to write one of the great anticolonial tracts, *The Case for West Indian Self-Government* in 1932, 30 years before a single West Indian territory had become independent! C. L. R. James and cricket were way ahead of West Indian politics, then and now. The same C. L. R. James was to write the first *History of the Pan African Revolt* in 1934. The same C. L. R. James was to write the history of the only successful slave revolt in all world history, which took place in Haiti in 1804. James in 1938 wrote this magnificent historical work, *Black Jacobins*, as the book itself says, in the cause of African freedom. James was among a small few who thought in terms of African freedom. It is therefore not accidental that the same doyen of twentieth century thinkers is also the doyen of cricket writers. In C. L. R. James, the pan-African struggle and the international struggle combine with cricket in one world historical figure.

Here is James, writing on 18 April 1933, in the *Manchester Guardian* of the first of the great West Indian batsmen, George Headley:

> He is a Negro, finely built but short and small, and only a careful judge of physique would notice him in a crowd. *But at the wicket no one can miss his mastery.* He is that type which uses a bat as if it is an extension of the arm. Ease, poise and balance, he has them all. Good as his footwork is for defensive play, it is even better in the way he makes ground to the ball.

In the same piece of 1933, James concludes with this about Headley:

> In Australia (1932–1933) he failed to get runs against Grimmett. 'I have to make a century against Grimmett' he told his friend St Hill. Batting very carefully he made it in the third test. 'Satisfied?' asked St Hill. 'Not yet. I have to master him now.' In the fifth test Headley made another century in a little over two hours, playing so brilliantly that even Bradman, Kippax and the rest joined in the applause. 'Satisfied?' asked St Hill. 'Ye-es,' said Headley hesitatingly. He had been brilliant but it galled him that he had to treat Grimmett with some respect. It is the genuine artistic instinct faithful to an inner ideal.

But Headley's determination to master Grimmett was part and parcel of the pan-African ideal of absolute equality. Headley's instinct was most faithful to that ideal and its realization.

The declaration of cricket independence for West Indies cricket in 1928, with independent test status, more than made the case for West Indian independence. But arch-conservative opinion in cricket as in West Indian society at large still held the region. The cricket captaincy had to be white, as were the commercial, industrial and legislative leadership in West Indian society.

Even independence in cricket came in neocolonial garb. The MCC, then the rulers of world cricket, sent one of their most experienced committee men, R. H. Mallet, to guide the West Indies on its independent course in cricket. R. H. Mallet not only advised on the formation of the WICBC established along the lines of the MCC, but himself attended the first meeting of the WICBC at its inauguration in 1926.

Incidentally, as Michael Manley in his very fine *History of West Indies Cricket* noted, it was the same R. H. Mallet from England who served as the manager of the West Indies team on its first two test tours to England in 1928 and Australia in 1930–1931. Thereafter, we managed ourselves.

Needless to say, the management and leadership of West Indies cricket continued to be pro-colonial in its sentiments, character and behaviour. H. B. G. Austin, rightly considered the father of West Indies cricket, and its first test captain, was openly pro-colonial in his sentiments. It would be embarrassing to quote him. It is far better to put this in a larger context of the social milieu in which cricket was played and administered in the West Indies at the time, because it is dangerous to judge the 1930s with the eyes of the 1990s.

C. L. R. James, in his justly celebrated magnum opus, *Beyond a Boundary*, explains the social and political context this way:

> . . . our (school) masters, our curriculum, our code of morals, *everything*, began on the basis that Britain was the source of all light and leading, and our business was to admire, wonder, imitate, learn: our criterion of success was to have succeeded in approaching that distant ideal – to attain it was of course impossible. But masters and boys accepted it as in the very nature of things.

"In the nature of things" is a wonderfully apt phrase from a fine passage. The phrase reminds us that the West Indies was *born* in colonialism, the *only* place in the world where that is true, and that the colonial way of seeing and being was the only way of seeing and being, there being no native civilization on which to rely, there being in consequence 'too much nothing here'. At first we would 'admire, wonder, imitate, learn'. Eventually we would come into our own. Becoming is the thing.

The great western philosopher G. W. F. Hegel, in a great discovery of philosophic thought, discovered that it is by 'making the thing' that the slave becomes conscious of himself as being *other* than the master. And then it is by fighting it out with the master that he or she comes into full self-consciousness, or an awareness of himself as a distinctly separate being, and as a result demands freedom.

I am sure you can take a difficult passage from Hegel because it is impossible to divorce philosophy from life, and cricket is a part of life, if not a way of life. That passage is this. Hegel said: "The truth is the whole. The whole, however, is merely the essential nature reaching its completeness through the process of its own development." We are then embarked on a course to see how the ex-slave, through cricket, through actually playing it, 'making the thing', became aware of its racism, its colonial assumptions of superiority and inferiority, and rejected it in favour of equality and liberation, that is to say, the pan-African ideals. Therefore, we are embarked on a course to see how through cricket, West Indian people find their own 'essential nature' and how, "through the process of (our) development" we find identity or completeness – that is, the truth of our own nature – through our national self-expression in cricket.

In a most remarkable essay, contained in a collection of essays, *An Area of Conquest*, Trevor G. Marshall points out one of those authentic and signifying moments in West Indies cricket, 'in the process of' our own development, our own becoming, or, better put, becoming our own, seeking full expression of the national personality in cricket. Marshall writes:

> Mitchie Hewitt's formation of the Barbados Cricket League (BCL), in 1936–37, can be seen as a magnificent attempt at 'revolution from below', because 'Mitchie' not only created an islandwide structure enabling such hidden talent to gain visibility, but he went further, by creating the opportunity for other persons to gain experience with the theory and practice of leadership, at the club and parochial level.

This is one of the grand moments in Caribbean history, not just its social history, but history, for the Barbados example reproduced itself throughout the cricketing Caribbean. Through cricket, the ordinary people could get a sense of participation in an "islandwide structure". More importantly, they could administer and lead themselves in their own self-organization, their club or village team. It is not only the democratization of cricket, challenging the elitism which R. H. Mallet brought with him from the elitist MCC. It is democratization of a society that was rigidly authoritarian, by creating leadership from below. In time that leadership 'from below' would challenge leadership from above on and off the cricket field, for the liberation which pan-Africanism sought on the continent and in the black diaspora.

Two things need to be noted. Mitchie Hewitt was bringing the struggle for equality on the cricket fields, creating 'a revolution from below', in 1936–1937. The date is important. For at the very same time that Mitchie Hewitt was creating this 'revolution from below' in cricket, West Indian society itself exploded, in 1937–1938. Up and down the Caribbean, a 'revolution from below' tried to displace colonial authoritarian rule from above. The revolution in cricket succeeded. The nationalist upsurge of 1937–1938 failed as did West Indian Federation. All in fragmentation ends. That failure reverberates throughout the Caribbean as petty nationalism, in greater subordination to external control, thought and direction, independence or no independence. Cricket is the exception. Cricket, in fact, negates our political fragmentation.

But any revolution, in any sphere of human activity, such as the one Mitchie Hewitt led, must of necessity produce its great personage. That great cricketing personage was Herman Griffith. Again Trevor Marshall supplies the essential character sketch of this West Indian figure, who deserves to be the subject of a book. So does Mitchie Hewitt. West Indian historiography ignores both to its own peril. But this is not the place to expand on that. Here is Trevor Marshall on Herman Griffith:

> It was he – Herman Griffith – who between 1913 and 1944 was Barbados' major exponent of the fast bowler's art. He actually played first-class cricket between 1922 and 1935 but continued in the intercolonial games into the 40s, becoming the first black man to captain his island, in 1941 in a Goodwill series in Trinidad.

Continuing, Marshall wrote:

> Griffith gained respect for the black cricketers of ability and fought for the establishment of particular standards in selecting cricket teams and utilizing the skills of talented blacks in the game. He was the first to challenge racial discrimination, the negative self-image, and the unhitherto unchallengeable 'colour bar' . . . His single-handed fight over three decades served to prepare the society for the revolutionary ideas and challenges of Frank Worrell in the 1950s.

Hegel would have said that Herman Griffith embodied "the seriousness, the suffering, the patience and the labour" which confronted the negative, namely, "the discrimination", "the unchallengeable colour bar" and "the negative self-image" of blacks. Griffith, in short, embodied the pan-African ideal. Cricket was his battle ground.

Herman Griffith bowling the great Don Bradman for a duck in the fifth test in 1930–1931, no doubt had the same effect on the consciousness of people in the Caribbean, as had the Headley century in that same test. The latter had mastered the best – Grimmett. The former, Herman Griffith, had bowled down the best, Bradman. And both had struck a decisive blow against the negative self-image which kept Africans and Indians, as West Indians, from becoming. Not to see Herman Griffith as the cricketing and spiritual father of Viv Richards is simply not to see.

I need only add, in a sort of parenthesis, that in the small islands black captains had emerged long before 1941. Sydney Walling had captained Antigua in Leeward Islands cricket since 1931. I contend that the very emergence of blacks in leadership and in near total representation on cricket teams in the Leewards and Windwards had everything to do with these islands being excluded from intercolonial white-administered cricket and, therefore, from test match cricket. Alfie Roberts, Grayson Shillingford, Irving Shillingford and Mike Findlay would break down that barrier for the Windwards, while Elquemedo Willet, Andy Roberts and Vivian Richards would do so for the Leewards. Alfie Roberts, the first of these, was and is himself a pan-African thinker and activist of great note. Andy Roberts, an all-time great West Indies fast bowler, was the first of the 'country boys' to play for Antigua from the parish league, and was the first West Indian test cricketer to refuse the South African rand, to break the ban on cricket in the land of apartheid. A very fine Antiguan, Mr Ephraim John, had done for Antigua cricket what Mitchie Hewitt had done in Barbados, the Herman Griffith-Mitchie Hewitt revolution in cricket. Pan-Africanism, in essence, was spreading to all parts of the cricketing Caribbean.

Herman Griffith is a historical figure through cricket. Put another way, through cricket he became a historical figure. But when the history of the Caribbean is written as the story of a people trying to find their 'essential nature' and doing so in "the process of [their] own development" and not as the object acted upon by external forces, Herman Griffith, Mitchie Hewitt and Sir Learie Constantine will have a chapter to themselves as cricketers, and at one and the same time as contributors to the mighty current of pan-Africanism.

It is Sir Learie Constantine who was most explicit, the most conscious of the cricketers. The great philosopher Hegel, the founder of the modern dialectic, would have characterized Constantine as a "consciousness [who] comes to find that what formerly to it was the essence [i.e. playing cricket] is not what is per se or what was per se". I am not being difficult by quoting these philosophic passages. For it is these passages that led me to understand both West Indian cricketers and the cricket they played. It is a gross misconception of our time, born from the narrow specialization of our time that cricket is cricket, and philosophy is philosophy and the twain shall never meet.

But now listen to Learie arriving consciously, at this judgement about West Indies cricket. "Cricket in the West Indies", wrote Sir Learie, "is the most glaring example of the black man being kept in his place, *and this is the first thing that will have to change* "(emphasis added). This pan-African consciousness was coming from a West Indian cricketer, about cricket, in the West Indies. It is not external. It is internal. It is the overcoming of traditions within an organism which is the basis of all movement and therefore, all progress. Learie Constantine recognized the essential contradictions in West Indies cricket per se, and as such it was per se. He did not set about to change it directly. Herman Griffith, Mitchie Hewitt, C. L. R. James and Frank Worrell did.

Nor did Sir Learie leave the matter there. He wrote, too: "The heart of our cricket [West Indies cricket] is rotted by racist politics. I only hope that before I die, I see a West Indies cricket team chosen on merit alone, and captained by a black man, win a rubber against England." The statement is as clear as can be, so much so that it is both lucid and pellucid. It is a concentrated expression of the pan-African ideal in West Indies cricket.

It was not just a question of a black captain, it was the equality that Learie wanted – a team chosen on merit alone. It was not just the emancipation from black subservience in cricket that Sir Learie Constantine wanted through black leadership. It was also the overcoming of that English dominance over all aspects of West Indian life, which a people born and bred in colonialism had to overcome in cricket by victory in a rubber over England, and in particular, under black leadership.

In 1950 when the West Indies, led as usual by a white captain, John Goddard, defeated England, with Ramadhin and Valentine, Indian and African integrated in cricket, the batting built on the great batsmen – Weekes, Walcott, Worrell – was but prologue to that great event. Sir Frank Worrell, in 1963 would achieve Sir Learie's pan-African hope, in a most thrilling series, but symbolized by the great Wes Hall bowling all day, off his long run, in a magnificent, perhaps unmatched, feat of athleticism and skill, with Colin Cowdrey, with a broken hand, coming in as the last batsman to save England from defeat. With Worrell, a fine black man, as captain, the West Indies romped over England in the series. A people, in a way, had a new identity. There was the dash and elan of Kanhai, the power and mastery of Sobers, the athleticism and skill of Hall, the uncompromising Griffith deadly serious about his own self-expansion in cricket. And there was Frank Worrell, brilliant and astute, welding the several parts into a whole. Under Worrell the West Indies team was no longer a group of gifted individuals, but a splendid team. It was a homecoming and a new beginning.

There is no need to sum up what Sir Frank Worrell meant to West Indians as the first black captain.

When I grew up in Antigua, most of the cricket *cognoscenti* did not back the West Indies in cricket. They backed any and every team against the West Indies. They ranged from Dr Alfred Blackett, a fine classicist, a man most learned not only in Latin, but in the history of ancient Greece and Rome. Like many another he taught, he left me with an enduring interest in the democracy of ancient Athens. There was too, Stanley 'Mankad' Joseph, a non-established worker; Sammy Davis, a baker; Bertie Gonsalves, played for Antigua, also a baker; as was J. Joshua, as well as 'Weasel' Stevens. There was too Ivan Barrow, a fine cricketer and I think the first to make a century for Antigua in the Leeward Islands cricket tournament. Nearly all that I know about cricket, before 1950, I did not get so much from books, but from these men with whom I was privileged to talk cricket from about age seven. I did not include my grandfather, Sergeant J. E. Hector, who could tell you all of Challenor's scores, and for whom Challenor, Headley and Worrell, all belonged in the same category as Zeus, Jove and Yahweh. He, obviously, backed the West Indies through hell or high water. But all of the other men, who were a library of knowledge about cricket and loved the game above all else, did not back the West Indies. The West Indies did not have a black captain, secondly no 'small-islanders' were on the West Indies team, they therefore could not, would not, and did not, support the West Indies.

In other words, keeping the West Indian captaincy as a fine white preserve, and excluding the small-islanders, made these very fine people into antinationalists. It was a current which ran through most of the small islands and I suspect all of the English-speaking West Indies. I want to suggest to you that these men, and many others, were left in a condition that psychologists call schizophrenia, but which we will call a 'duality'. They relished the performance of Headley, the three W's, Ram and Val, of G. N. Francis, Learie Constantine and Martindale, but they were against the side on which these men played – and for good reason. It was an approach avoidance complex.

Frank Worrell, as captain of the West Indies, in Australia in 1960, returned these men to themselves. It is fair to say that the fact of his captaincy, his strategic and tactical sense, not to speak of his tactile presence, but more so his high sense of conduct on and off the field, made these men truly West Indian for the first time in their lives. I would posit that it did the same for the entire West Indies, as nothing else had done before. Frank Worrell, then, returned a nation to itself.

Pan-Africanism sought to make nations out of colonies, not just in a formal sense of flag and anthem. But, through George Padmore, C. L. R. James,

Du Bois, Frantz Fanon, there is the common theme of how to avoid the pitfalls of national independence, where new nations are really old colonies, only writ larger. Worrell, in the style and content of his leadership and actual play on the field, achieved that genuine national independence in cricket. Worrell went further. When he plumbed for and campaigned for Gary Sobers to succeed him, he was ensuring that the ordinary West Indian rose to the highest heights, by virtue of his ability and in this case extraordinary ability, squared, which is normally described as genius.

But I would be remiss if I did not point out something else of world historical importance, and directly related to pan-Africanism.

As I said before, Padmore belongs to that distinguished group of men, very few in number, who before 1930, worked systematically, patiently, and continuously for African freedom. After all, not a single colony had been freed by 1930. In fact the first was freed in 1947. To most intellectuals the world over, at the time, Padmore, James and so on, were brilliant men, but their idea of African emancipation from colonial thralldom was, at best, a pipe dream, if not downright madness. We now know who had no grasp of reality, historical or political. Obviously then the creators of pan-Africanism were men of unusual foresight, with a firm historical grasp.

Padmore in 1928, headed the Profintern, in Moscow, in charge of all agitation for colonial freedom, with specific reference to Africa. On May Day, he would be on the reviewing stand with Stalin and Molotov. He lived in the Kremlin. He had vast sums of money at his disposal for his political work. He was easily the most important and powerful black figure in the world at the time.

At that time too, the overwhelming majority of intellectuals in the world including Bertrand Russell, Arthur Koestler, George Bernard Shaw, Silone and so on, even the Edmund Wilson of *To the Finland Station*, fed up with the deepening inequities and iniquities of Western society, looked upon the Soviet Union as a new civilization, often excusing its every twist and turn, even the sham of the Moscow trials.

However, in 1934, George Padmore was told that he could no longer direct his great anticolonial work at Britain, France and the United States, because these were the 'democratic imperialists'. But his anticolonial work should be directed at Germany, Italy and Japan, 'the fascist imperialists'. This sudden change of line was made because the Soviet Union under Stalin, was entering into alliances with the 'democratic imperialists' as the world moved towards World War II. Theory and practice changed according to the needs of the Soviet Union. The great Padmore would not put up with that! Socialism, for him, was not the handmaiden of nation states, but the efforts of the international working people.

Padmore at once gave up all his positions in Moscow, returned penniless to England, and there continued his great work for the emancipation of Africa, through the African Service Bureau, arming African colonies with information, ideas, organizational methods, and influencing world opinion by his resolutions on all serious matters arising from or occurring in the colonies. Padmore was indefatigable. There was no anticolonial leader of note who did not meet with Padmore.

Padmore thus made a complete break with Stalinism, seeing its frequent shifts of line as inimical to any kind of socialism and a threat to African freedom.

That this world historical event is not a chapter written in any history of the Caribbean only reminds us of how far West Indian historiography has been turned into its opposite by the Cold War. It is a most decisive event.

I need only say that, had the leaders of the Grenada Revolution (1979–1983) been aware of the experience of Padmore and his historic response, they may not have followed the ways and byways of Stalinism. And the *Fundamentals of Stalinism* by Stalin would not have been a text, let alone a guiding text, of the Grenada Revolution. This distortion and abortion of socialist theory led directly to a bloodbath, prompted from within and aided and abetted by its Jamaican guru from abroad. In sum, the Grenada Revolutionary collapse reminds that we need to return to our own historic and historical experiences, or there will be the persistent inauthenticity in which we all live in this region.

Do not by any means think that this is a digression from pan-Africanism, West Indies cricket and Viv Richards. At the very same time that Clive Lloyd was building the West Indies cricket team into a mighty fortress for our people, in Grenada, the Revolution (which announced itself as the first government in the Caribbean 'to bring the people in', into direct administration of their own affairs, from National Budget to sanitation in the community) jettisoned its own profound objective by casting itself in the mould of the other. It proclaimed 'democratic centralism', a concept which Lenin himself repudiated as inapplicable to any but Russia with its feudalism at one pole, and the advanced capitalism of the Putilov works at the other. When the Grenada Revolution embraced Stalinism, as in the Soviet Union it replaced the Revolution with the Party Class, a self-serving bureaucracy over and above society. In Grenada it came tumbling down, in blood, but with lightning speed.

At the heart of the batting of Lloyd's mighty fortress was the greatest batsman of his time, Isaac Vivian Alexander Richards.

He had come from a small state – Antigua and Barbuda – until 1973 excluded from West Indies test cricket. At 17 he was playing for Antigua, and was the subject of a cricket riot. Here it is not the riot that concerns us, it is that from so early an entire nation saw him, in the immortal words of Jimmy Durante, "as my boy". From the inception of his career, Vivian Richards was the embodiment of the hopes and aspirations of the people of his twin island nation, and he was expected to express the national personality on the world stage. If he was cheated as they thought he was when given out to bat-pad catch off the wiliest leg-break googly ever in these parts, Coury, they were cheated. Hence the invasion of the pitch and their insistence that he must bat again. As he did! I cannot say what influence this had on Viv's career. What I can say, is that he always 'walked' thereafter.

Doubtless, too, no other figure in the history of Antigua and Barbuda, before or since, has enjoyed that symbiotic relationship between the individual and his community.

On that foundation, I can now say that if ancient Greek democracy rated as its significant achievement not the grandeur of its art, architecture, tragic and comic drama, or its military glories under Pericles, but the harmony of the individual with the community, then Viv Richards, in his relation to Antigua and Barbuda, and I believe the West Indies, is the living proof that a new society and, therefore, new possibilities are in the womb of the present decay. Cricket, you will note, is the incubator, if not the cradle, of this new beginning – the harmony of the individual with his community.

I go further: the entire crisis in the world today, with its relentless barbarism in this century in particular that has seen over 187 million slaughtered in war, has as its basis the disharmony between individual and community. Cricket, through Vivian Richards, was showing the alternative to that twentieth century barbarism.

A very fine modern historian, E. B. Hobsbawn, writing on the history of the short twentieth century, *The Age of Extremes 1914-1991*, had this to say:

> Since this century has taught us, and continues to teach us, that human beings can learn to live under the most brutalized and theoretically intolerable conditions, it is not easy to grasp the extent of the *unfortunately accelerating, return* to what our nineteenth century ancestors would have called *the standards of barbarism* [emphasis added].

And again this from one of the finest modern historians writing in English today, the same Hobsbawn, in the same book, writes, that one of the major forces transforming modern life:

> and in some ways the most disturbing, is the *disintegration* of the old patterns of social relationships, and with it, incidentally, the snapping of the links between generations, that is to say, between past and present. This has been particularly evident in the most developed countries of the western version

of capitalism, in which the values of *an absolute a-social individualism* have been *dominant*, both in official and unofficial ideologies, though *those who hold them* often deplore their social consequences [emphasis added].

It is a passage that deserves both study and contemplation. But what is most noteworthy is the "absolute *a-social* individualism" which has become dominant in most developed and least developed societies alike. All that was holy is now profaned, as the break between individual and community produces this exaltation of the standards of barbarism. In consequence, the twentieth century is the bloodiest of all centuries. We are supping deep of horrors.

The contention then that Viv Richards was a departure from the worldwide trend in himself producing a new unity, a new harmony, a new symbiosis between individual and community, is to say in words what he actualized with bat in hand. I have to be economical as "time marches on and in a little while our lips are dumb".

Let me encapsulate Richards at the wicket, for our eyes must be on the ball. Here is Manley writing on Richards in the first test at Nottingham in 1976:

> Indeed the entire match was dominated by the batting of Vivian Richards. He made 232 runs in 7 hours and 18 minutes, in an innings in which restraint alternated with abundant, sometimes almost extravagant, stroke play. Built like a middle weight boxer, with powerful shoulders and arms, Richards on the go will always be remembered as one of the exhilarating sights of cricket. At this point of his career he was twenty-four and hungry for runs with the appetite of a Bradman, a Hammond or a Weekes. If Weekes was a shade more brilliant off the back foot, the young Richards was overpowering on the front foot.

What a portrait! On the go Richards determined the length of bowlers, by back foot play equalled only by the great Everton Weekes, and at the same time, he had no peer on the front foot. Time and time again, he hit the length ball off the back foot, making it difficult for even a great master such as Bishen Bedi or Imran Khan or Dennis Lillee to determine where to pitch.

At this time, remember, cricket, or rather batting, especially in England, had degenerated to front foot prodding with the occasional drive at the rank half-volley. Richards, like Sobers before him, cut through that no-risk, plodding accumulation, bred by the welfare-state, with its no-risk habit of mind.

But above all, as Manley himself was to write, Richards was "not to be dictated to" by any bowler, however fast; by any spinner, Bedi, Venkat or Chandrasekhar, the best of the age. Viv Richards was not to be dictated to. It is the pan-African rejection of dictatorship in all its forms, and a move beyond the totalitarian democracy, which passes for democracy, Westminster or

Congressional style. Perhaps you will demur and say I see too much in too little. But wait.

Perhaps this is best summed up by the finest of all pan-Africanists, with whom, be it noted, Vivian Richards shared the world stage and who was always in his bags on or off tour – Bob Marley. Marley was to express his own spirit and the spirit of Vivian Richards in some memorable, if not immortal, lines in the following:

> Bars could not hold me
> Force could not control me
> Now they try to put me down
> But Jah want I around.

This is how Richards walked out to bat and that is how he batted. That none can dispute. Bob Marley and Viv Richards are inseparable. They are part of a piece, piece of a whole, the struggle for pan-African liberation. Taken together, they are two of its epochal moments and colossal figures. We will explore this further.

The story of Viv Richards, pan-Africanism and West Indies cricket is intimately connected with his own beginning in Antigua and Leewards cricket. It goes back a long way. In 1964 a group of us including Robert Hill, a Jamaican, now a distinguished professor; Dr Hugh O'Neal, a brilliant economist from Grenada, who was to die in his prime; Alfie Roberts of St Vincent, who played for the West Indies in New Zealand in 1955–1956 and a fine pan-African scholar; Rosie Douglas of Dominica; Franklyn Harvey of Grenada; Henderson Simon of Antigua and myself, had formed the Caribbean Conference Committee in Canada. We had tremendous support from some excellent women who did a great deal. We brought speakers and activists from Africa, the USA, Cuba and from across the Caribbean. The great Caribbean figure, George Lamming, was the first guest speaker, at the first conference in 1964, C. L. R. James at the second in 1965, Orlando Patterson at the third and Walter Rodney at the fourth – the now famous Black Writers Conference – in 1968.

However, it is not the conference of 1968 but of 1967 that is of immediate concern here. We made a departure. We not only invited intellectuals, but also that year we invited Gary Sobers and David Holford. Naturally, in the course of discussions, the issue of the exclusion of the Leewards and Windwards from test cricket, and until 1960 from intercolonial cricket, came up. It transpired that all save Alfie Roberts and I were of the view that we small islanders did not have what it took to make it in test cricket. Whatever 'it' was, we just did not have it. I bristled. Smallness it seemed was the bugbear. That I would not abide.

I resolved to do something about it. As chance would have it, on my return to Antigua, a row broke out in the Antigua Cricket Association (ACA) as to whether or not cricket should be played on Sunday. All the old stalwarts, including the great Sydney Walling, one of the finest batsmen produced in the West Indies, arguably the fourth W – Worrell, Weekes, Walcott, Walling – and a most distinguished and principled Antiguan, resigned his position in the Cricket Association. The late Sammy Henry, who himself had led Nevis into the Leeward Islands Tournament, expanding it in 1954, was then secretary of the ACA. He too resigned, as did others.

As the leader of the Young Turks, so to speak, I was elected secretary. The Sunday issue was important not only as theology but as cricket. This imitation of MCC not playing cricket on Sunday was to me 'not cricket' but neo-colonialism. More than that, I had in mind that if cricket was to advance, local cup cricket in Antigua had to move from being played on Thursdays to Saturdays and Sundays. Actually I had in mind three-day matches, played over Thursday (a half-day in Antigua then), Saturday and Sunday. I was out-voted on that. And it became Saturday and Sunday games. That was the first reform.

Another very fine Antiguan, Leo Gore, perhaps the best captain the Leewards ever produced, a great slip-fielder – I have not seen any better – and a batsman of test class in his day, and even then in 1969, holder of the Leeward Islands batting record for the highest individual score (200 not out made in 1957 with the present Prime Minister Lester Bird as his last batting partner), became president of the ACA.

Leo Gore and I determined that to produce a test batsman we would have to change the entire Leeward Islands Tournament. Two-day games were out. Then there were two two-day games, and the winners would play in a final of three days. Then too, the Leeward Islands Tournament was played in a single island with all the teams assembling there.

Our proposed change was that all matches would be of four days' duration and each territory would play all others, providing players in Antigua, Mont-serrat, Nevis, St Kitts, with three four-day games. We were proposing to change an institution, the Leeward Islands Tournament, which was then 56 years old. Certainly the oldest inter-island tournament in the region.

Leo Gore as president and I strategized and he sent me off to the Leewards Cricket Association meeting in Montserrat, in 1970, to secure this reform of the Leeward Islands Tournament. Mr Gore's parting words were "If you do not come back with this reform of the Leeward Islands Tournament, stay in Montserrat. Your mother is from there so they have to accept you." It may sound or read like a joke, but it was not. Leo Gore was deadly serious. A war veteran of World War II, he is a strategist of a high order. As a cricket captain, he was both tough and astute. He had, unbeknownst to me, telephoned every member of the Leeward Islands Association and secured their agreement. Of course, Mr Gore had forgotten that his tremendous prestige in Leeward Islands cricket, and his stature as a man, would make no one in Leeward Islands cricket openly disagree with him on a long distance call. In a meeting, it was an entirely different matter!

Cricket is a conservative institution, invariably run by conservatives. I would need a series of lectures to develop this idea, but accept it as gospel for now. Even though the planters had moved out of cricket administration in the Leewards, the black administrators felt that they had to be as good as their planter predecessors, and, therefore, were no less conservative.

Then there was an even more serious complication. I had returned to Antigua in 1967 and immediately plunged into politics. Immediately after my involvement in the new opposition trade union, the Antigua Workers' Union (AWU), as an executive member, the tempo in politics in Antigua intensified. I edited and wrote the opposition paper – *The Trumpet* – and events culminated in a general strike, state of emergency and resignation of the government on 19 March 1968, the same day as Sobers' famous declaration at Queen's Park Oval, a declaration which I supported then as now.

Dr Eric Williams, writing in his biggest historical tome, *From Columbus to Castro*, dubbed the uprising in 1968 in Antigua as the "first of the Black Power revolts in the region". British and American intelligence agencies dubbed me as "the prime mover behind the scenes" in these events, and circumscribed me as "a dangerous pan-Africanist and communist, a devout follower of Padmore and C. L. R. James", with Garvey thrown in to complete the picture. The point was that Tim Hector, known as a fervid enemy of the Soviet Union, saw it after 1924 as counter-revolution. Besides, describing me as a 'communist' and a devout follower both of Padmore who had made a celebrated and historic break with Soviet Communism, as well as of C. L. R. James, whose *World Revolution* of 1938 was a systematic attack on Soviet Communism and its counter-revolutionary assault on Marxism, was an obvious contradiction in terms. Nevertheless, fiction is stranger than truth more often than not, and this fiction of Tim Hector, the flaming red communist, no doubt given to violence and mayhem, stuck. Perception, I am told, is more real than reality, until reality overtakes it.

I have encapsulated a lot in a little, to make a long story short. The point is the members of the Leeward Islands Cricket Association felt they had to resist me. I was on my best behaviour. I made the case for the change in the Leeward Islands Tournament. I recalled the greats of the Leeward Islands Tournament from Dr Ross, Austin Eddy of St Kitts, through McMahon, and Kingsley Rock of Montserrat down to Len Harris, Hubert Anthonyson, Winston Soanes,

Gilbert, Coury, Gonsalves and Matthews and so on, showing knowledge of the history of Leewards cricket and its players. I even recalled that in 1955 the *Trinidad Guardian* headlined "Earl Michael Candidate for New Zealand". Nothing came of it. I was careful not to be insular, leaving out the contentious. The point was it was the nature of the two-day, sometime one-match-a-year cricket we played which was the biggest impediment to our players in the Leewards, especially batsmen, not getting into test cricket. We were, so to speak, our own worst enemies. No siree, said they. Not I think with reason, but simply resisting change and above all resisting this flaming communist–Black Power–pan- Africanist–radical.

Fortunately, my training had given me some diplomatic skills. Recognizing that I could not win I retreated to second base. I secured an agreement that the proposal would be considered at the next meeting, after study by the individual territories. I retreated too, from the cricket argument, making a new case that it would be good for the economics of Leeward Islands Cricket. With a match in each territory, and in the second year two matches, every territory in the Leewards would be financially viable. I suspect, but cannot prove, that my recognition of the value of money showed a sufficient respect for capitalism. Besides, I did not, like Kruschev at the United Nations, pound the table with my shoe when I could not win the argument. The imposed perception was different to the reality of their experience of me.

Anyway, I did not apply for Montserrat residence, and had to return to Antigua to face Mr Gore. Luckily too, I had got the support of Mr Eugene Walwyn, then the attorney-general of St Kitts and also the representative of Nevis on the Leeward Islands' board. In the break, he had agreed that it was not my personality – which he said was in striking contrast to the propaganda about me – but the propaganda which was responsible for the resistance to reform. He and I agreed that an emergency meeting should be called to discuss the reform (or was it the revolution?) in Leeward Islands Cricket. Astutely Eugene Walwyn piloted this resolution ever so successfully. At least I had got half a loaf to return to Mr Gore, who though furious about the delay thought, to my relief, that I had "achieved the impossible". He even flattered me that I had displayed the "patience of Job" which he would not have done. Mr Gore, gracious as ever, took the lead in congratulating me for my efforts at the next ACA executive meeting. In a while, the emergency Leeward Islands meeting, one of the few in its history, was called. The meeting lasted about half-an-hour – if so long. The apparent conservatives, the president, the late Mr Wade of Wade's Inn in Montserrat and Mr Heyliger, a former St Kitts player and established jeweller, spoke in support of what they called the "Hector Reforms" and Leewards cricket was never to be the same.

Four-day games replaced two-day games, with each island playing three matches each year, allowing the quick runs mentality to be laid to rest. There would be better pitches. And, not least, more money for the development of cricket in each island.

Thus Viv Richards began his career in Leeward Islands cricket, in a new format, allowing for development of an innings, different bowling strategies, and field placings – in a phrase, modern cricket.

Simultaneously and internally in Antigua, cricket was to go through a thorough change. Leo Gore did it, and not me as legend has it. Gore determined that all the old players who represented Antigua had to be dropped. Not that they were not good players, but they were set in the old mould. Antigua fielded a brand new team. All in blazers as official garb. Mr Leo Gore has never admitted it. He said the blazers were a contribution from a 'rich Mill Reefer'. In my own mind, I am certain that this was none other than Leo Gore himself who as usual did not wish to attract attention to himself, and preferred to leave this as one of his little, unremembered acts of kindness and love for cricket.

On top of that Mr Ephraim John had organized the Parish League bringing in players from the rural areas, hitherto excluded, except for the incidental. Leo Gore himself looked more at the Parish League games than at Cup games in Division One cricket. So too did the selector Carlton Roberts, a former Antigua and Leeward Islands player, an architect by profession and a devout pan-Africanist by conviction. They discovered Andy Roberts in the Parish League.

By the first Leeward Islands Tournament in the new format, Leo Gore was certain that Andy Roberts, Elquemedo Willet, Jim Allen, Vernon Edwards, Viv Richards and Gene Gould would all play test cricket. He resigned the presidency of the ACA. To this day I am certain it was because he could not endure the tension of the wait. He expected it in 1972, but it came in 1973 with Willet, then Andy Roberts, then came Vivian Richards. I quit in 1975: mission accomplished.

Lester Bird, the current Prime Minister of Antigua, would regard me as a revisionist if I did not include him in the reform or revolution (take your pick) in Leewards cricket.

During the Rowan Henry, Leo Gore presidencies of the Cricket Association in Antigua, with a view of producing test cricketers I had the new young Antiguan players playing against Trinidad and Barbados teams. Lester Bird as president and I went further: we began to invite English teams. Mike Brearly came as did Underwood with the Mendip Acorns, with Len Creed of Somerset as manager. Lester Bird, the late Danny Livingstone and I persuaded Len Creed to take Viv to Somerset. Creed had preferred Viv's younger brother, Mervyn, who had outclassed him that game.

Both Leo Gore and Lester Bird have together and separately reproached me for allowing the baseless myth to be noised about and even printed in books, that it was Richards and Roberts going to Alf Gover in England that made them. Tony Cozier, meaning well, gave the myth wide credence, when he wrote that Gore retorted that if Alf Gover could produce test cricketers, "England would be the greatest team on earth". Lester Bird felt that once again, the West Indian was ascribing to England (Alf Gover) what we ourselves had accomplished in our own cricket revolution. "We were always denying ourselves," said Lester Bird.

Later and in 1978, Lester and I would part company over both pan-Africanism and cricket. Through *Outlet* I had exposed how Lester as a deputy premier had masterminded Antigua being used as a conduit for nuclear and non-nuclear arms going to the racist Botha government in South Africa. I was then chairman of the Sports Council. There Guy Yearwood, as vice chairman, had organized a Combined School team, which produced Richie Richardson and Eldine Baptiste. I had wanted to organize tours through Barbados, Trinidad and Guyana, starring Enoch Lewis, Richie Richardson, Eldine Baptiste and so on, hoping that success would lure Enoch Lewis, the best Leewards batsman never to have played test cricket, from banking to test cricket. This was not to be. Having exposed the Antigua government's military links with South Africa, I was fired by the government as chairman of the Sports Council. Pan-Africanism and cricket had collided. Lester Bird and I – close, close, friends till then – never spoke to each other from 1977 to 1989. He had negated his own role in the cricket revolution. My plans for youth cricket died on the vine, as with youth football, where as chairman of the Sports Council I had had coaches trained in Mexico. In the words of Derek Walcott, "All in compassion ends / So differently from what the heart arranged."

But I would be greatly remiss too, if on my subject I did not say what part the old Leeward Islands Tournament played in the new players. When the Hesketh Bell Shield was established in 1913, the Leeward Islands Tournament became one of the most passionate arenas of cricket anywhere. The mono-crop sugar did not provide an identity for the people of the Leeward Islands. Bananas for sure, being a small farmer crop, did so in part of the Windwards. Cricket was the source of identity for the Leewards. A final between St Kitts and Antigua had everyone, however wise or ignorant, bursting with enthusiasm. If both St Kitts or Antigua had armies and air forces, the reports of bad umpiring *would*, not could, have led to war. Montserrat felt exalted if it got the better of St Kitts or Antigua. And in time Nevis began to win. All the islanders got a sense of identity and belonging from cricket and the Leeward Islands Tournament in particular.

A Leeward Islands Tournament brought out the island in all its social variations. Arabs, from Lebanon or Syria, who knew nothing of cricket by culture, learnt it and became patrons of the game. Nothing else, save business were they involved in. Cricket in the Leewards included them. The Leeward Islands Tournament, and not carnival, was for more than 50 years the centre-piece of social and cultural life in the Leewards. It contained both our Being and our Identity. The best ontologists would quickly agree.

Something of the passion and intensity with which Viv Richards played cricket was entirely a Leewards phenomenon. It was the same with Andy Roberts, only that Andy Roberts, like Richie Richardson, was more shaped by the Puritan tradition, which masks passionate intensity behind what the French would call *sang froid*, and what my last but one son, Amilcar, calls the ice man. Richards was not an ice man. But under his passionate intensity lies an ice man, who could single-mindedly pursue a strategy – never to lose a test series, because the Afro/Indian people of the English-speaking Caribbean needed these triumphs to negate their marginalization in global history, trade and politics. To Viv Richards more so, cricket and anti-apartheid struggle were inseparable. West Indies winning against all comers, particularly England and Australia was, to him, an extension of the struggle against apartheid. It was a consciously held view by Isaac Vivian Alexander Richards, and it was con-sciously executed. Therein lies his immortality. Not the first man of pan-African views to lead the West Indies. Worrell was. But the first West Indian captain to see cricket and to play cricket with the view uppermost that cricket played by West Indians was part and parcel of the global struggle against racism and, in particular, apartheid. This was Viv Richards.

Further, Trollope, the foremost Victorian English intellectual in 1860 had written this: "The West Indian Negro knows nothing of Africa except that it is a term of reproach." In 1960, it was nearly as true as it was in 1860, in spite of Garvey, Aimé Césaire and George Lamming.

So much so, that another pan-African, all-time great figure, Frantz Fanon, writing of West Indians in the imperial armies of World War II, made this all-important observation: "The West Indian, not satisfied to be superior to the African despised him . . . But what a catastrophe if the West Indian should sud-denly be taken for an African!" However black, he despised his African roots. Viv, like Bob Marley was part of that generation who came to accept their African roots as essential to their very being, and to being Afro-Caribbean. His oldest brother Donald 'Donnymicth' Richards was a founder of the Afro-Caribbean Movement, later to become the Afro-Caribbean Liberation Move-ment in Antigua.

Viv Richards was part and parcel of that historical current which linked the

US Civil Rights struggle of the 1960s and 1970s with Black Power movements in the Caribbean, extending to the African liberation on the continent, all of which energized the Rastafarian movement, which till then, had remained *Jamaican*, but which through Bob Marley became universal. Marley attained universality and universalized reggae, with its emphasis on liberation, in Zimbabwe, in Trench Town, in Soweto or Tokyo. Viv from Nottingham, Melbourne or Islamabad, sought to impact on racism in England, Cape Town or Brooklyn, and to resist dictatorship, in whatever colour. He was not to be dictated to, by Lillee or Thompson, Chandrasekhar or Bedi, Willis or Underwood. Others should follow suit in their field of endeavour. Richards spoke his pan-Africanism with a cricket bat, like no other ever has or will. He attacked, so that others would attack with trumpets or whatever, the walls of Jericho that imprisoned them.

Like Marley, Vivian Richards, batting, bowling or fielding, was a "Buffalo Soldier in the heart of America / I and I come to break down depression / rule with equality / wipe away transgression and set the captive free." It was pan-Africanism in song and cricket. Viv himself, along with Andy Roberts, had set the small islands of the Leewards, long excluded from West Indies and test cricket, free. Free from their small island sense of inferiority; he had helped to free an entire region from the notion that 'African' was a term of reproach. Vivian Richards had helped free a people through cricket, he helped them come to the next stage of freedom from structural adjustment, which had been determined internally or externally to the detriment of the mass of the population. Vivian Richards, bat and ball in hand, proved that politics was *not* the art of the possible, but the extension of the limits of the possible for oppressed Africans everywhere. Vivian Richards did this by his own superlative achievement, and by his clear and unmistakable stance. He was not to be dictated to by anyone, however good – not Lillee or Thompson. This was Richards, the pan-African in cricket, the inheritor from Constantine, Headley and Herman Griffith. Vivian Richards, as cricketer, as captain realized their pan-African hopes and aspirations in cricket – he beat all comers and none beat the West Indies in a series under him. It was a triumph for West Indies cricket as well as pan-Africanism.

The Packer World Series and the Professionalization of West Indies Cricket

Tony Marshall

"Cricket is first and foremost a dramatic spectacle. It belongs with the theatre, ballet, opera and the dance." In addition to being a dramatic spectacle, cricket is also a visual art. Mike Marquesce, writing in *Anyone But England*, says, as purveyed by the test match special team in the 1970s:

> English cricket was a world where norms of an imagined nineteenth century still obtained. It was a world of deference and hierarchy, ruled by benevolent white men, proud of its traditions and resentful of any challenge to them. Cricket as they portrayed it did not live in the same world as the welfare state, feminism and giant trade unions and certainly not in the world of sex, drugs and rock and roll.

"Cricket is supremely creative," he asserts and goes on to note "the oddity of a professional sport being managed by earnest amateurs".

In the 1860s novelist Anthony Trollope observed that "cricket has become such a business, that there arises doubts in the minds of amateur players whether they can continue the sport".

Cricket brought the rulers into contact with a cross-section of the ruled but it allowed them to make this contact within a circumscribed social space -- the cricket field – under controlled conditions, embodied in the laws of cricket.

For decades women struggled to find a place in English cricket. The Women's Cricket Association was formed in 1926, a byproduct of the suffrage movement. But it had never been granted a voice in the cricket hierarchy, even after the Cricket Council, the Test County and Cricket Board (TCCB) and National Cricket Association (NCA) had replaced the MCC in 1968. Women invented the Cricket World Cup in 1973 – two years before the first men's cup.

Women's cricket experienced difficulty in getting sponsorship mainly, as they were told, because they did not attract enough television coverage. In fact, they were advised that they would get more television exposure if they played scantily clad. Because of this dearth of sponsorship the 1993 World Cup almost did not take place.

Despite the coming of age of women's cricket, women are still denied full membership in the MCC and the use of the pavilion. Yet they attracted a larger crowd than most county games. At the end of the match, presentations were made by Dennis Silk, president of MCC, who told the women that the 'spirit' of the game was everything we like about cricket. "The lady cricketers have provided us with a day we shall never forget." But he did so on the grass in front of the pavilion, not on the balcony in accordance with ancient custom.

Now in most sports across the world, particularly in the USA, rule changes or alterations in structures, equipment, uniforms, take place with little public dissent. Teams move from city to city, yet there is no human outcry. In cricket, however, radical change forces administrators to tremble in fear that something will be lost. Something that may cause them to say 'that is not cricket'.

In 1744 the first full 'laws of cricket' were published by the London Club, whose president was Frederick Louis, Prince of Wales who played cricket. We are told that Frederick died in 1751 following a blow from a cricket ball.

By the 1760s we saw the introduction of overarm bowling and the disappearance of underarm. This gave bowlers a greater scope for developing their skills and batsmen their technique.

In 1774 the first 'leg before' cricket law was published and by 1780 a match was of three days' duration. Next followed the formation of the MCC in 1787. Cricket was taking shape. So that by 1800 there were standardized laws – governance was in the hands of a single body: the MCC.

It had a permanent stage – Lords – and a small group of professional players, even though we are told many of these were personal servants of the rich patrons. The home of cricket is attributed to Thomas Lord, a wine merchant. He quickly worked to enclose it, not only to keep out ordinary folk, but also to enable him to charge an entrance fee.

By the 1890s rules governing qualification for county sides were entrenched. Unlike football, where eligibility is governed by the transfer system, cricket preferred to focus on place of birth and residential qualifications. And here perhaps we see the first signs of rigid control as players' freelance status was undermined and consequently bargaining power stifled. This was clearly demonstrated by the 'separation' of professionals from amateurs.

Cricket professionals were not born in the 1790s as I have shown earlier. Wealthy patrons employed, as gardeners and so on, men of talent not merely on account of their talent but because it was fashionable to make healthy wagers on the game. From the early days the different facilities provided amateurs as opposed to the professionals placed a stigma on the latter group. It is therefore not difficult to understand why the leadership in English cricket administration was provided from the amateurs.

It took until 1962 for the MCC to reluctantly abolish amateur status in county cricket. This led to a more explosive realization. Suddenly it was recognized that cricketers were being grossly underpaid. There was a sudden move to increase fees and this in turn diverted the focus of those in authority to the parlous state of club finances.

Suddenly the county committees started to note that gates receipts were declining. Competing as it did with soccer and even basketball, cricket seemed to have lost its spectator appeal. Thus the birth of 'one-day' cricket: the Gillette Cup in 1963, followed by the John Player league in 1969; the Benson and Hedges Competition in 1972 and, to crown it all, the Prudential World Cup in 1975.

But this was not all. We also saw substantial appreciation in the value of these sponsorships. In 1963 Gillette put up £6,500. In 1969 sponsorship of county cricket by John Player Ltd was worth £90,000. Prudential, which provided £30,000 in 1972 for one-day cricket, tendered £100,000 for the 1975 World Cup, followed by £250,000 in 1979. These events led to the awakening of county and English cricket administrations to the realization that gate receipts could no longer sustain the game. And so the commercialization of cricket had its birth.

You will recall the West Indies toured Australia in 1975 under Clive Lloyd's captaincy. The West Indies lost the first test by eight wickets and won the second test by an innings and 87 runs. Fredericks got 169 – a gem – and Clive 149. The West Indies lost the next four tests to finish 5–1.

This humiliating experience caused Lloyd to impress upon this team that, as he saw it, the way to success was through fitness. Australia had outbatted, outbowled and outfielded the West Indies. To support his view he got the WICBC to see the need to appoint a physiotherapist, and thus began the reign of Dennis Waight.

With the death of his father in 1974, Kerry Packer took over the family newspaper and television empire. One of his first decisions was to carry out an analysis of future marketing trends and he decided that the most exciting potential rested with sports. If these programmes could be so packaged as to produce a mass audience, they would attract large sponsorship. But there was a drawback. Packer recognized that sponsorship would only be attractive if he could offer exclusive coverage. Advertisers would be motivated, provided he could deliver a large enough 'head count'.

The centenary of cricket was in 1977, and Packer saw the time ripe to attempt to break the monopoly of employment exercised by established cricket boards. What Packer sought to do was to bludgeon his way into the inner sanctum of the sport of cricket.

This idea for the introduction of the World Series Cricket was new and innovative, but the cricket establishment and cricketing journalism politely named it the 'Packer Circus'. There can be no doubt that part of their pain was the embarrassment to the establishment that this entrepreneur, whilst they were minding their own business, stealthily put together a group whose actions would ultimately shake the formerly secure cricketing world to the foundations.

The first notice of the oncoming earthquake was provided in April 1977 by the South African *Sunday Times* which announced that four South African players had signed lucrative contracts to play around the world. It was nevertheless difficult to pinpoint exactly when the idea which led to the World Series Cricket came into being. Two years before, according to Henry Blofeld in his book *The Packer Affair*, Packer wrote the Australian Cricket Board of Control seeking exclusive rights to cover the series against the West Indies in Australia. The board acknowledged his letter but without giving him the chance to make an offer, sold the rights to the Australian Broadcasting Commission.

Packer's next move was to bid a half-million dollars for the sole rights to the next year's series against Pakistan as well as the Sheffield Shield matches. Of course this bid was also turned down. Blofeld writes that Packer left the room saying, "Well damn, I don't know why we don't put on our own cricket tests."

At that very time and by coincidence there were two men in Sydney who for different reasons came to a similar conclusion. One was John Cornell, a television actor and entrepreneur, and journalist Austin Robertson. Cornell had recently joined Channel Nine and so he put to Packer his idea of one-day cricket for television. Packer's response was, "Why don't we go the whole way and produce our own test series."

The biggest surprise about Packer's 'coup' was that he was able to contain such a massive project as a secret. Packer's key men, Ritchie Benaud and Tony Greig, anticipated the hostility they would encounter from the authorities and paid great attention to confidentiality. Approaches to players and administrators were made on condition they first agreed that whether they came on board 'the circus' or not, like bankers, everything they saw or heard was in strict confidence. Still further, on signing their contracts players were given solid cheques which was viewed by some as an element of hush money.

By 4 May 1977 the Packer Revolution was in high gear. Thirty-five players had signed on. Among this number were 13 of the 17 Australian tour party. It is felt that Alan Shield, a former South Australian player then working for the

Murdoch Group, thus obtained the story and, on realizing Peter McFarlane of the *Melbourne Age* also had details, broke the news in the Australian Press. Immediately, the *Bulletin Magazine,* owned by Packer, released full details.

England thus learnt for the first time on 9 May that Packer had 35 of the world's leading players under contract in most instances for three years and for an average £25,000 a year.

The question that everyone started to ask was "How was he able to do this?" Well, put simply, Packer realized that, compared with top figures in other sports, cricketers were undervalued and badly underpaid. Clive Lloyd, as reported by Trevor McDonald, had this to say:

> The principal thing which operated in my mind was the financial security offered by my World Series Contract. Here it was; a few months after leading the West Indies to a creditable performance against England, I was being offered three times what I had been paid for that series. Many of us never imagined such sums of money were possible in cricket. Several West Indian players at the end of their careers in the big time either played on in minor leagues to keep going or tried to get coaching jobs with Governments and so on. I simply could not see myself doing that when I gave up the captaincy. I was giving my all to cricket; it was not unreasonable to go for something which rewarded people according to their talents. Neither did I feel I was in any way 'letting down ' the West Indies Board. Certain decisions about one's future have to be taken, with a view to doing what is best for a player and his family. The campaign against Mr Packer was quite outrageous. It just made many of us more determined. Instead of making World Series Cricket weaker, it made it much stronger.

To West Indian players, World Series Cricket offered almost everything they longed for, perhaps more so than to other cricketers in other parts of the world. The careers of West Indian players, as you well know, have always been secured on less than firm ground. Because there is no full-time professional cricket in the Caribbean, those making the game their living must seek job opportunities in England. At the end of their playing days they then embark on a new life in search of employment; since, up to then, cricket had never afforded them a comfortable retirement. Packer, shrewd as he is, saw Clive Lloyd as just the man to play a pivotal role in signing up the best West Indian players. Thus by 1977 Clive Lloyd had begun to learn to treat "those two impostors, triumph and disaster, just the same".

Getting back to the Packer drama, the ICC and the TCCB immediately placed a ban on all those cricketers who had signed contracts with Packer. This ban was forthwith challenged by the players and with spectacular success. Justice

Slade was influenced no doubt by the line taken by North American judges, who had ruled repeatedly that organizations could not legally establish monopolies in such sports as basketball, football and ice hockey. And so the British Court ruled that neither the ICC nor the TCCB could induce cricketers to determine binding contracts they had signed with Packer, especially since their commitments to Packer did not in any way infringe on agreed commitments to the ICC and the TCCB.

This ruling, therefore, was the watershed in the professionalization of cricket, and brought home to cricket administrators worldwide that they had to function in a professional manner. Packer had taught them two of the rudiments of business, namely, the value of television and that a good product has real value to businessmen.

Packer demonstrated, without any doubt and certainly by his guts in investing millions of dollars in cricket, that the game, well organized if not packaged, had tremendous value to television and to major sponsors. There can be no doubt that he sensitized the cricketing world to the value of television rights. Cricket therefore could never be the same again.

As testimony to the above the TCCB charted a new course by significantly increasing the cost to sponsors of exclusive advertisement. Cornhill Insurance Company agreed in 1977 to pay some £1 million over five years, which TCCB saw as the answer to the £250,000 bill incurred in their defence of the court suit. Cornhill also sponsored test cricket and by 1982 had doubled its stakes for advertising cricket. Still further, and with sponsors competing against each other, some £2 million was being fed into the bloodline of English cricket.

Let us look at the direct benefits to countries thereafter. In 1962 MCC reported profits of £600,000; by 1983 TCCB proudly announced profits of over £3 million. These figures seem to gallop but are small when compared to the £7 million derived from the Pakistan tour of England in 1992.

The professionalization of cricket did not end at attracting major sponsors. We next saw subsponsorship – whether by man of the match, prize money, or highest individual score, or even the greatest number of sixes. These developments gnawed away at the foundations of established cricket and led most deliberately, even if embarrassingly, to the need for a complete overhaul of cricket's traditional administrative structures. Even the MCC, that very conservative institution, grudgingly acknowledged the old way could no longer do. It underwent radical reform and is today a very professional organization, employing a full-time staff of over 50 persons, led by a highly paid secretary. By the time of the annual general meeting of 1993 its finance director was able to report a surplus of over £700,000.

Overtaken by a climate of excellence and combined with an awareness of the fact that the customer – the spectator – is king, the TCCB over the last few years has turned its face squarely away from tinkering with the laws to contain four-prong fast bowling combinations and towards bonuses, fines for slow over rates, intended to provide more attractive cricket.

The next major development was that cricketers became aware of the new commercial possibilities available to them and started through personal managers/agents to exploit the financial plums to be had from product endorsement (Lara and Coca Cola) for foods, sports equipment and clothing or sports gear, as well as memorabilia.

It had been unknown and definitely unheard of, for cricketers to band themselves into players' associations. Not only did this come about, but in the 1970s the game saw the establishment of a tribunal to settle disputes between county clubs and individual cricketers.

I cannot help but comment here that given recent events there is definitely a need for a tribunal in West Indies cricket and I would urge the WICBC to 'think on these things'. In fact it was the cricketers' association led by John Arlott that negotiated the final settlement between Kerry Packer and the TCCB in 1979. The association did not stop there either: it next secured agreement for a minimum wage for cricketers starting at £4,500 in 1979 and by 1985 the average county player realized £12,000.

Let us now turn to the game itself. One saw a new spirit of professionalism with cricketers looking to the game as a first career, opening windows and corridors to rewarding possibilities after retirement. Look at Ritchie Benaud of Channel Nine and previously BBC; Geoffrey Boycott, Sky TV and, more recently, our own Michael Holding who, thinker that he is, said in his book *Whispering Death*, "I've also got into radio and television commentaries and enjoy it immensely. It has kept me in touch with the game and given me a different perspective on it." It is an area that has provided a comfortable living for several players, of whom the most outstanding example is Ritchie Benaud, the former Australian captain, who has made a reputation for himself on television in England and Australia.

The Packer 'thing' led cricketers to see the game as a first career and following World Series Cricket, professionals began to take the game more seriously than their predecessors. Both Clive Lloyd and Michael Holding commented upon the fierceness of World Series Cricket. There is a story that, following a poor performance by the West Indies, Packer visited the dressing room after the game and gave the team a roasting. Holding says, "He told us he wasn't impressed with our display and that for the kind of money we were getting, he expected a more professional performance." Players became conscious of proper diet and exercise. We saw the advent of physiotherapists and psychologists as part of the team and last year England even had a 'man of the cloth' among their number.

Cricket has become a business and not merely a sport. The game is far more scientific and fieldsmen are no longer concerned whether their 'flannels' remain unsullied. Batsmen are concerned with defending (Lara excepted) until the bad ball comes along, while seam bowlers concentrate relentlessly on the 'corridor of uncertainty'. Fast bowlers have perfected the art of swing without surrendering speed and so result-oriented have players become, that latest rules require the ball to be handed to the umpires at water breaks lest the seam is lifted miraculously or one side gouged by long fingernails or a bottle stopper.

It is clear that the professionalization of modern cricket post-Packer has left its most profound impact on West Indies cricket. But I need to make the point that its genesis can be more rightly attributed to 1961 and the late Sir Frank Worrell. Next came Clive Lloyd with his physical fitness mania and uncompromising four-prong pace attack. The measurement of Clive's generalship is manifested by the views of those who said, "If Clive and Andy have signed then it has to be OK." Also after the Georgetown selection debacle, all Packer 'sign-ons' followed their leader's footsteps and withdrew from the team.

Thus West Indies players became tough, uncompromising professionals playing with ruthless efficiency and every man knew his job. Press and commentators no longer were able to label the team with a silent chuckle 'calypso cricketers'. The use of the word in that context, to my mind, is pejorative. It suggests that because the Caribbean failed to market the art form as a serious business, then just the one word, encapsulated all that characterizes a two-day festival of gay abandon. Perhaps the excellence and ecstasy of panorama is unknown as is the creativity of a Peter Minshall. But back to the matter at hand.

Due to harsh economic realities, the Caribbean, a region with few natural resources, a higher than desirable unemployment problem and an almost certain destiny for inescapable poverty, forced the young aspiring cricketers of the region to recognize that one sure escape was through cricket. Most had seen, read or heard of the 3Ws, Sobers, Kanhai, Hall, Griffith, Holding, Roberts, Haynes and Greenidge, and today Brian Lara. They could not have asked for better models of professional cricketers. Many if not all of these men had sought their living in the leagues/counties or even Australia and so it was not surprising when the West Indies Players Association closed its ranks against the WICBC in 1978 in support of a few players who had signed up with Packer.

Prior to the 1960s first-class cricket in the Caribbean was irregular and it was not until the birth of the Shell Series that one could say West Indies cricket had a regular first-class season. It was also from the 1960s that we saw professionals taking over the captaincy of the West Indies, starting with Frank Worrell, followed by Sobers, Lloyd, Richards and now Richardson.

A further consequence was that because of the players' recognition of their worth and therefore their stronger demands for pay, the WICBC was forced to seek sponsorships. And so we saw Benson and Hedges, Geddes Grant, Red Stripe and Cable and Wireless (a current sponsor of the Australian Series). We now have for the second time sponsorship of the West Indies team on an away series, this time by Sandals and Shell jointly.

The general approach to cricket itself has taken on a more professional structure and is more professionally run. It now has a chief executive officer (Steve Camacho), a finance officer (Richard Jodhan), an executive secretary (Andrew Sealy), as well as a separate marketing committee headed by an outstanding and competent Jamaican, Pat Rousseau. This committee, I am pleased to say, is doing an excellent job. In Barbados we have also seen a step in the same direction with local cricket attracting sponsorship by Barbados Fire and General, Barbados External Telecommunications (BET), Cave Shepherd and Co. Ltd, Mount Gay Distilleries, and Barclays Bank PLC.

I do not know and am not prepared to argue, but it is of some significance that since the 1980s South Africa Cricket Authorities, through the several cash rich corporations there, have sought to hire outstanding West Indies stars. The primary objective may have been to secure South Africa's passage back to test cricket but even so I am suggesting they learnt from the Packer hijack – *the power of money*.

Malcolm Marshall, who previously turned down an offer of £50,000, is there today. We heard of Viv Richards refusing 'blood money' of US$1.5 million. Further across the cricketing world, players from England and Australia sell their services in South Africa year after year. The fact is professionals, post-Packer, are prepared to sell their skills and services to the highest bidder, ignoring political, national and other considerations.

Let us turn an eye to England for a moment and here we see that country attaching such major importance to the task of team selection – although results of the game do not substantiate this – that they now have a paid selection and the teams include managers and coaches who are paid professionals.

Since 1990 the West Indies have adopted the system of two managers for away teams, one to look after cricket, the other to look after all other matters; whilst at home one manager seems adequate, bearing in mind the support available to him on the ground through the local secretariats.

Let us take a glance at scoring. Today the game has become so professional, so scientific, that managers and captains as well as the players – the craftsmen – need every tool to assist them in the construction of their art. And thus we have seen the emergence of a scoring system (known as the Boxhill Scoring System, pioneered by a young man Darnley Boxhill, a former umpire and wicketkeeper for Barbados), which is capable of producing every piece of information required.

Sport has been a vehicle of personal advance for a number of oppressed groups in societies all over the world, because the premise of sport is that everyone is subject to the same rules, everyone starts at the same line, and is timed with the same stopwatch. Cricket, like the law and the market, is supposed to be colour blind.

In the good old days before the West Indies started beating England regularly – and before there was a large West Indies population in that country – West Indies cricket was dammed with faint praise. Cardus summed up the prevailing view, "The erratic quality of West Indies cricket is surely true to racial type. At the moment these players are eager, confident and quite masterful; then as circumstances go against them you can see them losing heart."

But with the rise of Clive Lloyd's all conquering side of the late 1970s and 1980s – post-Packer, that is – the tune changed. The carefree amateurism had been replaced by a hardened professionalism and command for respect, and the England who gave professionalism to the world did not approve. At the start of the 1984 season Robin Marlar belittled Lloyd's army of weary mercenaries. Then came the 5–0 blackwash, one of the most powerful displays ever by a touring test side, featuring exceptional batting, bowling and fielding from a host of West Indian stars.

The next objection was to 'slow play'. TCCB had pressed for a higher minimum number of overs per day but the West Indies did not bite the bait. Lloyd's rotation of four fast bowlers did mean fewer overs were bowled. But where West Indies bowlers averaged 13.5 overs per hour throughout the series England bowled 13.4. But the West Indies won most of the tests within five days – a matter that Tony Cozier has always defended for the West Indies.

John Woodcock was next to take a turn denouncing "chilling West Indies pace bowling". "Its viciousness", he warned, "was changing the very nature of the game." Yet another commentator said he was sickened by the downright thuggery of fast bowlers working in relays to remove batsmen by hurting and intimidating them.

For many English commentators West Indian 'exuberance' had been replaced by a boorish aggression. The English had seemed so happy with the old rules until someone else started to win under them. Michael Holding put complaints about West Indies 'intimidating' fast bowling in perspective.

> All the press stems from the fact that one team has been very successful with
> a particular mode of attack, perfectly legal, that the other teams have been

unable to combat. Opposing captains have admitted that if they had such bowlers, they would employ them similarly.

It is an old story. Learie Constantine recalled the West Indies 1933 tour:

> When we played Nottinghamshire during that tour, Larwood sent ball after ball so near our men's faces that presently some of them kept away and their wickets began to fall. We did not complain. If we could not make fours off that sort, it was our fault, not Larwood's. But we did resent the blindness of some of our critics who professed to see danger in those balls when we put them down and none when English players bowled them.

The myth of the West Indies natural ability and spontaneity is a powerful one, on and off the field, but it does not suffice as an explanation for West Indies achievements and professionalism. You cannot spontaneously invent something as complex as a square cut or a fast inswinger to the ribs.

Each of the West Indies quickies, Roberts, Holding, Garner, Croft, Marshall, Ambrose, Walsh, worked to create his own style, varying bounce and angle of delivery, line and length. They were successful everywhere, proving themselves to be adaptable.

The glory of cricket is its difficulty, its unnaturalness (the Kanhai sweep). If West Indian cricketers often manage to make it look natural, it is their expression of freedom, of uncoached talent, of pure artistry – Frank Worrell, Lawrence Rowe, Carl Hooper.

Back in 1960–1961 Worrell, the first black man to captain the West Indies, had instilled unity, integrity and mutual respect in a side previously known for inconsistency. C. L. R. James described this: "Clearing the way with bat and ball, West Indians at that moment made a public entry into the comity of nations."

Clive Lloyd took West Indies professionalism to its highest pinnacle, developing perhaps one of the greatest test sides in history. The cricket fields of the world were their home and this gave them an independence. Distinctively and powerfully individualistic, they transcended insularity and division by organization and professionalism.

As you read the several books written by former West Indian stars, particularly those of the 1980s, there is a common thread. They all acknowledge that being West Indian and black – in a world storm tossed and buffeted by a sea of inequality – has been itself a powerful motivation for success in international cricket. Their consciousness that they were playing on behalf of the West Indian diaspora, not just the islands but a diaspora that sees itself West Indian, rose to unprecedented heights. This cannot be better articulated than by Ambrose following England's rout for 46 chasing a total of 194 in Trinidad in March 1994. Ambrose said:

I understand how important it is to play my cricket hard. I do it for the people. They expect nothing less and we're very conscious of them wherever we go on the field. Their love is very strong. It is demanding on you but it also makes you strong.

So there we have it, the post-Packer impact on West Indies cricket. Kerry Francis Bullmore Packer did what no one else had seen up to then. Coloured clothing for the advent of colour television was beyond imagining. One-day cricket has a very big place and those who neglect it will clearly be poorer for it. The West Indies in the 1980s revelled in it.

Many of the changes introduced by World Series Cricket were stylistic rather than substantive. It did not look at the game, it looked at the consumers and the revenue generating potential. But Packer saw that the players had to be professional.

After the first World Series Cricket, Packer set the players certain targets to achieve for the following year – weight reduction, mobility, stamina, wind and speed. He was responsible for radical change in pay. He exposed the fruits of a marriage between cricket and television.

What he will not be remembered for is the fact that he gave cricketers *player power*. There can be no doubt that for two seasons the best players in the world played some remarkable cricket whose 56, 126 runs and 2,364 wickets, for reasons best known to the ICC are not first-class status.

West Indies cricket faces a multitude of challenges as it goes into the twenty-first century and to treat the World Series Cricket as though it never happened would be a waste of its lessons.

Here are some thoughts for a new approach – a new direction. Like basketball and football in the USA, in cricket there could be the emergence of rival leagues to take up those players presently knocking on the door of the West Indies test team, culminating at the end of season in a new cricket superbowl.

Still further, in harmony with the current development of trade blocs throughout the world, how much longer will Sri Lanka, Pakistan, India and the West Indies be willing to have the supreme controlling body for cricket headquartered in London – a body perceived to take care primarily of the needs of its foundation members England and Australia.

In keeping with the new 'player power', should we not expect the players to rally and band themselves together, forcing sponsors to negotiate directly with them and to pay handsome fees for them to wear logos or even 'pyjama' apparel? This scenario, to my mind, seems a strong possibility the longer they continue without contracts from the WICBC which would assure them of year round employment.

One can envisage the possibility of another maverick appearing on the horizon owning the West Indies team (à la the USA basketball or football system) and forcing Caribbean people through the WICBC to have to hire the members of the team to represent our nation. If the WICBC is to head off these possible developments then I suggest it should turn itself on its head so that the players take a leading role in shaping the destiny of cricket, while the board takes on the mantle of facilitator. A pleasing first step would be to have the president of the players' association sit on the board and relevant sub committees.

The 'Packer explosion' can thus be categorized as a catalyst for change. I therefore put the challenge to you out there that we *do not* have to wait for someone to come from somewhere else to determine our destiny and forge new directions. We do not have to wait for someone from outside the region to make the sport more dynamic, rewarding and profitable. The answers are right here in our communities. One or a group of you must have the courage, vision and resources to make the impact as Kerry Packer did.

We have impacted as world champion players. What will be the challenge for us is to be equally effective in influencing and changing the game on an international scale in the professionalization of the sport.

Cricket and the Artistic Tradition
West Indian Cricket as a Performing Art

Rex Nettleford

Reports and commentaries on, critiques of, discussions, arguments and debates about cricket – the now ancestral expression of the creole Commonwealth Caribbean's sense of place and purpose in the universe – are laced with one recurring word: 'performance'.[1] This or that player, whether batting, fielding, bowling or wicketkeeping, is judged by his 'performance'. Each 'man of the match' wins the title on his overall performance, which goes beyond the realm of quantifiable indicators into that of the qualitative, the mysterious, the surprise-filled signifiers of excellence called art.

Cricket is more than a sport, more than the vehicle it has served as social protest for a long subjugated people, as strategy of demarginalization, or as defiant celebration of self in the face of persistent denigration.

Cricket is art, with an aesthetic distinctive to the Caribbean cultural context and served by a repertoire of technique(s) corresponding to the craft that underpins all great art. That technique must be learnt and mastered and should serve as source of liberation rather than of constraint. Such has been the experience of the West Indian in his joyous centuries of survival and the unending quest to sustain that survival by whatever means possible.

Cultural resistance utilizing the creative intellect and creative imagination has been a foremost strategy. It was that ownership of one's mind that suggested alternatives to the denigrated self in circumstances where chatteldom denied humanity to the vast majority. Taking on the master's God and reshaping the Deity in one's own image gave the West Indian early apprenticeship for the embrace of cricket a century or more later. So much for religion.

But the secular and even more personal/private weapons of war in the battle for space came almost from the beginning in the performance of music and dance created in the image of self. Incorporated into religious rituals as they were in the so-called syncretized religions down the archipelago, a serious means of self-empowerment developed from very early. How could cricket, when it finally came on the scene, not benefit from such powerful forerunners? It is to the West Indian cricketer's lasting credit that he drew on the strategies and stratagems long evident in the performing arts practised by the people from below, to respond to the pervasive obscenities of imperial rule. As such, he played constantly beyond the boundary even while confined to the crease, pitch and outer field. C. L. R. James has long pricked our consciousness into structured appreciation of the cultural role of the game in the history of West Indian liberation and decolonization this past century.[2]

The political role of culture, especially of the performing arts, is part of our historical experience and our contemporary reality. How else can one explain the weight of social response borne by the magnificent calypsonians of Trinidad and the latter-day reggae composers of Jamaica in their poetic and forceful ambush of their respective communities and the bloated personages of power and influence presiding over them?

Earlier festival arts – whether jonkonnu/masquerade or pre-Lenten carnival – had long taken pot-shots at oppression under the guise of miming, recreation and play. Cricket entered the fray in the late nineteenth century. It was a perfect gift to the colonized just as Christianity, from the late eighteenth century, lent itself to dialectical manipulation producing West Indian ways of worship ranging from pocomania and zion revivalism through Shango and cumfa to modern-day Rastafari. The process is the same, only the product is different. The West Indian is a born (or is it socialized?) performer: he has long had to sing (and dance and play) not only for his supper but for his survival.

On this broad canvas of historical reality, James in his magisterial epic *Beyond a Boundary* could not be caught in the slips or made to run out for failing to hit a series of sixes. In some matters of detail, he may well be faulted as Kenneth Surin in a brilliant critique recently did, taking him to task for restricting his analysis too rigidly to Hegelian and Weberian notions of social reality.[3] There is, admittedly, something to the point that the Hegelian notion of the 'world-historian individual' could well be regarded as contradictory when plotted against the myriad forces and textured experiences that constitute West Indian historical reality. No one person or type of person could possibly encapsulate such contradictions, insists Surin in disagreement.

But as the performing arts have long illustrated and James, for all his clinging to respected theoretical constructs for intellectual legitimacy must have realized, political Messianism, like Weberian charisma, is also part of our reality; hence the urge to single out individuals as embodiments of the West Indian collective unconscious at given times of our chequered history. The superstar has long been a feature of all West Indian 'performing arts'. Note the king and queen for a day in festivals, the pocomania shepherd or Shango priest in the creole religious ceremonies of the region, the Mighty Lordships of the calypso, the revered Rastafarian icons of reggae. And then there are the heroes of our mass politics, ranging from Bustamante, Bradshaw and Gairy, wonderful showmen in their own right, to Eric Williams crooning dulcet tones into the microphone at the University of Woodford Square, Forbes Burnham seducing the crowds with courtroom oratory at Bourda, and Michael Manley, complete with rod of Joshua, wooing audiences throughout the region with verbal virtuosity and matinee-idol visage and physique.

Why not a Gary Sobers, a Viv Richards, a George Headley, a Frank Worrell, a Constantine or a Lara in cricket. These are the undoubted stars of the art by whatever yardstick we use. There are scores of others, of course, for as the saying goes, every nigger is a star. "Perhaps more than any other team sport," writes Michael Manley, "cricket provides outlets for individuality and individual performance [while in other sports] formidable athletes on the team tend to sink in the collective anonymity of the team effort . . . cricket . . . provides for each player ample opportunity to star."[4] Before Hegel thought of the absolute-spirit embodied in some human frame, humankind, of which the West Indians have never had any doubt they are a part, named their own icons. W. G. Grace, Pelham Warner, Don Bradman and Gary Sobers are by no means the inventions of C. L. R. James. It is the nature of a performance culture that brilliant exponents of consummate skill get singled out, even when teamwork is understood to be paramount.

It is the rigorous use of the Hegelian/Marxist paradigm that may give trouble, since it is admittedly always dangerous to push analogies too far. In any case, inconsistencies abound in human existence as a matter of course. As a performing art, cricket must make allowances for the play of circumstances unforeseen, for the unexpected creative input and output by individual 'players', for changes that constantly challenge the text and context of the game. If Clive Lloyd's team failed to fit into the theoretical schema of C. L. R. James, it made Lloyd no less a significant performer to the art of cricket – certainly no less than the virtuoso musical rendition of a Schoenberg piece is to music as against a traditionalist performance of compositions by Mozart or Chopin. In any case, playing to win on the basis of highly technical manipulations of the virtuoso skills of bowlers did not diminish, on James' own account, the feline grace of a fast bowler like Michael Holding. Technique and creative engineering are not without their aesthetics in the field of the performing arts, whether it be music, dance or drama.

On this score James had no doubt. To him cricket is a "dramatic spectacle"; and true to his generation and intellectual orientation, his declaration drew on European classical sources. Cricket, he wrote,

> . . . is so organized that at all times it is compelled to reproduce the central action which characterizes all good drama from the days of the Greeks to our own: two individuals are pitted against each other in a conflict that is strictly personal but no less strictly representative of a social group. One individual batsman faces one individual bowler . . . The batsman facing the ball does not merely represent his side. For the moment to all intents and purposes, he is his side.[5]

Athens was indeed a 'performance culture' not unlike our contemporary Caribbean. Greek tragedy was a theatre of, by and for the polis, and, along with other public fora, was a place to confront matters of import. Greek theatre in this sense was deemed to be integral to the life of the city, as cricket certainly is to Bridgetown. In other words, it was a theatre focused on the audience.[6] That audience for cricket is more than the exuberant inflammable participatory hordes of humanity to be found with each match at our parks and ovals. It takes in the entire society divided into television viewers, radio listeners and the communities of souls locked in ongoing combat over the pros and cons of play in this or that test and one-day encounter and, like the plays of Aristophanes, a cricket match is less a text for reading and more like a fluid libretto for performance.[7]

On this James need not have journeyed back to ancient Greece. The audience at a West Indian cricket match is an integral part of the drama. Every ball played is commented on with wit, raucous humour and that inventive infectious orality which is part of 'the West Indies way' of play enjoyed not only in the region itself but at Lords or Old Trafford when invaded by the fans drawn from the West Indian diaspora inhabiting the Motherland.[8]

That audience/player organic interaction is a feature of the performing arts as well. The poet or painter who boasts that he writes poetry or paints for himself and for none other will soon be starved of both funds and spirit. But many West Indian poets now perform their poetry – from Derek Walcott and Kamau Brathwaite to Louise Bennett and Mutabaruka. Writers like Lamming are a joy to hear when they perform their lectures. And like the cricketers they are of their side as much as their individual selves. The 1992 Nobel Prize for Literature belonged not just to Walcott, nor to St Lucia, but to the entire

Caribbean. And even Walcott acknowledged the debt he owed to the Antillean collective without loss of his right to individual existence.[9] He is no less 'West Indian/St Lucian' for residing in Boston among the glitterati and literati of New England. How less West Indian, then, is Clive Lloyd, a great West Indies cricketer, for becoming a British citizen or a celebrity supporter of Margaret Thatcher, of all people? Lloyd, in his introduction to Michael Manley's *History of West Indies Cricket*, betrays no doubt in his mind that the game he presided over, with professional precision for ten years, 'is the ethos around which West Indian society revolves'.[10] He was echoing James' thesis but also joining in the celebration of the performing arts as a mode of 'apprehending the world, history and society'.[11]

I am reminded by none other than George Lamming himself that in my own efforts to define the performing art I have grown to know a little about, I had asserted that

> the dance is not only a performing art, but also an art of community effort that proclaims the virtue of co-operation over unrestrained individualism. It is self-evident how this relates to self-government, nation-building, and social organization. Traditional government leaders have dismissed the sensitive intellectual gifts of peasant experiences, precisely because they have been regarded as too mundane or folkloric to guide affairs of state. Yet it is the peasant who realizes that the individual dancer usually has little to offer outside of community ritual.[12]

The parallel in cricket is richly described by Michael Manley in his 1988 *History of West Indian Cricket*.

> A great batsman is not unlike a great tennis player in the individual attention that he necessarily commands . . . [but] at the same time if his individual effort is to be the jewel in the crown of victory, there have to be levels of team discipline. It is the interaction between individualism and collectivism that are to be found on the two sides of cricket's coin.[13] C. L. R. James was dead right: the cricketer is not only of his side, he is his side!

Other parallels are to be found among the established arts themselves as, say, between literature and the dance. George Lamming concludes:

> Both passed through phases of scornful hostility, then a softening of attitudes, conveyed by the news of international approval and curiosity; and settling later into a more critical, native evaluation of the work under scrutiny. It has been a rough road of question and argument about social relevance and artistic standards.[14] No Caribbean artist has escaped this plague of historic self-doubt and cultural dependence.

Nor has any West Indian cricketer who has been exposed to the not always subtle distinctions made between gentlemen and players, amateur and professional, those fit to captain the team by reason of predetermined racial legitimacy and those not, for having come from the canepiece.

It is not by accident that the performing art that cricket comes nearest to resembling, and with which it shares most characteristics, is the dance. In both art forms—cricket and dance—it is the human body that is the chief instrument of expression.

> Dance is an art performed by individuals or groups of human beings existing in time, space, force and flow, in which the human body is the instrument, and movement is the medium characterized by form and structure . . . commonly performed to . . . rhythmic accompaniment. . . [It] has as a primary purpose the expression of inner feelings and emotions, although it is often performed for social, ritual, entertainment, or other purposes.[15]

Surely this could be a definition of cricket as well, for cricket shares with dance the uniqueness in art of the dancer's double role both as the creator and as the instrument extending the creation.

The bat and the ball, the pads and the gloves are but extensions of that body, as props and costumes can be to the dancer. In both dance and cricket the "physiological raw material is transformed by its social environment and embodied with social meaning".[16] The cricketer constitutes a 'social body' as well as a West Indian aesthetic energy.

One gets glimpses of similar correspondences elsewhere, as in the references to the marvellous sharpness of eye among the batsmen of India and the sense of balance in the overall approach in the game from our Asian brothers. As it happens, eye movement and balance are major attributes of kathakali and bharantanatyam dance forms in Indian culture. These correspond to the lithesome, fluid muscularity and polyrhythmic signatures that are features of both Caribbean dance and West Indian cricket.

If it is true that the human body is always treated as an image of society as expressed in Caribbean dance, theatre or Caribbean sport, and especially West Indian cricket, then it follows that by examining people's attitudes to the human body, and their definition of its boundaries, we should gain some understanding of the use of that body in an art form like dance or cricket.

> West Indian batsmen escaped the geometric rigidities of the best coached exemplars of the English and Australian game. Instead they moved in a more poetic manner, the stroke seeming to begin with the toes and to move in a supple, flowing line through the legs, arched back and whiplike arms.[17]

What a graphic description of the West Indian dancer! Actually it is of the West Indian cricketer by Michael Manley, himself an ardent devotee of the dance and kindred arts.

At least one anthropologist is of the view "that the human body is ugly and that the natural tendency is to debility and disease. [So] incarcerated in such a body, man's only hope is to avert these characteristics through the use of the powerful influences of ritual and ceremony"[18] — in our case such rituals and ceremonies as cricket, dance, carnival jump-up and just plain dressing up.

It is Lamming again who acknowledges the centrality of the West Indian body to our rituals of liberation in his stirring defence of Carifestas in general and of the one held in Barbados in 1981 when others lashed out at West Indian governments for indulging circuses rather than giving sustained commitment to the arts. Lamming insisted that the Carifesta celebration gave the region a chance to "heal and restore the rhythm and beauty of that battered black body which [many] argued and continue to argue is ugly, graceless and without history".[19] He was talking about that black body so central to all our performing arts. He could have been talking as well about the cricketer's body, which was once felt to house only 'players' and not 'gentlemen', only minstrels in the form of bowlers and batsmen and not true creative artists in the form of captains with the intelligence and vision to plan strategy and apply tactics as the choreographer does in creatively assembling steps or the composer does in organizing disparate sounds into 'musical' patterns that conductors help audiences to understand and enjoy.

Pere Labat speaking in the early eighteenth century had this to say,

> I have travelled everywhere in your sea of the Caribbean . . . from Haiti to Barbados, to Martinique and Guadeloupe, and I know what I am speaking about . . . You were all together, in the same uncertain sea . . . It is no accident that the sea which separates your lands makes no difference to the rhythm of your body.[20]

I elsewhere once observed that,

> the Puritan ethic – which condemned the expression of the body, the very instrument of dance – had an especially negative influence on the acceptance of the art by even the educated Caribbean population. This was particularly true of the educated male population who confused eloquent body movement with Anglo-Saxon fears about effeminacy and homosexuality, a fear of great import to a male population reared on concerns about sexual prowess and the emasculation of their manhood especially under slavery.[21]

The West Indian cricketer in his macho maleness has undoubtedly responded to all such nonsense with an exuberant, brawny, rapid-fire vigour that once was, and still is, regarded as atavistic aggression. And he coupled it with a rippling rhythmic grace that once attracted the sobriquet 'calypso cricketer'. But like the calypso, irony, wit and layers of meaning constitute the West Indies way of play which, with technique and discipline has after all resulted in 'winning' a key factor in competitive games. West Indies cricket also signifies a path to excellence via poetic transformation of the received vocabulary, technique and style of this intensely English game. The West Indian cricketer, like the West Indian dancer, takes the chance, when at his best, 'to reach human heights whilst at the same time using his animal body to the full extent, not suppressing its needs, but relieving, balancing them in the most coherent way'.[22]

The body belonging to the oppressed is a powerful means of communication; and personal control over it places it beyond the reach of the oppressor. Cricketers and dancers without a command of the scribal language can nonetheless communicate. So the early West Indian cricketers, even when they were losing, were brashly and defiantly beautiful to behold! The celebration of the male body as hot-blooded power and authority in itself, as icon of athleticism, line and form became a psychic threat to opponents in colder climes but a source of visual joy for West Indians, and especially for the tens of thousands of West Indian women whose love for, and expertise in the understanding of, this chauvinistically manly sport is nothing if not astounding. Many will confess to be totally bowled over or caught silly off-guard (or mid on) by the arrogant sensuality of the striding men in white against dark skins advancing with stylish swagger towards the crease. The three Ws were famous for their physiques, I am reliably informed. And Gary Sobers 'walked a way' in his pads according to one still ecstatic female informant. Brian Lara's height (or lack of it) makes no difference to his animal magnetism, to the women spectators. Bob Marley and Francisco Slinger (The Mighty Sparrow) have had the same effect as star performers. The English may well have sacrificed the power of such bodily communication in preference for the power of speech. And though Shakespeare still stands supreme, a hot-blooded Greek could, in *Zorba the Greek* say to his English friend, "While you are talking I watch your arms and chest. Well, what are they doing? They are silent. They don't say a word. As though they hadn't a drop of blood between them."[23] Many drops of blood flow between the arms and chest of West Indian cricketers, allowing them to 'dance like natives', as the anthropologist would say, and to restore to self and society the full complement of the communicative powers needed, as James would have said, in times of a threatened formlessness under old-time colonialism or homogenization under the new-style globalized economy. Our bodies can here lead us to discovery of self and to safe positioning in the world by using them as performing agents.

Cricket and the dance, as either is performed by cricketers or dancers, are each a unity of succession, a cohesive moving form. "Dance", it is said, "is not only a kinetic phenomenon which . . . gives itself to consciousness; it is also a living, vital human experience . . . for both dancer and audience . . ."[24] The same with cricket!

So the phrase 'dancing down the wicket' is often used by journalists and broadcasters because they clearly understand cricket and the dance to experience a shared aesthetic base. 'Dancing down the wicket' actually refers to a batsman's leaving his crease or area of safety to attack the bowler as if by preemption. The bowler-batsman encounter and the rhythms involved are reminiscent of the point/counterpoint phenomenon in both music and dance.

Jimmy Carnegie, the Jamaican sports writer, is of the view that in cricket, as in several other sports, the most elegant performances are also, in them-selves, art objects and represent 'poetry in motion', in short, dance.[25] And he further cites Brian Lara at bat, Carl Hooper in the field, bowling and also at bat, Jeffrey Dujon of yore with bat, and behind the wicket, Alvin Kallicharan, Lawrence Rowe, Rohan Kanhai, the great Gary Sobers, Seymour Nurse, Roy Fredericks and Conrad Hunte, and, perhaps the father of them all, the late Frank Worrell. He describes Bernard Julien as being like Lara in the 'sagaboy' trad-ition (a well-known performance tradition) of their native Trinidad and Tobago. The great 'dancer-players' with the ball he feels to be Michael Hold-ing, Sonny Ramadhin, and Gary Sobers, who shared that panther-like fielding style with Kanhai, Clive Lloyd, Viv Richards and Roger Harper.

James Adams and Curtley Ambrose need not have danced that post-victory waltz shown worldwide in a Reuters photo on celebration of "the fall of another New Zealand wicket as the home team failed to save the follow-on on the third day".[26] Adams and Ambrose, like all their colleagues, danced their way to victory in the normal course of play. The congratulatory 'high fives' after a brilliant ball, a resulting catch or a high scoring stroke make for a beautiful choreographic design during a game.

The shared characteristics between dance as performing art and cricket are evident at the level of player and team in much the same way as they manifest themselves in the individual dancer and the company to which he or she belongs. At the level of the team, the game of cricket is reminiscent of a choreographed dance work in which individual players are utilized by a captain to create a unified and technically adept instrument analogous to that by which the choreographer gives effect to his creative imagination.

A well-captained team in the field often seems to move like a *corps de ballet* when it is doing well, as the fieldsmen crouch and/or move forward, as the bowler approaches and the players cover for one another. Similarly, when things are not going well or when the team is badly captained, the team often looks like nothing more than a group of novice students of the dance.

In dance, the choreographer needs a stable and committed group of dancers, trained to share and transmit his or her ideas. The same thing can be said of the captain of a cricket team who articulates through his players, the strategies and nuances of the game that he would have them perform. Like dancers, players are important collaborators in the creative act and through improvisations, individual strengths and devices they assist in formulating and forging the captain's particular idiom. Thus, just as the choreographer will assign dancers to roles and arrange them in positions which will best utilize their respective abilities, technical and artistic, the competent captain will position his players on the field in a manner which will utilize their unique strengths to achieve the maximum result. The specialist batsman and bowler can be equated to the lead or principal dancers in a dance work, whilst the other team members are representative of the corps. The overall team success is directly related to the linkages forged between the individual players in much the same way that a choreographic work achieves success through the interconnections of the dancers involved.

The dancer surrenders his or her instrument to the choreographer totally, but only temporarily, for the shaping of the dance work. In effect the choreographer draws the outlines. The fleshing out must be done by both the dancer and choreographer. But it is the dancer who takes total control in the performing. The dancer is the dance. The individual batsman or bowler becomes the game. A judicious division of labour is here the basis for democratic participation in the process of creating and the enhancement of the performer's sense of place and purpose. Surrender is here a basis for rebirth rather than for self-denial; and no one knows this better than the dance performer, as do the best of our cricketers.

Like dance, the game of cricket possesses its own vocabulary, a distinctive and sometimes esoteric lexicon, which one must master in order to achieve any level of technical proficiency in the game. It is this vocabulary that is central to the survival of the styles and forms present in both dance and cricket.[27]

At the individual level shared characteristics are even more immediate. An analysis of these two art forms and the individuals comprising them reveal the following:

- An emphasis on placement of the body in general
- The use of positions in respect of the feet and arms
- The use of the shoulders, wrist, back and pelvis in the execution of movement for enhanced form as well as accentuated force
- The need for control and technical training

- An emphasis on form and line
- An emphasis on fluidity, agility and flexibility
- An emphasis on strength and endurance
- The subjection of the body to intense levels of training and discipline
- The drama and pageantry of the spectacle as projected by the individual

These characteristics are best illustrated in the several strokes played by the batsmen even though they are just as prevalent in bowlers and fielders alike. It is also the emphasis on form and line that makes cricket into the performing art that it is.

Take the cover drive, which is said to be the classical stroke in the game of cricket. Deriving its name from the position to which the ball is directed by the player, namely, cover, it is played off the 'front foot' (left foot in the case of a right-handed batsman and a term used by choreographers in staging movement). The orthodox placement of the feet is in parallel position usually a few inches apart, which is the first position parallel in different forms of dance. This classic placement is, however, not popular with a player like Desmond Haynes, who more often than not will go into this shot with his legs in a parallel position apart and bent, so typical in some African sculptures. Here individual preferences are allowed a performer, albeit within limits.

In this stroke the toes are usually pointed towards the direction of cover and the shot is initiated with the left foot sliding across the right foot with the weight being transferred on to the left foot (front foot) at the point of execution of the shot. The shot is completed with the right leg trailing behind the left foot, as if in preparation for an arabesque in dance.

Although the shot is usually one in which there is much use of the wrist (as in the case of players such as Jeffrey Dujon and Lawrence Rowe), there are some players who prefer to execute the shot by adjusting the placement of the shoulders to give an added degree of force to the shot, as is the case with Gordon Greenidge and Viv Richards. Dujon and Rowe were characterized as 'graceful', whereas Richards and Greenidge were described as 'explosive', words well known to dance critics.

Translated into dance, this stroke begins with a *chassé* (gliding) movement and ends in a transfer of weight. The arms are in a restrained ready-to-hit fourth position *en avant* and the chest opens to provide the needed leverage to effect the stroke. On completion of the shot, the pelvis is in contraction and the elbows and wrists are supported as they are in dance.

Another popular shot which is sheer dance is the hook shot. This is usually played off the 'back leg' with the ball going towards backward square and fine leg. In this movement, the torso actually spirals and the legs are made to follow

Vice Chancellor's XI in action, Sabina Park, Jamaica, 1996.

in much the same way that the spiral movement is effected in dance, from the base of the spine centred on a firm pelvis. In the case of a proficient and graceful player given to form ad style, this shot can culminate in an exaggerated position where the left leg is raised midway between 45 degrees and 90 degrees (*développé* position in classical ballet, or a cantilevered lift-of-leg position or extension in modern dance and Caribbean contemporary dance).

The placement of the shoulders tends to vary in this shot depending on the objective of the player. In a case where the batsman is seeking to raise the ball to a six, the right shoulder tends to drop under the ball and the left shoulder is elevated towards the ear. This placement is just as evident in the case of a dancer preparing to execute a double or triple spiral turn. Where, however, the aim of the batsman is simply to avoid the ball being caught, the right shoulder will be elevated and turned over to give added spiral and contraction to the back.

With the square cut the right foot slides across and out (*chassé*) and the shoulders open up and out in preparation for the shot. The batsman, in some instances, will go to the balls of his feet – *échappé relevé* to the dancer – so as to effectively dominate play of the ball; and just before contact he will transfer the weight onto the right foot (back foot) – *tendu* or stretch of the foot in dance. The movement is completed very often with the front foot (left foot) raised at a 45 degrees angle off the ground – in an attitude position.

The full shot is usually played through square leg and, like the hook shot, involves a spiral of the torso. The shot culminates in a hunching of the upper body (a contraction in dance) with left leg leaving the ground in a position preparatory to a spin (a *passé* position in dance). For the more flamboyant player this shot will actually move beyond a hunched position to an actual *pirouette* (whirl), which, as in the case of dance, represents a facet of brilliance in terms of the player's performance. Let us face it, we like to look 'pretty'. For the West Indies it is cricket to indulge flair and ostentation.

The late cut, called a 'daub' in Barbadian parlance or a 'caress' in general cricket terms, is a shot which is characterized as subtle and stealthy. The player's weight is on the back foot (right foot) and the shot is played at the last minute, in an attempt to 'steal' the ball from the keeper's gloves. It is executed outside the line of the player's body and the ball is redirected away from the fielders and the keeper, usually to a position between slip and gully or first slip and the keeper. The player is crouched over in this shot and often his right shoulder will drop towards the right leg. The cut is reminiscent of that small change of the upper back in dance which characterizes the initiation of a lay-out position in jazz-dance or the 'break' in Haitian dance (*yenvalou*).

The flick stroke can be off either the front or back foot, something of a variant of the on-drive. Usually a response to a full toss or an attempted yorker, the shot operates to take the ball off the pads and redirect it to a point between square leg and fine leg. This shot can very often see the player on his toes (*relevé* to the dancer) just before he makes contact with the ball. The wrist is essential for the proper execution of this stroke. Described in dance, the player is in an open *relevé* position with a contraction of the upper back over the legs.

And with the drives, whether square drive, off-drive, straight drive or on-drive, these shots are each played to a particular direction. The difference in the shots is derived from the angle at which the ball is struck. The square drive is usually struck between point and cover and is executed with the weight placed on the front foot (left foot) in a lunge position. The lunge position is a frequent attitude in dance. The off-drive is played towards mid off whilst the on-drive is directed towards mid on. A straight drive played off either front or back foot, is directed down the wicket towards the bowler. The movement in this case captures the fluidity of the dancer in motion.

Finally, where a player is required to play a ball delivered by a spinner (a slow ball) the exceptional batsman will initiate this shot by chipping or 'dancing' down the wicket (two gallops in dance) towards the ball to avoid it bouncing or turning. This shot, characterized by movement and energy, is illustrative of the kinetic and kinesthetic elements which give to the game of cricket that quality of dance.

The emphasis on weight in the negotiation of and the shaping of many a movement pattern find kindred association with the fall-recovery, tension-relaxation complexes of some schools of American modern dance as does the contraction-release complex usually identified as a Martha Graham invention but organic to all African dance which predates (American) modern dance by a few centuries. Movement (in our cricket as in our dance) is moulded more often than attenuated (note the spiralling torso on top of contracted pelvis). It is as though the material being worked is clay rather than steel. Arms flow like rivers and torsos undulate like the outlines of rolling hills or the ebb-flow of the surrounding sea . . .[28]

The overall choreographic nature of the game is complemented by the grace, rhythm and timing of the bowlers and fielders. In the case of fast bowlers, much of their success directly relates to their demeanour during delivery, in the same way that a dancer will assume a character and stance indicative of his role in a dance work. Bowlers are masters of the wrist corresponding to those dance idioms where the hands and wrists are almost entirely expressive of the dance. Delivery of the ball culminates in the working leg in attitude position.

The bowlers have a rhythm to their run-up and seek line, length, curve, spin, swing and turn in preplanned choreographed ways. The total effect is created when the fielders execute a catch or save with the innate flair, panache and grace which they bring to the game.

Cricket has drama involving crowds and mass appeal defying Europe's snobbish division of art into 'fine' and 'popular', 'classical' and 'ethnic'. It has flowing movement and sudden movement. It has music of bat on ball and the cacophony of broken stumps. And when the batsmen are running well between the wickets and there is a clear understanding between them the site is reminiscent of dancers prancing from wing to wing across the stage.[29]

The television, admittedly no substitute for the real thing, nevertheless confirms this beyond the shadow of a doubt.

So these two great performing arts have a special place in the development of the West Indies. The claims made by C. L. R. James for cricket as an agent of empowerment have often been revisited. There are devotees who hang on to his every word within and beyond the boundary. But Surin has some reservations. He boldly declares, while acknowledging a possible misreading of James, that James "fails to realize that the real reconciliation" he claims cricket can bring to West Indians is by no means "structurally guaranteed anywhere".[30] Such reconciliation, he insists, depends on the abolition of poverty and dispossession and therefore "is still very much an unfinished project".[31] To him "James has by no means given us a final position on the place of cricket within that ceaselessly dynamic process which is capitalism"[32] and one might add, that process which is also the resistance to the viler consequences of that very capitalism.

Well, here is yet another characteristic shared by cricket and the performing arts. The dance is always 'unfinished', and is itself 'dynamic and ceaseless' in its quest for excellence and truth. The ephemeral nature of any performing art would not allow otherwise. One is, in any case, only as good as one's last work. Yesterday's performance belongs to yesterday. One never quite knows what tomorrow will bring. While one must understand the future, one cannot predict it. A magnificent Lara century today can be followed by a miraculous duck tomorrow.

In the wider context of liberation politics via cultural resistance or artistic affirmation, *a la lucha continua,* indeed! The stereotypical perception of beautiful black bodies given to titillating trivia called calypso, reggae or sensuous cricket, has taken a hold of Western consciousness, even in the face of proven expertise and excellence. Moreover, 'performance culture' can be easily dismissed as lacking any capacity for thought and intellectual formulations in the face of a heady hedonism. A Lord Learie or Thatcherite Richards remains, to many, an idiosyncratic departure from a 'historical norm'. And knights of the realm selected from the cricket pitch corresponding to the titled actors from the British theatre stage make sense only if such conferments are made not too long past the peaks of performing careers.

So one's performance skill must in the end rest on the creative mastery of whatever craft underlies the particular art – whether it be cricket or dance. This is what is meant by being truly 'professional' and not simply the command of lucrative remuneration which should be logically the result of that mastery.

Only so will the art form be able to rid itself of the binary indulgences of those who see the English way as the norm and every other way as an aberration. The 'West Indies way' may well fall into neither category and this is as true of Caribbean dance as it has come to be of West Indies cricket for the past quarter of a century at last.

Perhaps it is the encounters between the West Indies and Australia which present us with something in which the beauty and poetry of cricket as an art can best receive full play between evenly matched teams in terms of bottom-line technique, style and tactics. Perhaps there is something liberating, exciting and particularly poignant about the descendants of convicts performing with the offsprings of slaves. Such peculiarities are, after all, the stuff of Caribbean life, art and cricket.

Notes

1 Tony Becca, sports editor for the Jamaica *Gleaner*, uses the word 'performance' frequently in his assessment of local, regional and international cricket matches. In his appraisal of Jamaica's lacklustre display in regional competitions he headlines his article "Emphasis on performance", *Gleaner*, 1 March 1995. Both C. L. R. James and Michael Manley write their 'histories' from the point of view of spectators of a performance event which is cricket.

2 C. L. R. James, *Beyond a Boundary* (London: Stanley Paul, 1963).

3 Kenneth Surin, "C.L.R. James' materialist aesthetic of cricket", in Hilary McD. Beckles and Brian Stoddart (eds), *Liberation Cricket: West Indies Cricket Culture* (Kingston, Jamaica: Ian Randle Publishers, 1995), 313–41.

4 Michael Manley, *A History of West Indies Cricket* (London: André Deutsch, 1988), 381.

5 James, 192–93.

6 See Rush Rehm, *Greek Tragic Theatre* (London: Routledge [Theatre Production Series], 1994).

7 See Carlo Ferdinando Russo, *Aristophanes: An Author for the Stage* (London: Routledge, 1994).

8 The size and reaction of the crowds in the stands are critical to the game. C. L. R. James in his 1960 article "The proof of the pudding" made several references to the size of the crowd of 30,000 ("out of a total population of 800,000") attending the test match against the MCC at the Queen's Park Oval in Port of Spain on January 30, 1960. Cricket, originally regarded as an exercise in upper class gentility, has become in the West Indies a popular cultural endeavour with great mass appeal. Paradoxes abound when East Indian members of audiences in multiracial Trinidad viewing West Indies versus India are required to be 'West Indian' rather 'Indian'. Evenly matched teams such as Australia and the West Indies, arguably the best teams in the game at the time of writing, are able to evoke objectivity from West Indian spectators, it is felt. Its increasing professionalism has not lost to players and audience the sense of fun with which the game is associated in the West Indian mind.

9 Derek Walcott, *The Antilles: Fragments of Epic Memory* (The Nobel Lecture) (New York: Farrar, Straus and Giroux, 1992). Walcott said, *inter alia*, "It is not that History is obliterated by this sunrise. It is there in Antillean geography, in the vegetation itself. The sea sighs with the drowned from the Middle Passage, the butchery of its aborigines, Caribs and Aruac and Taino, bleeds in the scarlet of the immortelle, and even the actions of surf cannot erase the African memory, or the lances of cane as a green prison where indentured Asians, the ancestors of Felicity, are still serving time. That is what I have read around me from boyhood, from the beginnings of poetry, the grace of effort . . ."

10 Clive Lloyd, "Introduction" in Michael Manley, *A History of West Indies Cricket*, v.

11 C.L.R. James, "The proof of the pudding", in Hilary McD. Beckles and Brian Stoddart (eds), *Liberation Cricket: West Indies Cricket Culture*, 307. The full statement reads: "All art, science, philosophy, are modes of apprehending the world, history and society. As one of these cricket in the West Indies at least could hold its own."

12 Rex Nettleford, *Dance Jamaica: Cultural Definition and Artistic Discovery – The National Dance Theatre Company of Jamaica 1962–1983* (New York: Grove Press, 1985), 21. Cited by George Lamming in his review article "Jamaica's National Dance Theatre – A celebration: an artistic work of excellence", *Caribbean Contact* (September 1985), 13.

13 Manley, 382.

14 Lamming, 13.

15 Richard Kraus, Sarah Chapman Hilsendager and Brenda Dixon, *History of the Dance in Art and Education* 3rd ed. (New Jersey: Prentice Hall, 1991), 24.

16 Ted Polhemus, "Social bodies", in Jonathan Benthall and Ted Polhemus (eds), *The Body as a Medium of Expression* (New York: E.P. Dutton, 1975), 27.

17 Manley, 383.

18 H. Miner, "Body ritual among the Nacirema", *American Anthropologist* 58 (1965), cited by Ted Polhemus, 13.

19 See *Caribbean Contact* (September 1981), 9-12.

20 Pere Labat, *Nouveau voyage aux Isles de l'Amerique* 1722, cited by George Lamming in "The new world of the Caribbean", Radio Script Programme 4. Mimeo, Georgetown, British Guiana Public Library Archives, 1957. The full quotation cited by Lamming reads: "I have travelled everywhere in your sea of the Caribbean . . . from Haiti to Barbados, to Martinique and Guadeloupe, and I know what I am speaking about . . . You were all together, in the same uncertain sea . . . citizenship and race – unimportant, feeble little labels compared to the message that my spirit brings to me: that of the position and predicament which history has imposed upon you . . . I saw it first with the dance . . . the *meringue* in Haiti, the *beguine* in Martinique, and today I hear *de mon oreille morte,* the echo of calypsoes from Trinidad, Jamaica, St Lucia, Antigua, Dominica and the legendary Guiana . . . It is no accident that the sea which separates your lands makes no difference to the rhythm of your body."

21 Nettleford, 25.

22 Roderyck Lange, *The Nature of Dance: The Anthropological Perspective* (London: Macdonald and Evans, 1975), 55.

23 See N. Kazantzakis, *Zorba the Greek* (London: Faber and Faber, 1961), 226, cited by Ted Polhemus, 30.

24 Attributed to Maxine Sheets-Johnson by Myron H. Nadel, H. Nadel and Constance G. Nadel in *The Dance Experience* (New York: Praeger Books, 1970), 46.

25 James Carnegie, "Dancing down the wicket: notes on cricket and the dance", prepared for Rex Nettleford, March 1995.

26 *Gleaner*, 13 February 1995, 1B.

27 I am grateful to Messrs Adrain Cummins and Ralph Thorne, attorneys-at law, of Bridgetown, Barbados who gave to this author invaluable guidance by way of 'tutorials' and notes which enabled him to better grasp the correspondence between the vocabulary of cricket and that of the art of dance. Mr Thorne, true to his Barbadian heritage, is a passionate afficionado of the game, while Mr Cummins adds to his strong knowledge of cricket his practical experience in the dance through his long association with the Barbados Dance Theatre Company (BDTC) both as performer and adviser. The BDTC has had in its repertoire, since the 1970s a dance work entitled "Cricket Lovely Cricket" inspired by the game and choreographed by Virginia Sealey. The 1994 Little Theatre Movement (LTM) pantomime in Jamaica "Anancy Come Back" featured a scene on cricket which was something of a show-stopper in that long-running musical play. The National Dance Theatre Company of Jamaica (NDTC) at time of writing is planning to add to its repertoire in 1995 a work based on cricket with Barbara Requa as choreographer. This author has long concluded that Caribbean dance theatre (in the Commonwealth) could benefit tremendously from a closer look at the movement patterns to be found in cricket for the expansion of its vocabulary in the way American Modern Dance has benefited from baseball (as in the choreography for the Broadway musical "Damn Yankees") and American football. Mark

Murphy, a British choreographer, created a dance inspired by cricket for his "idiosyncratic" company V-TOL at The Place in London, 4–8 April 1995. In a promo of it Tom Morris remarked that "English cricketers are encouraged to imitate the positive body image of the West Indian team." The English cricketer Mark Ramprakash reportedly enjoyed the work but was restrained in his reaction: "We don't say beautiful in cricket," he explained. "We say top drawer." Reference has, however been made to the "exquisite" drivers by David Gower, "delicate" late cuts by Sachin Tendulkar and "hypnotic" rhythm in the bowling of Michael Holding (see Tom Morri, "Lots of swing and silly legs?" in the *Sunday Times: The Culture*, 2 April 1995, 10).

28 Rex Nettleford, "Afro-Caribbean dance", *Dancing Times* (May 1990), Dance Study Supplement, Part 8, London.

29 Carnegie, *Notes on Cricket*.

30 Surin, 332.

31 Surin, 332.

32 Surin, 332.

'The Unkindest Cut'

West Indies Cricket and Anti-Apartheid Struggles at Home and Abroad, 1893–1993

Hilary McD. Beckles

The intention here is to illustrate the manner in which modernist notions of West Indian identity and nationhood can be understood by examining cricket culture as a social project. To do so it is necessary to conceive and analyse cricket history as constituted by a series of ideological contests within society, and to delineate their social effects as markers of political change and progress. Cricket in this region has functioned as a metaphor in the discourse of modernity, and much more. It is, in addition, a cultural technology that represents and expresses complex, and oftentimes contradictory, political forces. This general statement may require considerable specification, but its meaning is amplified when placed within the context of the compelling truth and seductive logic of C. L. R. James' assertion that "West Indians crowding into Test match venues bring with them the whole past history and future hopes of the region." Three questions immediately leap from this statement. What exactly is it that West Indians take to cricket? What, furthermore, have they given to cricket? Finally, what have they come to expect of cricket?

The answers to these questions require that we begin with a perception of social conflict as an agency or determinant in cultural transformation. Also, that we recognize how ideological representations of conflicting social relations are in themselves political instruments. These vistas enable us to see how different groups of colonial West Indians made enormous social investments in traditional English cricket culture for widely different reasons – and with diverse effects. The returns on these expenditures, however, have been the collective infusion of the colonial game with a new democratizing identity, a radical philosophical mandate, and a revitalized sense of cultural purpose. Freshly emerged from the scaffold of a slave-based dispensation, and frantically searching for cultural renewal and ontological recognition, the majority of West Indians confronted the ideologically backward Victorian activity with a demand for social inclusion and equity. In so doing, more so than other colonials, they provided cricket culture with an opportunity and an ability to realize in concrete social terms the game's highest moral vision.

Cricket had found its way into the West Indies at the end of the eighteenth century as a cultural import of the white colonial elite – soldiers, administrators, planters and merchants. The paramountcy of race ideology in slave society, and its implications for class relations, meant that cricket functioned initially as an instrument of ethnic social exclusion as well as a force of class cohesion for those with managerial responsibility for the colonizing mission. By the mid nineteenth century, however, an increasingly determined political struggle by the emancipated to remove social privilege and ethnic apartheid from public institutions could not be contained by the boundaries of the elite game; barriers were lowered and some walls breached. What was true of cricket also obtained for politics, commerce and the respected professions. By the end of the century, middle class coloured men, who brought with them some privileges from slave society, played for white clubs or formed their own. In turn, they would engage black teams in 'friendly' games – but these teams were not generally invited to the club houses. It was within this socially segregated environment that the institutional and ideological formation of cricket developed.

The establishment of a network of cricket clubs constitutes a principal expression of the transformations taking place in West Indian social life at the end of the nineteenth century. The convergence of an urban professional middle class of whites, coloureds and blacks challenged the traditional dominance of the planter-merchant elite within the cricket culture. In Jamaica, for example, St Jago, and Vere and Clarendon Clubs were represented exclusively by the planter elite, while the Kingston Club catered for their wealthy urban mercantile allies. While the Kensington Club maintained a largely upper middle class urban white membership, the Melbourne Club was the facility of the coloured professional classes who, from the slavery period, embraced the skin-lightening miscegenation approach to social mobility and respectability.

Not surprisingly, then, Melbourne Club harboured as many anti-black attitudes as the whites only clubs; the colourism that separated the different shades of non-white society was as potent ideologically as the racism which divided blacks and whites. No blacks are listed among the 58 members of the club in 1894.

Whereas in Jamaica, Melbourne used the technicality of a complex fee structure to rationalize the absence of blacks from the club, in Barbados, white officials categorized blacks as professionals and deemed them ineligible for participation in amateur competitions. The formation of Wanderers Cricket Club in 1877 represented the Bajan planter elite's social need for an institutional agency to distinguish their cricket from subordinate 'others'.

The Pickwick Club that followed in 1882 was the response of small planters, middling merchants and professional whites to whom Wanderers had closed the membership list. The Spartan Cricket Club (1893), like Melbourne in Jamaica, was the institution of the politically denied but socially respectable coloured families. With a few whites and blacks admitted to its membership, Spartan's presence was to democratize Barbados cricket and discredit the longstanding ideology of white superiority. Its first president was the distinguished mulatto lawyer Conrad Reeves, first non-white chief justice, whose sense of racial pride was matched only by his loyalty to the political agenda of the white elite.

In both Jamaica and Barbados the black working class remained locked out from these institutionalized arrangements, despite having established a reputation for producing very skilled professional players. "Barbadian professionals", noted Ronnie Hughes, "were groundsmen, young men employed as grounds bowlers, and occasionally helpers and hangers on, in other words, labouring class black Barbadians." These players, in spite of, or probably because of, their ability, were all excluded from Challenge Cup competitions in which white clubs played since 1892. White clubs, however, would occasionally hire them as individuals or as teams to play in 'friendly' games as a means of providing excitement for spectators or to sharpen their own game.

The impressive, and surprising, performance of the Trinidadian team (considered the weakest of the 'Big Four') against the touring Lord Hawke side in 1895 drew particular attention for one special factor. Pelham Warner, Trinidadian by birth, and star batsman in Hawke's side, studied the matter closely and concluded that Trinidad's victories were due to the inclusion of two black professional bowlers, S. Woods and C. P. Cumberbatch. This observation was a critical development in West Indies cricket. Black professionals were still excluded from colonial teams that competed for the Intercolonial Challenge Cup, though a few were included in 'all-island' teams for 'friendly' games. Without black players, it was recognized, the Trinidadian team was no match for Barbados, Demerara or touring English teams. Warner's final submission was that only the integration of blacks into colonial and West Indies teams could guarantee the raising of performance standards.

It was the illiberalism of white elite society in Barbados and Demerara especially, Warner argued in 1895, that promoted and defended the racism that was suffocating West Indies cricket. Furthermore, he said, only the fullest display of the talent of black players could "make the game more popular locally", and assure "great and universal enthusiasm amongst all classes of the people". The first West Indian team selected for a proposed tour of England, he insisted, should include "four or five" black players; it was the only way to prevent embarrassments against county teams.

The mid 1890s, then, witnessed the beginning of a serious call for the introduction of blacks into intercolonial cup competitions and West Indies touring teams. In 1896, nonetheless, Barbados stated its refusal to play against Trinidad in the Challenge Cup if they included black players. The following year Trinidad arrived in Barbados without its black bowling stars and was massively beaten by an innings and 235 runs; centuries were scored for Barbados by H. B. G. Austin (129) and Gussy Cox (161). White Barbadians, however, received an internal message in 1899 when Spartan, the coloured middle class team, won the island's Challenge Cup. The rise to dominance of Spartan within Barbados cricket vindicated Warner's argument that racism and apartheid in West Indies cricket were inhibiting and unacceptable.

The Trinidadians had initiated the policy of selection on merit. By 1900 it was obvious that ammunition for the future growth of West Indies cricket was to be found in large quantities within black communities. This recognition, however, raised a number of questions concerning the material disadvantages of black cricket. Responding to the debate over the relative facilities of black and white cricketers in Barbados, a feature writer for the *Agricultural Reporter*, the planters' journal, argued that "there is absolutely no provision of playgrounds attached to primary and elementary schools" attended by black children. Blacks, it was said, had established an innovative cricket culture about the 'gullies' of plantation villages and in urban ghettos. Their game was learnt at the community level rather than formally within the school system. Behind Spartan's success, then, could be found this spring of talent awaiting opportunity. Professional working-class black teams, such as Fenwicks and Carrington Cricket Clubs, represented this potential. It was popular knowledge that these teams often defeated established Challenge Cup sides. When it was announced at the end of the year that Lord Hawke had invited a West Indian team to tour England in the summer of 1900, working-class black players had good reasons to believe that their time had come.

P. F. Warner's brother, R. S. Warner, was appointed to captain the touring West Indies side. A selection committee representing all the West Indian cricket territories met in Trinidad in January 1900 with the mandate to choose a representative team. Shortly thereafter the news came that five blacks were selected to the touring party of 15. These players were Fitz Hinds (Barbados), W. J. Burton (Demerara), C. A. Ollivierre (St Vincent), and S. Woods and G. L. Constantine (Trinidad). Pelham Warner wrote:

> It has been decided to include black men in the coming team, and there is little doubt that a fairly strong side can be got together. Without these black men it would have been quite absurd to attempt to play first-class counties, and no possible benefit would have been derived from playing those of the second class only. The fielding will certainly be of a high class. The black men will, I fear, suffer from the weather if the summer turns out cold and damp, as their strength lies in the fact that their muscles are extremely loose, owing to the warm weather to which they are accustomed. Woods takes only two steps and bowls as fast as Mold! Englishmen will be very much struck with the throwing powers of these black men, nearly all of them being able to throw well over a hundred yards. On the whole, I feel pretty confident that the team will attract favourable attention all round, and my view is I know shared by many sound judges of the game. The visit of any new team to England is always an experiment, attended with more or less possibilities of failure; but that they will be a failure I do not for a moment think, and in any case West Indian cricket will be greatly improved.

The tour was not given first-class status; there was deep belief among English officials that the West Indians were not ready for the world of serious 'international' cricket. *Wisden,* the reputable cricket magazine, also described the tour as an 'experiment', but P. F. Warner was sure that by its end the West Indians would be ready for first-class status.

Following the 1900 tour, the concept of a first-class multiracial West Indies team was irretrievably established. The WICBC was formed in 1927 with a mandate to promote a representative cricket culture. The West Indies team was elevated to test status the following year, just in time for a three-test tour to England. Blacks, therefore, had brought their cricket to the international stage, and the West Indian team impressed wherever it went as attractive representatives of the modernized game. In so doing, blacks broke down the outer barriers of institutionalized racism in the West Indies and advanced the wider democratic discourse.

In this process of social transformation 1948 was seminal. It was the moment that witnessed simultaneously on both sides of the Atlantic great achievement and deep despair for black colonized communities. The WICBC, under 20 years of persistent pressure from a fractured but deepening democratic agenda, and fuelled by players like Herman Griffith (Barbados), Learie Constantine (Trinidad), administrators like Mitchie Hewitt (Barbados), and political activists like Marcus Garvey and C. L. R. James, succumbed and appointed George Headley – arguably the greatest player of his time – to captain the West Indies cricket team. Headley's tenure lasted for just one test match. It was, nonetheless, a significant breach in the walls of a homegrown, plantation-based West Indian apartheid in cricket culture. That a black man from the lower order could lead a prestigious public institution, and manage the cultural activities of white men of property, seemed at the time revolutionary within the ideological context of these societies.

However, while West Indians had made this crablike advance, 1948 also witnessed the constitutional imposition in South Africa of apartheid – a social system long established in custom and publicly promoted by whites. There is no need at this stage to go into the details of what transpired in South Africa prior to 1948; suffice it to say that, whilst the transformative democratic forces were gaining ground rapidly in the postwar West Indies, ideological fervour demanding the institutionalization of white supremacy was seeking constitutional recognition in South Africa.

South African apartheid required, as West Indian chattel slavery did, a constitutional framework within which social life could be regulated and controlled. This was systematically constructed over time as follows:

1949 — Mixed marriages illegalized

1950 — Racial classification of all inhabitants made statutory by the Population Regulation Act

1950 — Suppression of Communism Act: allowed the state to suppress any political or civic organization that questioned or opposed apartheid

1950 — Group Areas Act: mandated the spatial segregation of races

1953 — Primary and secondary schools racially segregated by law

1953 — Reservation of Separate Amenities Act: imposed racial segregation in public places

1957 — Native Laws Amendment Act: regulated racial segregation of civic organizations, sports clubs, schools, churches, etc.

1965 — Group Areas Act: amendments R. 26/R. 228 banned black crowds from white games

Finally, starting first in 1952, Pass Laws were codified, with amendments in 1956, 1957, 1959, 1963, 1964, 1966, 1967, 1968, 1969 and 1970. These laws obliged every African over 16 years of age to carry on his or her person at all times a pass book which could be demanded by security forces at any moment, and which indicated whether or not he or she was entitled to be present in a white zone.

The objectives of these legislative developments, according to the Minister of the Interior, Dr Donges, were that whites, blacks and coloureds were required to organize their sport separately; no mixed sports would be allowed within the borders of South Africa; no mixed teams could represent South Africa – at home or abroad; international teams playing against South Africa at home or abroad should be all-white. On the ideology of merit as a criterion of social engagement, Prime Minister John Vorster, in an address to Parliament on 11 April 1967, said:

> I, therefore, want to make it quite clear that from South Africa's point of view no mixed sport between whites and non-whites will be practised locally, irrespective of the standard of proficiency of participants. We do not apply that as a criterion because our policy has nothing to do with proficiency or lack of proficiency.

The logic of history, and the course of social change, then, were moving in the opposite directions within the Caribbean and South Africa at the same time.

How, therefore, would it be possible to interface these ideologically contradictory worlds at the rendezvous of a celebratory cricket culture? Under what political banner, and to what end, could the galloping pace of West Indian democracy come to terms with a society that represented anathema for those involved in the popular struggle? The entire world, it seemed, and particularly South Africa, knew that cricket was serious business. Indeed, everywhere it was recognized that sport, in general, was no 'sporting matter' – but a foundation stone of modern political discourse that sought to give meaning and life to political concepts such as national identity, nationhood and social justice.

The first signal of opposition to South African apartheid in sport within the international community came from the British Empire Games Federation (BEGF). In 1934, shortly before Learie Constantine had published his classic *Cricket and I*, in which he called for the removal of the last vestiges of institutional racism in West Indies cricket, the BEGF decided not to award its next games to South Africa. The reason advanced was that the government there had indicated that non-white athletes would not be acceptable. The Canadians led the protest, inspired in part because their black long-jump star, Sam Richardson, would have been debarred. Richardson went on to win a gold medal when the games were held in London.

The international attempt to reject South Africa for its racial policy, however, moved rather slowly after 1934. The major bodies of the cricket fraternity were perhaps slowest. In 1956, the International Table Tennis Federation expelled South Africa's all-white team; the government had refused passports to black and coloured players. In 1964, South Africa was barred from the Tokyo Olympics as well as the World Fencing Federation Games. Closer to the Caribbean, Mexico in 1967 refused entry visas to the South African white team for the Mini Olympics, and the following year South Africa was expelled from world boxing by the International Amateur Boxing Association.

Finally, at the end of 1968, 20 years after the establishment of constitutional apartheid, a scheduled cricket tour to South Africa by the English team was cancelled by the organizers, the MCC. Coloured England player, Basil D'Oliveira, who was born in South Africa, was declared unacceptable on racial grounds by the South Africans. The MCC objected to the attempt to determine the combination of its team, but was not explicit in opposition to the all-white policy of South African cricket authorities. In 1970, the Australians took a stance specifically against apartheid and cancelled their 1971–1972 tour to South Africa.

West Indian cricket institutions, however, long before the MCC took their decisions, had problematized relations with South African apartheid. It should be noted, however, that South Africa, a founding member of the Imperial Cricket Conference (ICC) (later renamed the International Cricket Conference and currently chaired by former West Indian test player Sir Clyde Walcott), showed no interest before 1948 in playing cricket against the West Indians. They played tests against Australia, England and New Zealand, white countries whose unofficial policy it was to avoid embarrassing them by not selecting black or non-white players. During the 1950s these countries organized no serious attempt to expel South Africa from the ICC. In fact, the South Africans were never kicked out; they merely lost membership when the Pretoria government withdrew from the Commonwealth in 1961. The WICBC, considerably marginalized within the ICC, and led by white men, some of whom seemed indifferent to the South African question, was divided on the adoption of a firm policy. It is true to say, however, that after 1961 West Indian cricketers, and the WICBC, played a major role in ensuring South Africa's ostracism.

In spite of formal opposition by the WICBC to South African apartheid, many West Indian cricketers held the view that they could make critical anti-apartheid contributions through the direct interface of the two cricket cultures. Those who articulated this opinion recognized and accepted that their ideas were cast in terms of a moral contest between political good and evil, social progress and reaction, and were confident with respect to the inevitable triumph of the good and progressive – altogether a perspective on social change that is intrinsic to a particular theory or philosophy of history. Evidence of this perspective could be seen at home in the bitter but successful campaign to secure for Frank Worrell the captaincy with tenure of the team, thus putting to an end the traditional assumption of white leadership. Worrell's appointment by the WICBC in 1959 represented the completion of a process that had begun in the West Indies with the 1900 tour to England. Furthermore, it signalled a structural advance towards full internal democratic governance and constitutional independence. It symbolized dramatically the final collapse of racist ideology in West Indies cricket, and the triumph of merit as the dominant organizing principle.

As was the case in 1948, 1959 carried within its bosom a complex and seemingly contradictory set of ideological possibilities. Mass celebration soon turned to private reflection when it was announced that Worrell, triumphant hero of the crowd, had agreed to lead a goodwill West Indies to South Africa in order to play eight matches, not against the white national side, but against black and coloured teams, though under the auspices of the South African Cricket Board of Control (SACBOC). Public opinion in the region was deeply divided; those who argued in support of Worrell stated that any West Indies cricket tour to South Africa would give encouragement and support to black and coloured players in spite of apartheid, a process that could only strengthen domestic anti-apartheid consciousness. Persons in opposition to this view suggested that such a tour would constitute a victory for apartheid in that it would legitimize an inter-black cricket culture, leaving whites to chart a separate, privileged course. They argued, furthermore, that it would suggest to the world that black West Indians, despite their own struggles against racism, had no deep-seated revulsion to a legal definition of themselves as second- or third-class citizens.

Learie Constantine, wrote C. L. R. James, opposed the tour. James supported Worrell and argued that the team should go. Apartheid, James argued, "sought the isolation of the Africans not only from whites but from progressive black voices in the diaspora". The tour would have had worldwide publicity, he continued, and the "African cricketers and the African crowds would have made contact with world famous West Indian cricketers who had played in England and Australia". "There might have been incidents," he said, "so much the better. A pitiless light would have been thrown on the irrationality and stupidity of apartheid." The proposed tour was cancelled as a result of 'wide and acute' public controversy, and Worrell, it has been said, subsequently agreed that this was a good thing because the project was premised on faulty and unconvincing political assumptions.

Worrell's reconsideration had much to do with personal experiences with persistent racist attitudes in Barbados' domestic cricket. On more than one occasion he expressed disgust with the traditional white clubs that continued to defend a policy of black exclusion despite the presence on the island of internationally respected black superstars. His decision to settle in Jamaica at the height of his career was in part a reaction to Barbadian white racism, and a refusal to accept the patronizing social politics of elite society.

In the immediate aftermath of the Worrell discourse, West Indians went about the negotiation of their constitutional independence at Lancaster House in London, divided with respect to action policies regarding the destruction of black life in South Africa. That Nelson Mandela and some of his African National Congress (ANC) colleagues were thrown in jail in 1963, while Trinidad and Tobago, Jamaica, and Guyana were breathing the fresh air of constitutional freedom, had no pressing political significance for most West Indian politicians. Identification with the criminalized ANC-Mandela vanguard was not publicly stated by the West Indian independista leadership, though support for trade embargoes against Pretoria was uniformly adopted. As a result, most West Indian cricketers and spectators, unexposed to public anti-apartheid struggles, had no political understanding of what was going on in southern Africa.

In 1967, the year after Barbados, according to Prime Minister Errol Barrow, had ceased to "loiter on colonial premises", and had severed constitutional links with 341 years of unbroken British rule, the Barbados Cricket Association (BCA), still under the management of the white elite, fired the first salvo against the ideological sensibility of black political governance. It extended an invitation to three white South African players, Colin Bland, Peter Pollock and Graeme Pollock, to join a Rest of the World Team to play a match against Barbados at the Kensington Oval, as part of a public celebration of nationhood. The Barbadian community, divided on the politics of this invitation, argued the case from all sides. The spirit of the 1959 debate was revived, but Sir Frank Worrell, clearer on the issue, opposed the game but on the grounds that it was sheer "poppycock" for Barbados, rather than the West Indies, to take on the world. For him Barbados was seeking to establish for itself a prestige greater than the West Indies – the arrogance of the part considering itself larger than the whole.

Popular debate, however, focused on the invitation of the three South Africans who were described as supporters of apartheid on account of their refusal to publicly denounce the system. Demonstrators attacked E. D. Inniss' leadership of the BCA in the press, and claimed that as a member of the planter-merchant elite he was generally politically insensitive to black suffering in South Africa. The debate, in addition to indicating considerable ideological divisions along lines of race and class on the question of apartheid, illuminated the extent to which the social majority had no concrete knowledge of apartheid. After three weeks of public protest, the BCA withdrew the invitation.

The publication two years later, in 1969, of Walter Rodney's seminal work, *The Groundings with my Brothers*, a statement that encapsulated his intense ideological work and struggle against racial and class injustice in the Caribbean and Africa, foretold what was perhaps the major postcolonial regional political crisis. Described as the 'Sobers Affair', the crisis occupied West Indian popular attention during most of September and October 1970. As an event it took credit for, among other things, establishing focused political discussions between Fidel Castro and many Commonwealth West Indian leaders who, for the first time, seemed prepared to publicly express support for the overthrow of South African apartheid.

On 7 September 1970, news originating in London swept through the Caribbean, and over the world, that Gary Sobers, the West Indies cricket captain, had accepted an invitation to play in a double-wicket weekend competition in Ian Smith's apartheid Rhodesia. No other matter, since the collapse of the British West Indies Federation, had mobilized regional public opinion in this way. The debate took place in the press, on the streets, in parliaments, in Trade Union Congress and within cricket organizations.

Persons defined as 'Black Power' nationalists provided a compelling local framework within which sections of society understood and judged this event. Revolutionary movements throughout Africa provided the global context, while the intensification of the civil rights movement in the United States energized them both. The American Olympic basketball team in Mexico had already provided West Indian youths with an iconography of struggle with the high fist; Mandela was languishing in jail, but Steve Biko was not; Malcolm X and Martin Luther King had been murdered, but Stokely Carmichael and the Black Panthers were trying to hold it together; Mohammed Ali had declared his hand and Fidel Castro's Cuba was defiant in the face of American counter-revolution intentions; Angela Davis had emerged the rebel woman of Black America and Winnie Mandela was 'Queen Mother' of African liberation. Within the ideological and political circumstances of this pan-African upsurge, West Indian cricket, forged in a crucible of anti-apartheid and resistance, seemed fractured in terms of its mandate and moral sensibility. Once again, however, it provided West Indians with an opportunity to examine themselves, to look into their history, and to choose a path.

West Indians reacted as if their cricket culture had met its nemesis. Frank Walcott, head of the Barbados Workers' Union, and a former first-class cricket umpire, condemned the decision of Sobers on the grounds that he "is an international personality and represents the heart and soul of millions of people in the West Indies who see their national identity manifested in cricket". Next door to Rhodesia, Forbes Burnham, president of Guyana, also a 'son' with Barbadian lineage, was visiting Zambia to attend the Conference of the Non-aligned Nations. Burnham pledged $50,000 to Zimbabwe Freedom Fighters and stated that unless "Sobers recants and apologizes for this foolish and ill-advised stand", he would in future be unwelcome in Guyana. The West Indies were scheduled to play a test match in Georgetown during the 1971 Indian tour.

On 15 September, Sobers returned to Barbados and indicated publicly that only good could come of his visit to Rhodesia, and that he had received an open invitation to return. He stated also that he had met Ian Smith and found him less sanguine than represented by the press. Joshou Nkomo, a senior leader of the Zimbabwe Liberation forces in combat with the Smith regime, expressed disappointment with Sobers. He stated that Frank Worrell, whom he knew and respected, had spoken highly of Sobers. *The Workers' Voice*, a newspaper in Antigua, reported that Sobers had abdicated his loyalty to Africans every-where, and described him as "a white-black man". It went on to say that "[Sobers'] deed was the unkindest cut to all those dedicated to the struggle against racism in all its forms".

In Barbados, the issue assumed an importance of the highest political nature, and dominated parliamentary debates for three consecutive days. Deputy Prime Minister Cameron Tudor declared that much of the criticism levelled at Sobers had been out of proportion to the offence, and said that "the people of Barbados will not even for friendship's sake countenance the implied denigration of Mr Sobers by those who now choose to divorce politics from common sense." On 21 October, Lionel Craig, opposition member of Parliament, tabled a resolution calling on the House to deplore Burnham's statement, and *The Barbados Advocate-News* in an editorial asked West Indian political leaders to "cool it". The prime minister of Trinidad and Tobago, Dr Eric Williams, sent for Wes Hall, who had been employed by his government in Port of Spain as sports commissioner. He instructed Hall to go to Barbados, meet with Sobers, and report back to him on the discussion.

Dr Williams had been in touch with Fidel Castro on the issue, and had also asked Indian prime minister, Indira Gandhi, not to cancel the forthcoming Indian tour to the West Indies. Williams needed information and guidance, and Hall functioned as his advisor. The WICBC, meanwhile, had asked Guyana for a "clarification" of the president's statement. Kenny Wishart, president of the Guyana Cricket Board of Control, said that it called for an "apology" from Sobers. A Guyana Sunday paper on 18 October, also called for an apology from

Sobers. In response to these published positions in Guyana, Vernon Jamadar, leader of the opposition in the Trinidad and Tobago House of Representatives, praised Sobers on 20 October for his "calm dignity in response to the savagery of West Indian gutter politicians".

Prime minister of Barbados, Errol Barrow, in New York to address the United Nations General Assembly, telephoned Sobers and asked him to do nothing until his return. After close consultations between Sobers, Dr Williams and Barrow, a letter was prepared clarifying Sobers' position to a specially called meeting of the WICBC. It was issued on 25 October. Those in Sobers' corner insisted that his letter to the WICBC was a statement of 'regret' rather than an apology to Mr Burnham. The statement said:

> Mr President
>
> When I accepted an invitation to take part in a two-day, double-wicket competition in Rhodesia I was assured that there was no segregation in sport in that country but I was not made aware of the deep feeling of the West Indian people. I have since learnt of this feeling and the wider international issues involved. I am naturally deeply distressed by and concerned over the tremendous controversy and bitterness which have arisen after my return from Salisbury. As I was not aware of the serious repercussions I may have expressed myself in such a way as to create the impression for indifference to these issues. Mr President, I wish to inform you that in all sincerity that is far from my true feelings as the prestige of West Indian cricket and the unity and dignity of West Indian and African people are interests I have always served. I therefore wish to convey to you and the members of the Board my sincere regrets for any embarrassment which my action may have caused and to assure you of my unqualified dedication whenever I may be called upon to represent my country – the West Indies – and my people.
>
> *G. St A. Sobers*

Two days later, President Burnham welcomed Sobers' statement, and said that the West Indies captain was now assured of a "great welcome in Guyana". Prime Minister Barrow insisted that no apology was given anyone, and certainly not to persons who seemed keen on African redemption mainly as an instrument to suppress popular aspirations in their own front yards. It was, however, a moment that indicated West Indian determination to problematize cricket links with Southern African apartheid, and to set its face against all those who did.

No sooner had West Indians adjusted to the political crisis that had tarnished the public reputation of Sobers, their greatest ever cricketing icon, than the issue of apartheid and West Indies cricket resurfaced. In 1974, a tour of the West

Indies by an International Wanderers team, organized by British entrepreneur Derrick Robbins, had to be rescheduled because President Burnham and Prime Minister Williams refused it entry into their respective countries. Robbins had carried a similar team to South Africa the previous year, and news of this preceded their visit to the West Indies. The team, however, was permitted entry to Barbados, Grenada, Antigua, St Kitts, Dominica and St Lucia. Lester Bird, now prime minister of Antigua, then president of the ACA, argued Robbins' case. He stated that philosophically Robbins was no supporter of apartheid, and that by taking multiracial teams to South Africa he was contributing to the "breaking down of apartheid".

Two years later, in 1976, a Shell Shield match between Barbados and Guyana scheduled for Bourda (Guyana) was cancelled when President Burnham refused entry to Barbados batsman, Geoffrey Greenidge, who had toured South Africa the previous year with an international team. The BCA recalled the national team, and the incident represented the first occasion that political intervention had led to the abandonment of a first-class regional cricket match in the West Indies. This event placed the issue of the relations between West Indian and South African cricket, or more generally, West Indies sport and apartheid, firmly at the top of the regional political agenda.

The Guyana government, unlike others in the region, was unequivocal in its support for the United Nations' resolution on nondiscrimination in sport. President Burnham went further, however, when he declared that "no South African who supports apartheid, and no non-Guyanese who participates in sport in South Africa, shall be allowed to enter Guyana". Guyana, the president said, "cannot accept any compromise or assault from this quarter upon the historic dignity of citizens of African descent". Guyana joined Jamaica in spearheading an effort to arrive at a common position among Caricom member states. By 1977 the Governments of Barbados, Guyana, Trinidad and Tobago, and Jamaica – the traditional 'Big Four' in cricketing terms – succeeded in sketching the parameters of a framework for a regional, national and international anti-apartheid policy.

In this development, Michael Manley's hand was evident everywhere. His anti-apartheid politics, consistent with those of his father, Norman Manley, had provided global leadership, and his love of cricket rivalled only his commitment to political decolonization. His task was to bring along the more reluctant West Indian states, and hold them in alliance with a Guyana position that seemed by global standards extreme and inflexible. When the policy framework was finally enunciated, Barbados had adopted what appeared to be a conservative approach, which fell short of the Jamaica and Guyana provisions. The core of the Barbados position was that it would: disapprove, and not support, any Barbadian, or Barbadian team, visiting South Africa; support a decision by sporting bodies that did not consider eligible for selection any player in future who went to South Africa; it would not, however, ban a national of any other country who had previously played in South Africa from entering Barbados to play if they were part of a country with which Barbados had sporting links.

Jamaica accepted these points but qualified the latter with a ban on national teams who played in South Africa. With respect to the ban, Guyana went further and extended the ban to all individuals, including journalists, coaches and administrators. The WICBC was ahead with regard to these policy positions. After its Annual General Meeting, 13–15 May 1976, in Port of Spain, the secretary of the WICBC issued the following statement:

> The West Indies Cricket Board of Control wishes to reiterate its total opposition to the system of Apartheid as obtains in South Africa and Rhodesia and advises that all players from Caribbean territories under its jurisdiction who play cricket or coach in South Africa or Rhodesia will not be permitted to participate in matches organized under the auspices of the Board at home or abroad. In addition, the Board reaffirms that no official team from any country which tours South Africa or Rhodesia will be welcome in the West Indies until there is complete multiracial cricket and teams are selected solely on merit in those countries.

Within the context of anti-apartheid policies enunciated by governments, and the declaration of the WICBC, the 1976 England young cricketers tour proved to be divisive. The team was debarred from Guyana, since many of its members had played in South Africa. Games were rescheduled, however, for Dominica, Barbados, Montserrat, St Kitts and Grenada, where anti-apartheid provisions were less penetrative. In June of the following year, Commonwealth Heads of Government, meeting in the United Kingdom, signed the Gleneagles Agreement which aimed at establishing further guidelines for determining steps by the Commonwealth to isolate South Africa in sports. The structure of the agreement reflected many of the opinions of West Indian political leaders, and the views of the WICBC were integrated into its ideological spirit and language.

The centre stage of West Indies opposition to South African apartheid, however, was not completely dominated by men's cricket culture. The West Indies Cricket Women's Team, playing under the auspices of the Caribbean Women's Cricket Council which had participated in staging the first ever Cricket World Cup in 1973, cancelled a test tour to England because some of the English women had played in South Africa. Vivalyn Latty-Scott and

Dorothy Hobson, veteran Jamaica and West Indies stars, supported the stance against apartheid even though the team was just coming on stream and desperately needed the international experience and exposure.

West Indians, then, had no reason to be surprised when in 1981 the second test against the touring England team scheduled for Guyana was cancelled. Robin Jackman, a member of the English team, was refused permission by the Guyana government on account of his having played and coached in South Africa. The tour, however, went ahead; matches were played in Jamaica, Barbados, Trinidad and Tobago, and Antigua. There were no surprises, furthermore, when the WICBC, also in 1981, informed the former West Indies captain, Alvin Kallicharan of Guyana, that he was debarred from all cricket organized under its auspices, on account of his signing a contract to play Currie Cup cricket in South Africa. Kallicharan had followed in the footsteps of Barbadian and West Indian all-rounder, John Shepherd, who held the record for being the first black man to play Currie Cup cricket in South Africa, an achievement for which he was vilified by the anti-apartheid movement in England and branded a traitor to the black cause and a self-hater.

The murder of Walter Rodney in Guyana took place at a time when the free Mandela campaign was gaining international momentum and respectability. Under political pressure globally, as well as at home, from a cricket/sports-crazy white populace, the apartheid government in South Africa was forced into a position of mediation. The murder by the state of Steve Biko accelerated the militancy of the youth in the townships, and the South African Cricket Union (SACU), playing its part in the defence of apartheid, went on the offensive and targeted West Indies cricket with a razzmatazz of political and ideological propaganda that stunned the world. While the bloodstained apartheid state insisted to the world that racial barriers were being removed, and that liberal reforms were taking place, the SACU planned a daring raid upon West Indies cricket in much the same way that the Cuban army was taking South African military strongholds in support of liberation struggles in Angola, Mozambique and Namibia. It was a torrid time for the West Indian mind; what greater political coup for the South Africans than a black West Indies team playing against white teams in South Africa while the system of apartheid remained intact. President of the WICBC, Allan Rae, had spoken of such a threat to West Indies cricket by money offers from South Africa as early as 1982, and had referred to it as a "policy of piracy".

The man who led the raiding party on West Indies cricket was Dr Ali Bacher, director of the Transvaal Cricket Union; his agents in the West Indies were Barbadian cricketers Sylvester Clarke and Gregory Armstrong. On 4 January 1983, news broke of a proposed tour of West Indies cricketers to South Africa.

Names called in this first report were Sylvester Clarke, Wayne Daniel, Collis King, Lawrence Rowe, Faoud Bacchus, Albert Padmore, Richard Austin, Jim Allen and Emmerson Trotman. CANA listed Sir Gary Sobers as manager and Padmore as assistant manager, and gave the team as Lawrence Rowe (captain), Everton Mathis, Collis King, Sylvester Clarke, Desmond Haynes, Hartley Alleyne, David Murray, Alvin Greenidge, Emmerson Trotman, Malcolm Marshall, Colin Croft, Alvin Kallicharan, Derek Parris and Winston Davis.

Panic broke out in the camp of West Indies cricket, expressed in a rash of allegations and accusations; it was clear that a sick and insidious hand had gripped West Indian cricket by the throat. Secrecy and distrust pervaded the air. Padmore, Davis, and Clarke issued denials; Sir Gary was in Australia, and his wife, Lady Prue, said she was "surprised and shocked" at the report. In a release to the press she stated, "I am sure Gary would want me to let all West Indians know that he would not be engaged in any such tour." On 5 January, the Barbados *Nation* carried a front page report in which a "former Barbados cricketer" who claimed to be the West Indies agent for the South African organizers, stated that the tour was planned for December 1985, and that players would receive up to BD$25,000.

South African officials confirmed that some West Indies stars were scared off by the leaked report, but remained confident in attracting top players. Insights into the nature of behind the scenes negotiations between Ali Bacher and West Indian stars can be found in Desmond Haynes' recent autobiography, *Lion of Barbados*. What Haynes tells us is that many West Indian players were open and vulnerable as far as making a deal with Bacher was concerned, and that they weighed potential financial benefits with contractual terms offered by the WICBC. The WICBC, though not surprised, seemed caught off guard by the depth of the South African penetration, but did very little to secure the loyalty of targeted players. President Rae, after receiving personal assurances from Jamaica captain Lawrence Rowe, and West Indies fast bowler Colin Croft, praised them publicly for their principled stance in rejecting South African offers. Rae, speaking at a function in Kingston, stated:

> I believe the cricketing fraternity of the West Indies ought to say a big thank you to those gentlemen who have put the temptation behind them. It is something in their favour that their pride is bigger than their right hands.

Four days later, WICBC secretary Steve Camacho learnt in Kingston that Rowe and Croft were booked to fly out to Johannesburg. In Barbados, the airlines confirmed that Clarke, Greenidge, King, Mosley, Padmore, Trotman and Armstrong, all distinguished national players, were booked for the same destination.

While the sense of implosion within West Indies cricket magnified under the heat of public debate, the centre received a significant strengthening when news circulated that Viv Richards, arguably the best batsman in the world, was offered EC$1 million to play in South Africa and that he had refused, describing the financial offer as "blood money". The provision of firm anti-apartheid leadership by Richards further polarized public opinion, and the weakness of political leadership seemed the more treacherous. Richards received a message from Mandela's ANC thanking him for his vision and solidarity. He was not alone, however, in making firm ideological statements in response to the South African offensive. Michael Holding, front-line West Indies fast bowler, in reacting to an offer received, said he could not "sell his birthright for a mess of porridge". Clive Lloyd, West Indies captain, seeing the reserve players of his dream-team being spirited away by the rand, told the press: "I know that some of them are out of work and the money is very tempting, but that is not all in life."

West Indian cricketers knew very little of South African society, despite some exposure to South African cricketers through contact in the English county circuit. On arrival in South Africa Captain Rowe declared: "We feel a bit jittery, but we are professionals, and we are here to do a job." Everton Mathis, the young promising stroke player from Jamaica, and still a West Indian test prospect, told the Jamaica *Daily News* before departure from Kingston: "I am a Rastaman. That is my philosophy. I am not supporting apartheid. I am dealing with survival. At one stage I did not want to go, but I had to think about my family." Rowe's team was dubbed by the local and international media as 'rebels'; some were banned for life, others for short terms, by clubs, countries and the WICBC. They were labelled 'cricket outcasts' and 'mercenaries', and described as traitors to the cause of African redemption. In Barbados, Minister of Sport, Vic Johnson, told a press conference:

> . . . there is no price for which self-respect or human integrity can ever be bought. Those who did not go upheld the honour of the whole region and signalled to the rest of the world that human dignity is not a commodity to be traded in the market place of expediency.

Veteran Barbados journalist, Al Gilkes, writing in the *Daily Nation*, disagreed. He stated:

> Lawrence Rowe and his rebel team had become, not the mercenaries they were being labelled outside South Africa, but 18 black missionaries converting and baptizing thousands and thousands of whites to the religion of black acceptance and respect from Capetown to Johannesburg, from Durban and right into the throne room of Afrikanerdom itself, Pretoria.

In South Africa, where cricket had been cultivated as a sport for whites, the small but important coloured elite and black professionals' responses to the arrival of the West Indian cricketers were mixed. West Indians were classified by the state, and welcomed by whites for the purposes of the project, as temporary 'honorary whites'. In the black townships, however, they were hailed as villains, and graffiti saying "West Indies traitors go home" was common enough. Their presence was interpreted as part of a strategic political move by the state to counter mounting global criticisms of apartheid. West Indians, once again, were divided in their opinions, but the clandestine manner in which the entire operation had been conducted drew disgust even from those who seemed willing to give players the most liberal consideration.

In a recent autobiography, Gladstone Mills, Jamaica cricket administrator, and university professor of Public Administration, records a discussion between President Rae and Jamaica's batting star, Herbert Chang. News had broken in the Jamaican press that Chang had signed a contract to join the 'rebel' party in South Africa. Rae sought clarification of the matter. Mills wrote:

Rae: Mr Chang, there is a rumour that you are going to South Africa
         to play cricket. If this is not true, let us know, and we will assist
         you in scotching it.
Chang: Mr Rae, I have no contract to play in South Africa.
Rae: I did not ask you if you have a contract. Are you going to
         South Africa?
Chang: Me going to South Africa? No Sir!

The next day Chang was on his way to South Africa. As a result of these events West Indians were called upon by forces within their cricket culture to examine themselves and to see what C. L. R. James meant when he stated that cricket beyond the boundary is but a manifestation of the current state of political consciousness. The debate over 'rebel teams' was recorded in every village, town and city of the region. In every workplace and public institution everyone had a view, and cricket, quite clearly, functioned as a mirror that reflected the images of identity and attitudes within the fragmented but hopeful West Indian nation.

In 1991, when West Indians rose in spontaneous celebration of Nelson Mandela strolling out of prison, as if he had gone there to pay someone a visit, they had no way of knowing that he, not yet president and with apartheid still intact, would soon be asking them to accept and embrace Afrikaner cricketers as their newest 'test mates'. Was the nightmare really over? Were West Indians waking up to a re-engineered, but even more obnoxious reality? All eyes in the West Indies opened as the WICBC announced that the South African cricket team would tour the West Indies in early 1992 – and play a test in Barbados.

Political leaders declared that ideally they had hoped the matter of democratic elections would be settled before such an enterprise was launched, but supported the WICBC, who claimed extensive consultation with the ANC, and boasted evidence of Mandela's support. The first encounter between the two teams had taken place during the 1991–1992 World Cup in Australia/New Zealand. The moment was at best a test of West Indian sentiment. The West Indies were defeated by South Africa, and Captain Richie Richardson incurred, perhaps forever, the wrath of a West Indies public who, he lamented, had misunderstood his meaning when he said that the defeat was "just another match". Would Viv Richards have said that, they asked? Was Richards not selected by the WICBC for the World Cup because his presence would have given ideological cast to the historic match?

South African cricketers, however, fresh from their success against the West Indies in limited overs cricket, were on their way to Barbados for the grand 'inaugural' test. The front page of the Barbados *Daily Nation*, 17 April 1992, carried the bold caption "Out of Africa" over a picture of Gary Sobers embracing Ali Bacher and Mike Proctor, manager and coach, respectively, of the visiting South African team. Next to the headline, a smaller caption says, "Traitors: pan-Africans come out against cricket tour." While declaring themselves united in opposition to South Africa's visit to the West Indies before the system of apartheid was fully disbanded, Barbadian pan-Africans were divided on the tactics necessary to effectively represent their position. Some were prepared to carry into the stands placards and banners that denounced apartheid while watching the game. Others were prepared to keep vigil outside under the watchful eyes of well-armed police contingents.

The test match was scheduled for Kensington Oval, 18–22 April. From the first week of the month pan-Africanists led the campaign against the event, but the effects of their protest were overtaken by a larger community effort fuelled by the belief and allegation that the exclusion of Barbadian player Anderson Cummins from the West Indies team for the match was a blatant injustice, constituting evidence of yet another strike against Barbadian cricketers by WICBC selectors. Protest action that started as a limited anti-apartheid campaign was soon transformed into the popular 'Andy Cummins Affair'. Those at the vanguard of the Cummins campaign called for a national boycott of the test. Cummins, they said, had performed well in the previous World Cup and did not deserve to be abandoned. His nonselection, they said, was the result of discriminatory regional politics that had taken root within the WICBC. Cummins' replacement, Antigua's Kenneth Benjamin, they claimed, was less tried and tested, and universally considered more unreliable.

After 40 years of trying to stage a successful boycott of a test match, a West Indian community had succeeded. The Barbados boycott was almost total. Rumour circulated that on the first day the Kensington Oval was inhabited by "2 teams, 2 stray dogs, 2 umpires and a depressed groundsman". Some blamed the success of the boycott on Prime Minister Erskine Sandiford's structural adjustment programme with the IMF and World Bank; others said it was a strike against the arrogance and unaccountability of the WICBC. Few, however, reported that success was due to the pervasiveness of ideological opposition to apartheid. Newspapers in neighbouring Trinidad and Tobago screamed denouncements of Barbadian boycotters with the following headlines during the week of the test:

"Bumptious Bajan boycott"

"Insularity may again be stepping into West Indies cricket"

"God don't like ugly"

"Bajan boycott opens new wounds in West Indies cricket"

"Destroying the single bond that unites us"

"WICBC lose over $1 million"

Only one headline echoed a different note. It called upon readers to "Praise Barbadians for South Africa Boycott". Over a letter in support of the anti-apartheid movement in Barbados by Dr James Millette, lecturer in History at the University of the West Indies, this headline stood in naked isolation during a week when West Indians were shocked by sights of empty seats at a Barbados test match.

Consequently, popular interpretations of the event revolved around what became the 'Cummins thesis'. Media debates, therefore, were conducted in terms of its validity as an explanatory model, and no alternative accounts were offered. Boycotters were lumped together as a homogeneous group of reactionaries acting to the detriment of West Indies cricket. Former Barbados ambassador, Oliver Jackman, writing in the *Barbados Sunday Sun*, 22 January 1993, stated that "The Boycott of West Indies-South Africa was a national disgrace fomented by a bunch of chauvinistic, small minded people, including the media."

The Cummins thesis, however, seems flawed against the background of the traditional behaviour of Barbados cricket crowds, their accumulated knowledge with respect to the eligibility of competing players and the general ideological contexts of the encounter. Many questions can be asked, but one that seems compelling is this: Would Barbadians, who have accumulated a respected understanding of cricket, even within the context of a prior disenchantment with selectors, have boycotted a match in protest over a player whose selection was far from obvious? In recent years many Barbadian players with considerable merit 'died on the vine' of nonselection. Would Barbadians have boycotted the test if it had been staged against respected adversaries – England, Australia, Pakistan and India? Were Barbadians not showing deep disrespect for an encounter against a team for whom they were not ideologically prepared? Were they reluctant to offer respectability to South Africa before the advent of universal adult suffrage and democratic governance? Where were the thousands of non-Barbadian West Indians who usually visited Kensington Oval? Did not the players themselves signal to the public their own reluctance to play the test at that particular political moment?

In 1994, England visited the West Indies for a five-test series. Students at the CCR, UWI Cave Hill, took the opportunity of the Barbados test to conduct a limited survey of opinion among regular cricket spectators. Of the 343 respondents, 325 stated that they had taken a conscious decision not to attend the match; 18 stated that they attended the match at various stages. An analysis of the reasons offered by boycotters indicates considerable diversity in motivational factors: 34 percent explained their action in terms of their disenchantment with the WICBC for its maltreatment of outgoing stars, and for not appointing Desmond Haynes as captain following Viv Richards; 26 percent stated their objection to the South African test which they considered a premature project; 8 percent offered miscellaneous reasons, such as the high cost of tickets in relation to the quality of the opposition, falling interest in cricket and the general contentious mood that surrounded the game.

While these data are at best crude aggregates, and are offered with no pretence to scientific validity, they do indicate the need to question the accuracy of explanations that surround the Cummins thesis. Furthermore, they suggest that wider issues beyond and within the boundaries of cricket were at play, and should be taken on board if the historic moment is to be adequately scrutinized and properly understood. What the event indicates, for sure, is that after 50 years, efforts to interface these cricket cultures that symbolized opposing ideological cultures were still considered in the West Indies as problematical. West Indians in Barbados, looking at their cricket through the lens of past history and future expectations, were dissatisfied and stayed at home. The social and political price was too high; no one should have been shocked by these developments.

West Indies cricket culture, then, constituted the main theatre within which an intense and transformative democratizing discourse developed with respect to the politics of anti-apartheid. The dialogue took place first within the context of the anticolonial movement in which white supremacy ideologies and practices were targeted by an aggressive political philosophy that located meritocracy at the vanguard of an egalitarian pluralist, ethnic culture. At once a class and a race struggle for justice, the opposition to elite domination in cricket culture sustained the democratic movement, and widened the base of the challenge to traditions of colonial governance.

The political and social results of this process by the 1950s constitute a significant part of empirical evidence that validated the call for nationhood as a project whose time had come. Between 1948 and 1958, when the leadership of West Indies cricket moved slowly and painfully from George Headley to Frank Worrell, it was understood that social apartheid in the West Indies was no longer a viable public institution. The weight of this understanding, and the momentum it gathered, meant that West Indian society fractured in an attempt to come to terms with global apartheid. South African cricket was encountered after the 1950s as a test of the depths of West Indian public opinion and political consciousness. As governments, seeking to reflect rather than lead on this issue, turned their faces against South African cricket, persons who considered themselves disenfranchised and marginalized as economic citizens challenged the meaning and significance of their positions by proposing and participating in cricket encounters with apartheid regimes.

Cricket, during the 1980s, therefore, presented a new context for sustained democratic discourse that focused on class alienation within the postcolonial dispensation. Conflicting understandings of social freedom emerged, with some working class black West Indians considering themselves no more privileged than their counterparts in South Africa. The nationalist project had left most behind, particularly those in the working class who rose up during the 1930s in defiance of colonialism and in support of political freedom. By this time, cricket culture had assumed new and contradictory characteristics, influenced by the blurred vision of the discredited postcolonialist political leadership. The attempt, however, to achieve rationalization between the democratizing inner logic and moral impulses of the game, and the social dislocations and crises beyond the boundary, continues to constitute a site for political tension and ideological fervent. The last ball has not yet been bowled.

Cricket and the Black Struggle
in South Africa

●

Alan Cobley

Introduction

The modern game of cricket evolved out of the innumerable bat and ball games that were part of the European folk culture associated with pre-industrial, peasant society. During the eighteenth century a version of the game was codified and propagated by the English elite at the same time as the systematic destruction of the free peasantry in England (through enclosure of common land) was denying space to alternative, more plebeian, versions. As a result, the elitist version of cricket came to predominate, and by the mid Victorian era the attitudes, values and aspirations that surrounded the game were also essentially those of the dominant English elite.1 However, cricket's origin as part of the popular culture was never entirely subsumed, so that the game remained attractive to, and was valued by, the subordinate classes. For them it was not seen merely as an expression of the hegemonic values in society (and for that reason worthy of imitation); it remained a meaningful and vital part of their own heritage. As a result, cricket in England has never been an exclusive pursuit, however hard the elite might have struggled to make it so. At some level, cricket has always been a common currency of pleasure. It is this critical ambiguity in the nature of cricket that has ensured its enduring popularity as a game, and has also ensured that it has become a site of struggle between the dominant and subordinate classes in every society where it has been played.

Cricket arrived in South Africa at the beginning of the nineteenth century, imported initially by British troops – as in so many other parts of the world. The first recorded match was held at Capetown in 1808. The influence of the British garrison at the Cape in the early part of the century was supplemented by arrival of larger numbers of British settlers in the Eastern Cape region from the 1840s. The first club was established in Port Elizabeth in the Eastern

Cape in 1843, followed by the founding of a club in Pietermaritzburg in Natal in 1853. From that point, "cricket followed the spread of colonial occupation", arriving in Johannesburg, deep in the interior, only a year after the discovery of gold had led to the founding of the city in 1886.[2] The penetration of cricket to all parts of South Africa by the 1880s also coincided with the inauguration of the county championship in England.

The Rise and Fall of Black Cricket

Cricket in nineteenth century South Africa was an overwhelmingly English pastime. Nevertheless other communities in the region quickly took up the game. The initial mode of transmission of cricket among the pre-existing Boer settler community (of Dutch origin) and the indigenous African population was informal and haphazard, based mainly on imitation. Nevertheless, cricket quickly staked a claim as part of the emergent popular culture of colonial South Africa, creating parallels with its ambivalent role in English society. As early as 1854 a makeshift game between Boers and Hottentots was reported to have ended in a victory for the Hottentots.[3] Informal transmission among blacks was complemented by formal transmission in the second half of the nineteenth century through missionary endeavour. Anglican and Methodist missionaries flocked to South Africa in the Victorian era, imbued with a muscular brand of Christianity which was peculiarly English, and which saw cricket as exemplifying a 'perfect system of ethics and morals'. In the South African mission field cricket took on added significance as part of the civilizing force of 'western civilization' and of empire. It was natural, therefore, that the early 'native training institutions' targeted at the 'native elite' – such as Lovedale (founded 1840), and Healdtown (founded 1856) – included sport, and especially cricket, as an essential part of the training they imparted to their charges. In the Cape Colony cricket was also part of the curriculum at many primary schools for Africans by the end of the century.

The enthusiasm and adeptness with which blacks approached cricket was a notable feature of these early days. One reason for this was that competitive sport was not foreign to African society, even if the specific games introduced by Europeans – such as cricket – were new. African society was replete with tests of strength, dexterity and skill, especially for boys and young men. One such activity was the ancient tradition of stick fighting known as *amalaita*, which persisted as a trial of manhood deep into the twentieth century. In the 1920s and 1930s municipal authorities throughout South Africa, fearing that *amalaita* was becoming the focus of a radical youth gang culture among the urban black community, sought to stamp it out by banning the carrying of sticks within municipal boundaries. During the 1940s, when it became clear that repression had failed to eradicate the practice, the Pretoria Town Council resorted to allowing *amalaita* fights under police supervision every Sunday afternoon at one of its sports grounds, before a large and appreciative crowd.[4] Apart from *amalaita*, African boys were practised in running, wrestling, the use of slingshots and a host of other physical skills. In light of this background it is not surprising that an observer of a cricket game at a mission school in Natal in 1857 noted that African boys "rarely fail to fling down the wicket from a distance"; he went on to suggest that their skill in throwing spears gave them an advantage over white boys at cricket.[5] Whatever the precise reason, black or mixed school mission teams seem to have held their own with ease against white school teams in this era, and a number of senior 'coloured' or black clubs had been formed throughout the Eastern Cape by the late 1880s. The importance of the game to the emerging westernized African elite in the region around this time is illustrated by the fact that it was the first African political leader of note, John Tengo Jabavu, who donated the first cup for inter-town black cricket. This was less than ten years after the first trophy in white colonial cricket had been presented, and predated the inauguration of the regional Currie Cup competition in 1888, the year the first English team came to South Africa.

However, it is important to appreciate that for the black elite rising out of the mission schools, cricket was never merely a game. As André Odendaal points out:

> Sports, particularly Cricket, served an explicitly political function for the black elite. They were intent on using it as an instrument of improvement and assimilation. By enthusiastically playing the most gentlemanly and Victorian of games, they intended to demonstrate their ability to adopt and assimilate European culture and behave like gentlemen – and by extension to show their fitness to be accepted as full citizens in Cape society. Through sport they could pay homage to the ideas of 'civilization', 'progress', 'Christianity', and 'Empire' that were so precious to the Victorians, and call for imperial concepts of fair play to be respected; through sport they could assert their own self-conscious class position.[6]

Thus their enthusiastic involvement in cricket, in the clubs and embryonic associations, in the competitions, in the matches themselves, must be seen in the context of a much broader struggle on the part of the elite to be considered and accepted as equals in colonial South Africa. Black cricket in the nineteenth century was both a popular recreation and an expression of black aspirations against white colonial domination. The latter aspect was very evident in the attitude of black spectators to the visiting English team in 1888–1889, and towards every other touring team to visit South Africa until the ending of apartheid a hundred years later. Invariably they cheered on the visitors against local white colonial teams.[7]

The high-water mark of black cricket in the nineteenth century came in 1897 when Sir David Harris, president of De Beers Consolidated Mines, donated the Barnato Cup (named for the mining magnate who was the co-founder, with Cecil Rhodes, of De Beers) for interregional black cricket "in the hope that it would foster and improve cricket standards".[8] By this time cricket had moved with the black elite to the new urban industrial centres in Kimberley and Johannesburg, where new economic and social opportunities spurred the rise of a new, urban based, black petty bourgeoisie. At the same time, however, black cricket was exposed to the growing tensions associated with the ending of African economic and political independence and the concomitant of a racially ordered industrial capitalist system in South Africa at the end of the nineteenth century. After several decades of parallel growth and some limited interaction between black and white cricket, these wider societal developments gave rise to a much less tolerant attitude towards black cricket on the part of whites. One example of this was the controversy over the proposed inclusion of a 'Cape Malay' (a subcategory within the 'coloured' group) fast bowler called T. 'Krom' Hendricks in the 1894 South African team to tour England, after he had performed well in a Cape Malay team against an English touring side in 1891–1892. In the end, "as a result of the greatest pressure by those in high authority in the Cape Colony" it was reported that "the committee after due consideration decided that it would be impolitic to include him in the team".[9] The souring of relations between black and white cricket continued in the early twentieth century. The restructuring of international cricket as a vehicle for hegemonic British imperialist values through the formation of the ICC in 1909 (with the MCC, Australia, and [white] South Africa as founder members) coincided with the formation of the Union of South Africa and the establishment of a comprehensive system of segregation in South Africa after 1910. As a result of these developments, in the first half of the twentieth century, black cricket was increasingly marginalized and subordinated.[10]

Another negative development for black cricket associated with the segregationist era in the early twentieth century concerned its fragmentation and subdivision into racially defined associations. At an early stage white cricketers had been grouped in the exclusively white South African Cricket Association, but the pioneering Griqualand West Coloured Cricketers Union formed in 1892 had included African, Indian, 'Malay' and 'coloured' teams.

Segregationist pressure soon began to separate out these strands. A South African Coloured Cricket Board was formed in 1902; this split and the South African Independent Coloured Cricket Board (which was exclusively for coloured and 'Malay' players) was formed in 1926. African cricketers in turn broke away from the original body to form the South African Bantu Cricket Union in 1932. Indian cricketers, who had their own exclusive clubs from the turn of the century, formed the South African Indian Cricket Union in 1940. It was not until the SACBOC was formed in 1952 that the black cricketers from all of these communities began to play together in the same competitions once again. Separation from white cricket remained absolute until after South Africa was isolated by the international test ban in the 1970s.

Hostility or indifference to black cricketers on the part of the dominant white cricketing establishment starved it of resources, equipment, coaching, even pitches to play the game. It also encouraged the popular perception that cricket was a white game. Although it remained firmly established among 'coloureds' and Indians, who continued to produce some outstanding players, cricket declined markedly in support and general quality of play among Africans. Members of the African elite who continued to aspire to social and cultural assimilation with whites continued to play the game, but they were an increasingly embattled and isolated minority. Among Africans in the backyard slums, dusty townships and squatter camps (which were mushrooming on the fringes of the white urban areas), it was football that became the first modern mass sport, for reasons made plain by James Walvin:

> No other sport lent itself so easily and cheaply to the varying conditions of urban life. It was simple to play, easy to grasp and could be played on any surface under any conditions, by indeterminate numbers of men. It needed no equipment but a ball, and could last from dawn to dusk. Football could be played by anyone, regardless of size, skill or strength.[11]

By the 1940s football was not only a mass spectator sport among Africans, but supported considerable numbers of professional and semiprofessional players. Along with boxers, they were among the first professional black sports persons in South Africa's history.

African Cricket and the Role of the Mines

From the 1920s onwards, there was a growing influx of blacks into the urban industrial centres of South Africa in search of work and a better life. Whether they were migrant workers living on the gold mines along the Witwatersrand or permanent residents who settled in the burgeoning black townships, this growing concentration of Africans was a worry to whites, who feared black economic competition and black political radicalization. A growing black working class with a radicalized consciousness might ultimately threaten the hegemonic positions of whites in South Africa, which had been built on a racist political settlement in 1910. To prevent the 'swamping' of whites in the cities by an overwhelming tide of blacks, various legislative measures were taken, beginning with the Natives (Urban Areas) Act of 1923. Against this background the history of black cricket in South Africa took a new twist.

To combat black radicalization in the rapidly growing urban centres during the 1920s, missionaries and white liberals began to sponsor black sport. From the outset they argued that the provision of healthful recreation for blacks had benefits far beyond the physical. As one missionary advocate explained to a conference in 1929, it would have moral and social benefits also:

> Maladjustments to the social order would be prevented by the true adjustments that proper play would bring about. Proper and adequate provision for native recreation would mean better workers, keener mentally and physically, better citizens less likely to be criminals, better neighbours, less likely to be anti-white, more likely to possess a true sense of community values.[12]

In short, therefore, sport for blacks was viewed explicitly by those whites who sponsored it in these years as a means of social control. By the 1930s the message had reached municipal authorities along the Witwatersrand, who began to provide rudimentary sports facilities for blacks in the townships they controlled. Nor was the true purpose of the new official interest in the leisure time of blacks lost on politically conscious black observers. The ANC newspaper *Abantu Batho* commented in 1931:

> The biggest weapon to keep a native quiet is to give him sports and our present administration and employers know this and they want to use it to the fullest extent. When our intelligent young men are given sports they forget everything which is dear to them and their country. It is harmless to give him sports it keeps him contented they say, while they exploit the poor native to the fullest extent.[13]

The provision of facilities for cricket was a low priority in this general movement to encourage black participation in sport, in view of the space, equipment and level of training it required. Nevertheless, some cricket was played on grounds provided primarily for soccer and athletics, and some members of the black petty bourgeoisie began to form clubs and play the game competitively once again. The Bantu Men's Social Centre in Johannesburg, for example, had two teams by the 1930s. There was no comparison, of course, with the facilities available to whites, which were usually reserved for their exclusive use under municipal by-laws. It is interesting to note that for many years some private white clubs, such as the Wanderers Club in Johannesburg, as well as banning blacks, also banned Afrikaners from membership.

In the end, however, black cricket in the 1920s and 1930s did not depend on the missionaries or the white municipal authorities for its survival. The primary agents for promoting black cricket in these years were the gold mines. Mine owners had been the first major employers of black labour to appreciate the potential importance of sport among their workers. Even before missionaries were articulating the need to "moralize the leisure time" of blacks, organized sport had become part of the lives of the hundreds of thousands of black mineworkers who lived along the Witwatersrand, serving out their nine- or ten- or eleven-month contracts in austere single-sex barracks and prison-like closed compounds. The high level of control over black miners and their position as migrants accounted for the cheapness of their labour, on which the gold mines had come to depend for their inflated profit margins. But mine owners always feared that this cheap labour would be undermined and even lost to the industry if black miners were mobilized by unrest, alienation or political agitation in the compounds. Sport was seen as a way of directing the pent up emotions and energies of the workers into harmless channels, and, at the same time, was a way of improving their physical strength and productivity. Thus the majority of unskilled workers were actively encouraged to participate in athletics, soccer and 'war dance' teams. (Competitive 'war dancing' was perhaps the most blatant example of a sport designed for social control; not only did it burn up the leisure time energies of many in the black workforce, it also promoted ethnic identities within the mine compounds and so inhibited the development of a common black working class consciousness. By 1937 a 'War Dancing Union' had been created to oversee the development of the 'sport'. Latterly, war dance exhibitions by miners in specially built stadiums have been promoted as a tourist attraction in South Africa.) Cricket also had a critical role to play in the mines, but not among the unskilled migrant workers in the compounds. Instead, cricket was targeted at the small but vital class of black mine clerks.

Black mine clerks were employed in every mine along the Witwatersrand as the channel of communication between the white managers and the un-skilled black workforce. They were an educated, westernized elite whose position as permanent employees and higher level of pay set them apart from other black workers in the mines. Often they lived with their families in specially provided quarters – or sometimes in neighbouring black townships – and they were not subjected to the same confinement and the same indignities suffered by their brethren in the compounds. By the 1930s there were several hundred of them scattered along the length and breadth of the Witwatersrand. For the mine owners, 'native' mine clerks were a necessity, but also a constant worry. If they were ever to become radicalized as a class, they would be in a unique position to mobilize the workforce under them against their employers. It was cricket that provided a solution to this problem. Mine clerks were encouraged by the owners and mine managers to participate in competitive cricket, representing their mine company against others in the area. Apart from the diversion of the game itself, loyalty to the mine would be engendered through loyalty to the team, and the general ethos of cricket as a pastime imbued with elitist values would help to emphasize the status of the mine clerks as an elite, self-consciously distinct from the rest of the black workforce. The importance of playing cricket even seems to have influenced the recruitment policy towards black mine clerks, as Philip Q. Vundla discovered when he was interviewed for a job at Crown Mines in the mid 1920s. He was surprised to find that great store was put in the fact that he had been an excellent fast bowler while at school at Healdtown. His wife recalled:

> Philip always claimed that he only got it because he was a good cricketer. The mining communities take their sports very seriously and he was expected to play cricket for the mine that engaged him.[14]

In Vundla's case, active participation in cricket did not prove to be an inoculation against political radicalism, as the mine manager who employed him might have hoped.

> Philip's priorities during these years were simple. First came his burning desire to improve conditions for his people, and at this he worked night and day, for he was a committed revolutionary. A close second came his passion for cricket which took up most of his weekends. He was a good bowler and much in demand. On Saturdays and Sundays he would leave the hose at eight in the morning and return about six or seven in the evening. His family came in a poor third.[15]

Nonetheless the time and energy expended by mine clerks in playing the game is evident.

By 1932 the Native Recruiting Corporation (NRC) (the mines labour organization set up by the Chamber of Mines) sponsored the formation of the NRC Cricket Union on the Witwatersrand. Affiliated clubs included Crown Mines, Randfontein Estates, Simmer and Jack, Village Deep, and several other clubs sponsored by mine companies or linked to the mines, such as the Stone Breakers, Try Again, The Deeps, Hardcash and the Block Bs. The president, vice president, secretary and assistant secretary of the union were all mine clerks. Cricket clubs affiliated to the union played for two trophies, the NRC Cup donated by its patron, H. M. Taberer (who was chief labour advisor in the NRC), and the Piliso Cup, donated by its president, H. B. Piliso, headman at the Modder B Mine Compound. When the South African Bantu Cricket Board was formed in 1932 to govern interregional cricket, the mine companies again played a dominant role. Sponsorship again came from the NRC, which donated a trophy, and the first president of the Board was H. B. Piliso. Six of the ten interregional competitions over the next 20 years were won by the Transvaal team, drawn largely from the mines. The competition for the NRC trophy remained the main competition for black cricketers until 1976.[16]

Throughout the first half of the twentieth century, as we have seen, black cricket continued in relative obscurity. Notwithstanding the difficult conditions, several legendary players did emerge. Sometimes, as in the case of P. S. A. 'Oom Piet' Gwele, little is known of their exploits in statistical terms; however, Gwele was an active player from 1916 to the early 1940s and was remembered by subsequent generations as "a class player and an ace fielder". Others did leave some statistical evidence of their greatness. One example is Frank Roro, thought by many to have been the greatest African cricketer ever, who was described by one cricket history as the 'W. G.' of African cricket: "a man of small physique but one who possessed a quick eye and a stroke for every ball on the oft unpredictable pitches prevailing in his time".[17] A contemporary of Vundla's in the Crown Mines team during the 1930s and 1940s, he hit 100 hundreds in club cricket, including several double centuries, and had a career best of 304 against Main Reef in 1942. On the rush matting pitches of the era this was an astounding achievement. At the age of 43 he played for the national Bantu team against Indian and 'coloured' teams under the auspices of the new SACBOC in 1952, and was the only player in the competition to score a century.

Black Cricket in the Apartheid Era

The election of the National Party government in 1948 ushered in the era of apartheid. Under apartheid the black majority was more highly controlled and more systematically subordinated to white domination than ever before. In the sphere of sport the principle of segregation between 'white' and 'non-white' was rigorously maintained and reinforced with new legislation. The principle of using black sport as a means of social control was also maintained. To these traditional features was added a new feature in the 1970s, that of using black sport as a weapon against the enforced isolation of South Africa, which had been imposed by the international community in protest at the apartheid system.

Key apartheid measures that impacted indirectly on sport included the Group Areas Act and the Population Registration Act of 1950. The first extended the racial segregation of residential areas (already applied to Africans through the Native Urban Areas Act of 1923) to Indians and 'coloureds', while the second imposed statutory racial classification on the entire population. Updated pass laws ensured that the mobility of blacks around the country and from town to town (a prerequisite for competitive sport on any scale) was increasingly restricted. The Bantu Education Act of 1953 imposed a new curriculum on Africans specially designed to limit the scope of their education and their future life chances. Other measures impacted directly on sport. Amendments to the Urban Areas Act reserved sports facilities exclusively for one race group, while the Reservation of Separate Amenities Act of 1953 imposed racial segregation in stadiums and other public places. The Native Laws Amendment Act of 1957 extended segregation in sports organizations, clubs, schools and churches to limit the potential for interracial sport. Proclamation R. 26 in 1965 extended the Group Areas Act to allow the exclusion of black spectators from sport and other public entertainment involving whites, and also provided for the banning of multiracial matches in front of spectators, even on private land.

The extent of racial paranoia governing the separation of the races in sport can be illustrated by the fact that a government memorandum on the building of black townships in the mid 1950s directed that such townships should be separated from white areas by wide buffer strips of open ground, and that blacks should not be allowed to play sports on these buffer strips unless screened from white eyes by earth mounds and a line of trees, or both. At one of South Africa's cricket test venues, Newlands, in Capetown, separate entrances, separate lavatories and a wall two metres high were erected to screen white spectators from black; at most other sports venues blacks were excluded altogether.[18]

Under the SACBOC black cricket began to experience some important developments during the 1950s, despite the strictures imposed by apartheid. In 1956 a new stage was reached when a touring team of 'Asian' cricketers from Kenya was admitted to the country to play against a 'National Non-European South XI'. This was possible because the then Minister of the Interior, Dr Donges, had ruled that though local teams or international touring teams that wished to play against white teams in South Africa had to be exclusively white, and that no 'mixed teams' would be allowed, exclusively 'non-white' teams could compete with each other locally or internationally.[19] The South African team was led by a brilliant young 'coloured' cricketer named Basil D'Oliveira, and included five coloured players, five Indian players and one African, a six-foot three-inch bowler named Ben Malamba, who finished the three-match series (which the South Africans won 2–0) with 16 wickets at an average of 15.25 runs each. One of the 'coloured' players in the side, Cecil Abrahams, went on to play 15 seasons as a professional in the Lancashire League in the 1960s and early 1970s. Two years later D'Oliveira led his 'non-European' team to Kenya for a return tour, during which they outclassed all opposition, including a 'Rhodesian Indian XI' they played in Salisbury on the way home. A plan was developed by SACBOC to pit D'Oliveira's 'national non-European team' against somewhat stronger opposition in 1959. The West Indies were approached to send a touring team led by Frank Worrell to play a series of 'tests' against D'Oliveira's team. Apart from Worrell, the touring party was to have included a number of test players – Sobers, Hunte, Ramadhin, Valentine and Collie Smith, to name a few – and appeared much stronger than the current (white) South African test team, but when it became clear that, in line with Dr Donges' policy, they would not be allowed to play against any white opposition, the tour was cancelled. After this episode, D'Oliveira left South Africa to pursue his career in England, where he eventually rose to become a member of the English test team. After the D'Oliveira experience, it was clear that there was little scope for black cricketers under the tightening grip of apartheid. From this point on, aspiring black cricketers looked over-seas, rather than locally, for the opportunity to develop and exploit their talents. Apart from D'Oliveira and Abrahams, others who had successful careers overseas include Suleiman 'Dik' Abed (who played for ten years for Enfield in the Lancashire League), Owen Williams (who played club cricket in Australia), John Neethling, Rushdi Majiet, Goolam Abed (all of whom played in the Lancashire League) and Omar Henry (who played a representative game against Australia for Scotland in 1981). It was notable that among these names there were none of African origin. As a black spectator sport, too, cricket slid back into obscurity.[20]

Ironically, it was the controversy over the inclusion of D'Oliveira in the England party to tour South Africa in 1968 that finally exposed the depths of racism in South African cricket and the true nature of apartheid to the full glare of publicity throughout the cricketing world. After the cancellation of this tour, no further officially sanctioned international matches were played involving South Africa until the 1990s, when the end of apartheid was finally in sight. The international isolation of South Africa in cricket was part of a much more general isolation of South Africa in sport by 1970. To counter the effectiveness of these sanctions, the government of B. J. Vorster introduced the so-called multi-national policy in sport in 1971. This allowed international mixed teams to play against single-race teams in South Africa, but in theory continued to ban all mixed sport at a domestic level. However, black sports persons could compete as individuals with white sports persons inside South Africa in special 'multinational' competitions. One example of this was an international double-wicket competition held in 1972 in which pairs representing 'England', 'Australia', 'New Zealand', '(white) South Africa' and 'Africa' were included. The 'African' pair consisted of Edward Habane and Edmund Nticinka, two black South Africans, who were said to be representing their 'nation' in the tournament.[21] Under the 'multinational' policy three private tours of South Africa by a team of international players were organized (for the second and third tours the team was racially mixed) by a Conservative British industrialist named Keith Robins in 1972–1973, 1973–1974 and 1974–1975. The second Robins tour included Younis Ahmed from Pakistan and John Shepherd from the West Indies. The third culminated in another double-cricket tournament which included additional pairs said to be representing 'Pakistan' (Younis and Ibadullah) and 'West Indies' (John Shepherd and Geoffrey Greenidge). They were followed by an international 'Wanderers' team in 1975–1976. Several West Indians were imported in these years to play in local competitions and conduct highly pub-licized, though largely irrelevant, coaching sessions for local black players. They included Keith Barker, John Holder and Rohan Kanhai. This was also the era in which Gary Sobers went to Rhodesia.[22]

Such carefully contrived events were never more than a stop-gap response to South Africa's isolation, however, and the generally low standard of competition resulting forced the cricketing authorities to take more drastic measures. In September 1977, while South Africa was reeling from the inter-national condemnation surrounding the death of Steve Biko in detention, the South African Cricket Association (white) was formally merged with the SACBOC (black), and a smaller body called the South African Cricket Board (SACB), to form the SACU. The merger was portrayed to the cricketing world as a major step towards 'fully integrated cricket' in South Africa, but many black cricketers saw it as a cynical move to deceive international opinion without conceding the principle of a truly non-racial approach to the game. Inspired by the South African Council on Sport (SACOS) established to fight apartheid in sport in 1973 under the slogan of "No Normal Sport in an Abnormal Society", a small group of dissidents formed the avowedly nonracial SACB in 1978.

In the late 1970s and early 1980s the apartheid regime led by P. W. Botha sought to respond to its increasingly embattled position both locally and internationally by launching a carefully designed package of 'reforms' of apartheid, coupled with an aggressive international propaganda campaign to sell these reforms. In the sphere of cricket, the SACU made much of its sponsorship of coaching clinics in the black townships, which were often little more than photo opportunities in the campaign to sell these reforms. When this failed to weaken the international stance against South African cricket, the SACU resorted to buying in a series of 'rebel' tours, aided by sponsorship from the state-owned South African Breweries. An England XI which toured in 1982 was followed rapidly by 'The Red Lions', composed mainly of Sri Lankans. But the major coup was the 'rebel' tour led by Lawrence Rowe in 1983, dubbed by one enthusiastic white South African commentator as the 'Calypso Cavaliers' tour.[23] These, and subsequent, rebel tours (there were seven in all, culminating in a disastrous England tour in 1989), did little or nothing to develop black cricket in South Africa, and may in fact have harmed the development of the game among blacks by further alienating potential players and supporters, since cricket was now seen to be linked politically and ideologically to the defence of apartheid. A somewhat different effect of the tours was to introduce several black players from overseas to the domestic game in South Africa, where as honorary whites, they were able to eke out a living otherwise denied to them by their home associations. On the positive side, it may be that their undeniable influence in South African domestic competition over the past decade has had an effect in changing attitudes toward black cricketers among white cricket followers to some extent.

With the end of apartheid in the 1990s came the ending of South Africa's cricketing isolation. The SACU and the SACB were merged to form a new nonracial board controlling the game in South Africa. This is in line with the ANC's "Reconstruction and Development Programme" for the new South Africa, which asserts that there can be no real socioeconomic development without there being adequate facilities for sport and recreation in all communities.[24] But decades of neglect and the ideological baggage of white supremacy, segregation, and apartheid are likely to limit the future prospects of the game as a truly nonracial sport, especially since four decades of 'Bantu education' have left no infrastructure for development of the game in black schools. In these circumstances, despite broader political and societal changes, the white cricketing establishment is likely to continue to dominate the game in South Africa for many years to come.

Notes

1   Mike Marqusee, *Anyone But England. Cricket and the National Malaise* (London: Verso, 1994), chap. 2.

2 Robert Archer and Antoine Bouillon, *The South African Game: Sport and Racism* (London: Zed Books, 1982), 81.

3 Archer and Bouillon, 79. The Boers – or Afrikaners, as they became known – lost interest in cricket as it became closely associated with the oppressive force of British imperialism during and after the Anglo-Boer war (1899–1902). It was not until the South African Republic was formed in 1961 and South Africa took the important symbolic step of leaving the British Common wealth that Afrikaners took to the game again in large numbers.

4 E. Jokl, "Physical education, sport and recreation", in E. Hellmann, ed, *Handbook on Race Relations in South Africa* (Johannesburg: South African Institute of Race Relations, 1949), 455.

5 Quoted in André Odendaal, "South Africa's black Victorians: sport and society in South Africa in the nineteenth century", in James A. Mangan, *Pleasure, Profit, Proselytism. British Culture and Sport at Home and Abroad 1700–1914* (London: Frank Cass, 1988), 196.

6 Odendaal, 199–200.

7 Odendaal, 200. The complex relationship between cricket and nationalism is discussed in Hubert Devonish, "African and Indian consciousness at play: a study in West Indies cricket and nationalism", in Hilary Beckles and Brian Stoddart, eds, *Liberation Cricket: West Indies Cricket Culture* (Kingston, Jamaica: Ian Randle Publishers, 1995), chap. 11.

8 Quoted in Archer and Bouillon, 89.

9 Brian Crowley, *Cricket's Exiles: The Saga of South African Cricket* (London: Angus and Robertson, 1983), 112. Their decision was influenced partly by the fact that English amateur players in the 1891–1892 touring party had refused to play against blacks, although the professional players did so.

10 A decade after the controversy over Hendricks, blacks were still playing the game to a high standard despite the hostility or indifference of whites. Pelham Warner, who captained the first MCC team to tour South Africa in 1905–1906, employed several black bowlers to assist the team with net practice during the tour. He confided to his diary that "One young Malay with a fast left-hand action hit my middle stump nearly every other ball and Denton began his South African career by being caught and bowled by the first three balls and clean bowled by the next three." The bowler in question, C. J. Nicholls, never played first-class cricket in South Africa because of the prevailing segregationist climate, but worked as 'baggage master' and net bowler for numerous teams over the next 20 years. Cowley, *Cricket's Exiles*, 113.

11 Quoted by Tim Couzens, "An introduction to the history of football in South Africa", in Belinda Bozzoli, *Town and Countryside in the Transvaal: Capitalist Penetration and Popular Response* (Johannesburg: Ravan, 1983), 205.

12 *Report of the National European-Bantu Conference, Cape Town, February 6–9, 1929* (Lovedale: Lovedale Press, 1929), 196.

13 *Abantu Batho* (Johannesburg), 5 March 1931. For a full discussion of the move- ment to promote black sport as a strategy of social control see my article entitled "A political history of playing fields: the provision of sporting facilities for Africans in the Johannesburg area to 1948" in *International Journal of the History of Sport* 11, no. 2 (August 1994): 211–30.

14 Kathleen Vundla, *P. Q. The Story of Philip Vundla of South Africa* (Johannesburg: MRA, 1973), 17.

15 Vundla, 21.

16 Archer and Bouillon, 92. Apart from the Transvaal the other regions involved in the

competition were Western Province, Border, Eastern Province, Griqualand West (all in the Cape) and Natal.

17 Crowley, 114.

18 Archer and Bouillon, 44–47.

19 Archer and Bouillon, 46.

20 Crowley, 121–25.

21 Among the other participants were several international stars, including the Chappell brothers and Tony Greig. Crowley, 131.

22 Crowley, 131–35.

23 Crowley, 130.

24 ANC, *The Reconstruction and Development Programme* (Johannesburg: ANC, 1994), section 1.4.9, 9.

C. L. R. James and the Legacy of
Beyond a Boundary

●

Gordon Rohlehr

Home?

Beyond a Boundary is part autobiography and part social history. As autobiography, though, it provides only the barest outline of C. L. R. James' life,
thought and activity as a thinker, political philosopher, man of letters and
activist, leaving wide gaps in what it reveals of the man. Sticking rigorously to
its theme, it narrates a lifetime's engagement with the game of cricket and with
some of the men who were responsible for its development in England and in
the West Indies. James' account of great West Indian players such as George
John, Learie Constantine and George Headley, based on close knowledge and,
in the case of Constantine, friendship, is an intimate introduction to the ethos
of the West Indies of the 1920s and 1930s. We enter those decades through a
succession of anecdotes and leave with a sense of having vicariously lived in
that fascinating era of the last days of the old colonialism, with its unresolved
issues of race, colour, class, authoritarianism and mounting protest as self-
confidence grew among the underclasses.

   This magical evocation of time past abruptly ceases as James approaches the
year 1938, when he went to the USA on a lecture tour and remained for 15 years.
We learn nothing of those 15 years, which were, of course, years when James
neither played nor observed cricket. His account of the game after 1953, the
year of his return to England is nowhere as warm or as intimate as his
representation of the eras of Constantine and Headley. The game to which
James returned had altered in style and character. It had become more
conservative, less celebratory, a haven for mediocrities and antiheroic
practitioners. While James does recognize signs of revitalization in the West
Indies team of the 1950s and does, towards the end of the book, record his
intense campaign for the selection of Frank Worrell as West Indies cricket

captain, yet his actual account of postwar cricket is less intimate, and his nostalgia for a Golden Age, which was quite literally an age of Grace (W. G.), overwhelms the text.

It is at this point too that the spirit of the autobiographical subtext and that of the cricket text become one. For James' *Beyond a Boundary* is a text about the return of the native after 26 years of exile from his native land, and 15 years of separation from the game that he has loved as passionately as ideas, art, the Marxian dialectic or the notion of the eventual triumph of the common folk. But both the native land and the game have changed utterly. *Beyond a Boundary* was in its final stages just around the time that the irremediable rift opened up between C. L. R. James, the ideologue and editor of *The Nation*, the publication of the People's National Movement (PNM), and his former pupil, Dr Eric Williams, leader of the PNM and premier of a Trinidad and Tobago that was now on the verge of independence. The emergence of the PNM, which was in one sense what both James and Learie Constantine had campaigned for, ever since the days of James' *The Case for West Indian Self-Government*, would prove to be the greatest disillusionment in James' career. 'Home' no longer existed and, what was worse, could no longer be envisioned, not even as a mental construct of an attainable political state.

Similarly, cricket, whatever signs of rebirth there may have been, in first the three W's then Kanhai and Sobers, is a fallen game played in arenas from which all the giants have departed. While James keeps his nostalgia for 'home' and his anguish at its loss carefully hidden, refusing to discuss the collapse of his relationship with the PNM in *Beyond a Boundary*, he is much more open in his expression of disillusionment at the fallen state of the game of cricket. Insisting from early in the text that cricket is a creation of the 'puritanical' mind, with its laws, its moral code, its sense of ethics and honour, James traces the game's journey from the Garden of Eden – that is, the pre-industrial, pre-Victorian provincial village green or country club; the Pickwickian John Bull gusto of W. G. Grace – towards the Fall, that is, body-line, the incorporation of contemporary violence into the game, the possibility of a second coming, the birth of a redeemer who would be at once original and a reincarnation of the saving spirit and skill of an earlier Grace.

Beyond a Boundary begins with a construction of the memory of 'home'. Home is, first of all, the ancestral house in Tunapuna, Trinidad, from whose window the youthful C. L. R. James first watched cricket played. The first meaning of the title *Beyond a Boundary* is the quite literal one of the vantage point on the outskirts of what used to be the Tunapuna playing field, from which James observed the likes of Matthew Bondman and Arthur Jones, utterly unknown village green cricketers, but men whose mastery of particular strokes

– sweep, drive or imperial cut – evoked such pleasure in the spectator that they were able to achieve an acclaim, a stature and a prestige that far outweighed their demerits. Bondman, the surly tenant of James' lower middle class Aunt Judith, is described as having been a lout and a ne'er-do-well. But, we are told, Bondman could bat, a fact that brought him redemption in the eyes of the community, and seemed to soften even the stern condemnation in the eyes of James' censorious and puritanical aunt, for whom – as for her entire class – "respectability was not an ideal, it was an armour".

The early chapters do more than set the tone of the book. They establish its central themes and the metaphorical framework through which these themes will be explored. The house, the window, the anecdotes, the succession of characters are all part of the text's metaphorical design. The house and the window suggest James' stance as an observer, whose very observation provided him with the basis from which he would later become a keen participant in the game as player; avid, enraptured consumer of cricket literature; and critic whose earlier participation has sharpened his powers of precise, intelligent and informed observation. James makes the point that it was from that same room that his love of literature, art, fiction, the fine prose and poetry of the Bible and Thackeray's *Vanity Fair* was nurtured. The window, then, enabled his outward looking while the room itself became the venue for his introspection; and both qualities, close and accurate observation and introspective, reflective depth, will become manifest in *Beyond a Boundary* as it takes shape.

The house/home is a marker of identity. Towards the end of the book (chap. 19; 246) James circles back to the house and the family circle. It is the occasion of his father's death and, as had happened in Naipaul's *A House for Mr Biswas* and would later occur in Kamau Brathwaite's *Mother Poem*, death, the end of one cycle, evokes a deep sense of place and a longing to affirm one's sense of rootedness, of belonging to a specific structure of memories, of household objects, of familiar gods and spirits. James, an exile from Trinidad for 26 years, returns to his '*lares et penates*' that is, his household gods and guardian spirits, and tells us that the house, home of his family for over 150 years, still stands. In it and still in use there is a mahogany table and a wardrobe passed on to his father on the occasion of his marriage in 1900 by his great-grandmother. These had been presents given to her at her wedding 120 years earlier! The life of one generation flows into that of another. The James ancestors have been occupying the same spot in Tunapuna from the 1780s. Now, in the early 1960s, James watches his sister who had cared for his father for many years until his death, grow to resemble his Aunt Judith, who is still alive and an indomitable village matriarch.

Reinforced by such powerful examples of cyclic continuity, James asserts: "We are of the West Indies, West Indian" (246). It is not mere nostalgia that brings James to this utterance, which transcends the particular moment that it celebrates. The James family becomes representative of the aspiring ambitious folk of the entire pre- and postemancipation Caribbean; of their essential moral wholeness, restraint and faith; and of the everlastingness of the human quality that they have maintained in their lives. "We are of the West Indies, West Indian" is a claim James makes on behalf of all the people. *Beyond a Boundary*, nearing closure when James makes his claim and testament, has been in its celebration of the evolution of West Indian cricket, a statement of faith in the West Indian people and a recognition of the power with which the "inheritors of the middle passage" have consistently affirmed, expressed and discovered themselves. "We are of the West Indies" is, finally, the meaning towards which the text inexorably moves. It is also part of James' endeavour to reconstruct and reclaim the 'home' that, even at that very moment, he was again preparing to quit.

The Age of Grace

There is one further thing to be said about James' return to the image of the ancestral house and home, and his comment on the continuity of feeling and practice between successive generations, and it is this: intergenerational continuity, either as fact or ideal, is one of the great themes of the book, which gives it its organizational principle. Viewed superficially *Beyond a Boundary* might seem a rather erratic text in which one moves from West Indian cricket of the 1920s and 1930s back to a contemplation of English cricket between the 1860s and World War I, further back to the Greeks and the first Olympic Games, before one leaps forward to the postwar welfare state and ends in the middle of a bottle throwing riot in the 1960s.

What gives coherence to this welter of concerns is James' belief, everywhere visible, in tradition as an enduring link between past practice and present. Thus, while he chronicles the emergence of West Indian cricket from the 1920s to the 1960s, he is equally concerned with the Golden Age of the game's evolution in the twentieth century. According to James, cricket was pre-Victorian and pre-Industrial Revolution in origin, developing between the 1780s and the 1830s as the game of the artisans, "men of hand and eye" (158). The game was then appropriated by the emerging Victorian bourgeoisie, patronized too by an otherwise effete aristocracy, and eventually invested with puritanical rigour when it was introduced by Thomas Arnold into the public school system as a means of teaching young men the virtues of "loyalty ... self-sacrifice, unselfishness, cooperation, *esprit de corps*, a sense of honour, the capacity to be a 'good loser' or 'to take it' (162). James himself learnt these same virtues on the playing fields of Queen's Royal College in the early years of this century, and throughout *Beyond a Boundary* acknowledges their shaping influence on his adult life.

In the process of describing how the game became appropriated by the middle and upper classes, James excludes from his text the artisans who invented the game. These 'men of hand and eye' are replaced by the immense, gigantic figure of W. G. Grace, who becomes, in James' marvellous transformation, the representative spirit of a pre-Victorian age surviving unscathed throughout the central and latter years of Victorianism, the 1850s to the early 1900s. Grace, who died just around the time that James was born, is one of those figures whom James constructs, not from any memories of him, but from the literature in which the legend of the man is enshrined. Like Ranjitsinhji or C. B. Fry, he has become the prose in which his exploits have been celebrated. A golden aura surrounds the phenomenal statistics of his achievements, as he comes to represent for James, if not quite the purity of the code, certainly the energy, fervour and generosity of some earlier age.

James, as much a Romantic in his outlook as he is a Puritan, conceived of the game in terms that the Romantic poet William Blake would have understood. Blake conceived of man's life as a constant collision or negotiation between the contrary forces of Energy and Reason. Passion, joy, delight are properties of Energy. Restraint (that great Miltonic puritanical word), control and negation are properties of Reason which, Blake says, is the outward circumference of Energy and always seeks to contain and even inhibit the affirmative properties of Energy. W. G. Grace had Energy in abundance and strides through the central pages of *Beyond a Boundary* as a colossal figure whose very blemishes exude an aura of magnificence. For instance, James admits that:

> The records show that the family in its West Gloucestershire cricketing encounters queried, disputed and did not shrink from fisticuffs. To the end of their days EM and WG chattered on the field like magpies. Their talking at and even to the batsman was so notorious that young players were warned against them. (173)

Put in plain language, the brothers Grace were given to fighting, 'sledging' and coarse gamesmanship, the essence of old-time village green cricket. From this one may conclude that a quality has persisted in cricket: an earthy rugged substratum that had little to do with what C. L. R. James most admired in the appropriated bourgeois version of the game: the ability to be a good loser, to 'take it' with a stiff upper lip and a handshake, courtesy on and off the field, honesty and good sportsmanship. The evidence suggests that Grace was anything but a good loser, and that he disputed umpiring decisions, and that he could and did on occasions cheat. This much is admitted but when weighted against the qualities Grace brought to the game – passion, energy, gusto, independence, intelligence and an inventiveness that changed the nature of both bowling and batsmanship – whatever demerits Grace may have had are dismissed by James as unimportant.

> His humours, his combativeness, his unashamed wish to have it his own way on the field of play, his manoeuvres to accomplish this, his delight when he did, his complaints when he didn't, are the rubs and knots of an oak that was sound through and through. (174)

All is forgiven Grace who "did what no one had ever done, developed to a degree unprecedented and till then undreamed of, potentialities inherent in the game" (178).

Grace becomes a prototype of the popular hero whose energy is felt by the crowd to symbolize their own, who draws sustenance from and renews his strength on the acclamation of his public. As hero he earned "the spontaneous, unqualified, disinterested enthusiasm and goodwill of a whole community" (182) to whom he in his turn bequeathed an enrichment of their 'depleted lives' (183). "It was to bleak Sheffield, to dusty Kennington and to grim Manchester that W. G. brought the life they had left behind" (179). Grace, then, was culture hero, fertility god, life-giver who, emerging from written legends consumed by James since boyhood is endowed by him with a deeper mythology. His heroic qualities become the measure by which future greatness is judged. He is a product of the curious nostalgia with which James gilds the environment of nineteenth century cricket which, as presented in Beyond a Boundary seems to have been completely insulated from the class conflict and the 'dark satanic' grimness that much of the realistic literature of the age deplored.

One searches in vain for the artisan class who, like the Trinidadian proletariat of James' youth, are either erased from the centre of the game's arena, or reduced to the status of devitalized spectators, avidly seeking through their lower middle class hero and fertility god, the mythic vibrancy of 'the life they had left behind' (179). These inert shadows are certainly not the workers who, displaced from their cottage industries by the rash of factories, smashed machines with the Luddites, demanded radical democratic reforms with the Chartists and, after the 1850s, pioneered a system of cooperatives and working class associations through which they effected their own self-betterment. Such truer representatives of working class vitality have no place in James' romantic re-construction of cricket in the latter half of the nineteenth century, and their absence constitutes a major ambiguity in James' vision. For it was to the liberation of just such people that James dedicated the greater portion of his life.

Caliban's Version

Early in the Preface to *Beyond a Boundary*, James, assessing the task with which he was faced of unearthing the hidden history of the emergent Caribbean people, declares that :

> To establish his own identity Caliban, after three centuries, must himself pioneer into regions Caesar never knew.

Caliban, the surly earthy slave of Shakespeare's *The Tempest*, is invoked here as the archetype of enslaved colonized man entering the postcolonial phase of his history. Caesar is archetype of the conqueror, empire builder, and historian who, towards his own self-glorification minutely recorded his conquests over several military campaigns: how many were cut to pieces, how many were taken into captivity. James is expressing here a dissatisfaction with the historiography of the conqueror or colonizer as a text for understanding the historical experience of the colonized person. Caliban needs to do his own research and to construct his own version of the past if he is "to establish his own identity". *Beyond a Boundary*, then, is meant to be Caliban's version.

Caliban's version, as James envisions it in *Beyond a Boundary*, is inevitably a product of his long encounter as slave and survivalist colonial, with Caesar or Prospero. The question that arises is: At what point does Caliban achieve or assert a style of encounter that is distinctly his own, a voice, aesthetic and identity that have gone far beyond their colonial origins? *Beyond a Boundary* purports to answer this question with respect to West Indian cricket. So it presents us with sharply observed and clearly etched portraits of players James knew well: Wilton St Hill, George John, Learie Constantine, George Headley, the founding fathers of West Indian style. After *Beyond a Boundary* James recognizes the merits of Worrell, Sobers, Kanhai and Viv Richards, the last of whom James considered to be the only truly great player in the 1984 team that 'blackwashed' England.

The figure of 'Caliban', evident in the portrait of Matthew Bondman, is also discernible in James' depiction of Lebrun Constantine, father of Learie Constantine. 'Old Cons', as he was called, is presented as a man of fiercely independent spirit who met all men as equals on the field of play (106), and once objected to an umpire by leading his team out of Queen's Park Oval and forfeiting the match rather than play under that umpire's jurisdiction. Old Cons transferred that explosiveness into his batting and, on one occasion at Lords, participated in a partnership of 162 runs in 65 minutes.

George John was another 'Caliban' figure. Described as having come from "one of the most backward of the smaller/islands", John incarnated the plebs of his time, their complete independence from the values and ambitions that competed in the spheres above (79). In bowling he was "hostility itself" (81). On the playing field he was a dictator, virtually uncontrollable by his club captain, morose and yet possessing an inner discipline which allowed him to keep sight of his objective to think and bowl the batsman out. Admiring, yet never quite comfortable with Caliban's uncompromising spirit, James regrets "the inherent restraints of my environment " – that is, race, colour, class and caste snobbery – which prevented him from drawing closer to men like John beyond the boundary of the playing field.

C. L. R. James does not deal extensively with the Barbadian fast bowler Herman Griffith, who had the reputation of having bowled Bradman for a duck. But he too was an example of the Caliban syndrome in West Indian cricket. John Wickham writes thus about Griffith:

> The stories of the man proliferated . . . he was seen as always in arms against resistant establishment. He was the very embodiment of the little man who would not be bullied or gainsaid. Prowess at games, especially his fast bowling, was essentially an expression of his hostility towards those who would preserve the sanctity of their privilege at the expense of the self-respect of others.
>
> Fast bowling, I came to see from very early, was an instrument of destruction, the furious energy of the warrior hurling his arrow against the enemy, a proletarian weapon aimed at the aristocracy of batsman-ship (J. Wickham, *Sunday Express,* 30 March 1980).

Griffith, George John, and later Roy Gilchrist, are of a type. If James' aim in *Beyond a Boundary* is to write Caliban's version of history then it is individuals such as these whom he must locate at the centre of his text. And to a certain extent, James does achieve this end. There are, however, abundant signs in the text that James was rendering not only Caliban's version, but Ariel's. He confessed, for example, that his life as a man of letters "involved me with the people around me only in the most abstract way" (70–71). Abstraction is Ariel's essential quality; detached engagement in a rarefied atmosphere of pure ideas. Blood-and-sand directness is more typical of Caliban.

James was from the very start uncomfortable with the 'puritanical' rigidity, the moral sternness and, most of all, the uncompromising race and class consciousness of people such as Lebrun and Learie Constantine. This is first illustrated in his choice of cricket club on leaving high school in the 1920s. The Constantines belonged to Shannon, a club usually chosen by the black lower middle class, to which James belonged. James, from his own account a promising batsman and better than average medium-paced seam bowler, was expected by all his clan and caste to join Shannon. James, instead, after some mental agonizing, joined Maple (58–59) on the pragmatic advice of Clifford Roach's father that he should socialize with members of the class or caste for which his education had prepared him. James, too, lacked the high seriousness typical of the Shannon approach to the game. What little of Caliban there was in him was, even then, thoroughly under the control of the Ariel in him.

James, who describes himself as one who "moved easily in any society in which [he] found himself" (59), had through his education and his dilettante's interest in the arts, begun to relish the special space and flux that had begun to open up for what he was: a precocious and enormously well-read man of letters, a self-taught British intellectual who, by his own admission, had been brought up by his respectable Aunt Judith to shun black people of the category of Matthew Bondman. Bondman's only club would have been Stingo, a club described by James as "totally black and of no status whatever". "They were plebeians: the butcher, the tailor, the candlestick maker, the casual labourer, with a sprinkling of unemployed" (56).

In what is cruelly precise, frank and maybe confessional class analysis, James notes that the masses themselves gave more support to the clearly ambitious professional-minded black lower middle class team Shannon, than to Stingo, which contained mainly members of the proletariat. Of Shannon James says:

> They played as if they knew that their club represented the great mass of black people in the island. The crowd did not look at Stingo the same way. Stingo did not have status enough. Stingo did not show that pride and im-personal ambition which distinguished Shannon. As clearly as if it were written across the sky, their play said: Here on the cricket field if nowhere else, all men in the island are equal, and we are the best men in the land. (61)

Shannon stood for something: the democratic thrust of an underclass towards equality, race and class pride. Maple, by James' own analysis was the club of brownskinned middle class people who were generally prejudiced against 'dark' skins. The other clubs, Queen's Park and Shamrock catered for whites and off whites while Constabulary was a police club of black lower class players under the usual rulership of white officer captains.

Yet the James of the 1920s was more comfortable joining Maple than

Shannon. A mature James will come to the realization that it was Shannon, not Maple, that better represented what was possible in West Indies cricket. "The old Shannon club of those days," James writes, "is a foundation pillar of this book" (63). He also records Learie Constantine's belief "that the real West Indies team should be a team that would play with the spirit and the fire, the spontaneous self-discipline and cohesion of Shannon" (63). If James' social aspirations were symbolized by the imagined social freedom which Maple represented, his heart lay in Shannon. His sympathy for black lower class cricketers such as Piggott and Telemaque were genuine, though one feels he slightly undervalues what the 'Caliban' syndrome has contributed to the legacy of West Indies cricket.

Ariel's Text

This is no more evident than in James' presentation of the figure of Learie Constantine. Constantine, who left Trinidad when "the restraints imposed upon him by social conditions in the West Indies had become intolerable" (110), made his living in the Lancashire League and was grateful to England for the opportunity she had opened up to him for self-betterment. Yet Constantine never lost his Caliban streak of black pride. While James suggests a certain awkwardness in how they were received by the English during the early years, he seeks constantly to ignore or transcend the issue of racism. Not so Constantine. Unable to transcend or ignore the issue of race, he became even more racially conscious during the early years in England, until James could say of him: " I didn't know him very well. He had a point of view which seemed to me, unduly coloured by national and racial considerations" (114). James, more Ariel than Caliban, is commenting on Constantine, who was more Caliban than Ariel. James was at the time deeply immersed in Trotskyism, while Constantine was slowly compiling data for inclusion in *Colour Bar*, a text that surveyed racism worldwide and in its time became as influential as James' *The Case for West Indian Self-Government* in shaping the attitudes of West Indians on matters of race, colour and human equality.

Constantine would continue to take a harder line than James on the racial issue up to the early 1960s when *Beyond a Boundary* ends. Constantine was also resolutely against two white players from apartheid-ridden South Africa being allowed to participate in E. W. Swanton's goodwill tour to the West Indies. Clyde Walcott, who like Weekes had retired early from the West Indian cricket scene, was in complete agreement with Constantine's stand and that of the West Indies Board. According to Walcott,

> The edifice of apartheid will not be undermined in the least by tiny gestures of goodwill such as that which Swanton, McLean and Waite wished to make. Our Board wished merely to spare these players embarrassment, for they could have been the innocent targets of demonstrations against the greater tyranny. (Walcott 1958, 181–82)

Swanton's position was that "games and politics should never mix" (Swanton 1960, 281) while James, whose central thesis in *Beyond a Boundary* is that games mirror sociopolitical processes, felt that McLean and Waite should have been allowed to play in the West Indies (*Beyond a Boundary*, 228). This, he thought, would have been a means of turning sharp international scrutiny on the cloistered apartheid state, whose antidemocratic, discriminatory, and inhumane nature would be opened up to the scrutiny of world opinion. James also supported the idea of Frank Worrell leading a team of black West Indians to play against black South Africans in the townships, and liberate them from their solitude. He felt that out of such exposure, new and deserving talent might come, along with the unforeseeable impact of exposing a suppressed people to a, presumably, less suppressed one who were also supreme at the game.

For James, politics and sport were inextricably mixed; no more so than in the matter of selecting a captain for the West Indies cricket team. Traditionally captains had been Caucasian: Goddard, Stollmeyer, Atkinson captaining teams that contained players of the calibre of Headley, Weekes, Worrell and Walcott. The situation came to a head when Franz Alexander, a neophyte whose claim to leadership seemed to lie mainly in the fact that he was a Cambridge 'blue' and, if not fully white, hardly black, was chosen as captain of the 1960 West Indies team against the visiting MCC. Worrell, by now a veteran with over ten years' test experience, was playing under Alexander. James, echoing Walcott's *Island Cricketers* (1958), put the issue squarely in its racial context. He recognized that the plantation aristocracy, who had controlled West Indian cricket from its inception, dreaded Caliban's demand for participation in the game at its highest level, fearing,

> that cricket would fall into chaos and anarchy if a black man were appointed captain. (By the grim irony of history we shall see that it was their rejection of black men which brought the anarchy and chaos and very nearly worse.) (76)

The "anarchy and chaos" mentioned here is the 1960 bottle throwing incident which took place at Queen's Park Oval during the second test of the West Indies/MCC tour. The "very nearly worse" is the bigger social upheaval which James, recognizing the explosive mood of the people in that era of militantly nationalist politics, felt could occur. James' long experience with activist politics had taught him that whenever a people's patience becomes eroded through long and unavailing protest, then the possibility becomes imminent of that people abandoning all restraint and breaking out into open rebellion.

James' own patience, as one who along with Constantine had since the 1930s campaigned for a recognition of the just merits of the Caribbean people, was also eroded. For once he chose Caliban's version: that of outright rebellion, if not against the code of cricket, at least against the injustice with which the code had been manipulated by plantocratic Caribbean administrators of the game.

> According to the colonial version of the code you were to show yourself a
> 'true sport' by not making a fuss about the most barefaced discrimination
> because it wasn't cricket. Not me any longer. To that I had said, was saying,
> my final goodbye. (232–33)

James' masterful letter to the Queen's Park directorate apropos of the bottle throwing affair is an excellent illustration of how nimbly he could dance around the equally rugged rocks of race and class; of how, even when taking up Caliban's cudgel, he swings it with Ariel's delicacy.

The letter begins and ends on a note of apparent appeasement. First it notes the important role Queen's Park Oval, a private club, has played in the organization of West Indies interterritorial and test cricket, but suggests that, as with Carnival, the task has outgrown the abilities of those who have traditionally carried it out. This was a shrewd tap with the poui, since, as every Trinidadian knew, the Queen's Park/St Clair/ County Club clique had bitterly resented the appropriation of Carnival in 1957 by a Carnival Development Committee set in place by the new and democratically elected government. James' first recommendation for cricket administration was that it be similarly democratized; that a "democratically elected body representing the cricket clubs and associations of the country" (234) replace that of the Queen's Park Club as the local representatives of the WICBC. If, however, Queen's Park Club were to remain as managers of international cricket in Trinidad, they should develop "a vivid and active sense of public obligation".

Such are the opening blows of this stickfight: each one stinging and calculated to incense the opponent. What follows is a rapid listing of the sins Queen's Park had committed in the past, the chief of which was their insensitivity to public opinion in their choice of captain and manipulation of players. Caliban's patience, after so many years, had been exhausted and the bottle throwing at the Oval was only one symptom of this fact. James makes allusion to what he well knew was a nightmarish memory for the white and off-white ruling elite: the Butler riots of 1937, a class upheaval which, like the

1919 disturbances, had been characterized as having the makings of "another Haiti".

James, then, is not averse to playing on white ruling class hysteria to make his point about the desirability of opening up the captaincy to qualified black leadership. He bluntly states the popular "conviction now deep-seated that the Queen's Park club represents the old regime in Trinidad and that it is indifferent and even hostile to what the masses of the people think" (236). James, however, insists that the real issue is not one of race; or at least he does not regard race as the crucial issue:

> I do not bring prejudice to any of the charges. In the campaign I am carry-
> ing out against Alexander instead of Worrell as captain I shall exhaust every
> argument before I touch the racial aspect of it. (237)

From this point onwards, the tone of the letter becomes one of appeasement. James, Ariel rather than Caliban, the Maple rather than the Shannon or Stingo man, tries to soothe and assure the ruling elite that they have in the main been doing a good job; that there is room for all races in the new and evolving national community. "Here," James writes, "as everywhere else I am primarily concerned with the building of a truly national community, incorporating all the past that is still viable" (239). James assures Queen's Park that he is not anti-white, neither does he seek to exclude white West Indians from future West Indies cricket teams. He is aware of the contributions of H. B. G. Austin and the Challenors, and of that club which was "the originator of the great tradition of Barbados batting" (239).

James' campaign for black leadership is not a black nationalistic one, no more than his denunciation of traditional Queen's Park oligarchic practice should be construed as being anti-white. Far from this, since his Maple and Queen's Royal College days he has been friends with prominent Caucasian businessmen, a few of whom he has even taught at school, and umpired house matches in which they played. James tells us (confesses?) that one such businessman has underwritten his return to Trinidad. Others have been prominent sponsors of sports. In short, James' letter, for all its honest forthrightness, is as rich in apologetic appeasement as it is in veiled threat.

It is Ariel's text, not Caliban's. Ariel has a verbal contract with Prospero that if he works faithfully for a specific period of time, he will be released. Caliban has no such contract. Ariel respects the code to the letter and warns Prospero of Caliban's impending revolt. The main problematic of *Beyond a Boundary* thus becomes that of reconciling Caliban's drive towards self-expression through total rebellion, with James' belief in and glorification of the game's moral code. Both of these tendencies, rebellion and its containment through restraint, education, the rules of the game and the abstract culture of ideas, dwell within James and determine both his self-representation and his choice and analysis of situations in cricket. James saw the need for both Caliban's energy, open defiance and spontaneous unorthodoxy – what Viv Richards metaphorically terms "hitting across the line" – and Ariel's skill at negotiating and manoeuvring within the framework of accepted rules. Hence his unbounded admiration for Worrell and Sobers, but especially for Kanhai, in whom he recognized both Dionysiac enthusiasm and disciplined control, "the satyric passion for the expression of the natural man, bursting through the acquired restraints of disciplined necessity" (James 1986, 169). And Kanhai's batting at Edgbaston in 1964 typifies qualities that James recognized in the entire West Indies team, born again under Worrell's leadership, since the 1961 tour to Australia: "distinction, gaiety, grace. Virtues of the ancient Eastern Mediterranean city-states, islands, the sea and the sun" (James 1986, 171). James concludes:

> The West Indies in my view embody more sharply than anywhere else Nietzsche's conflict between the ebullience of Dionysius and the discipline of Apollo. (171)

He had recognized the same tension three decades earlier in the cricket of Learie Constantine.

Fall from Grace

The revival of the West Indies in the 1960s restored James' faith in a game in which in the 1950s, restraint, reason and inhibition seemed to him to have completely defeated Energy. What James in Chapter 17 of *Beyond a Boundary* terms "The Welfare State of Mind", that is a conservative, defensive and negative approach to batting and bowling, had killed the game as a spectator sport. This was most evident in the dreary MCC 1960 tour to the West Indies, when England bowled with seven men on the offside, directing at least three out of every six balls outside the off stump. Worrell, Sobers and Kanhai were determined not to sell their wickets cheaply to balls they had no need to play, and produced some of the slowest batting in the history of the West Indies game.

James, who had returned in 1953 after an absence of 26 years, describes the fall from grace:

> The cricketers of today play the cricket of a specialized stratum, that of functionaries of the Welfare State. When many millions of people all over the world demand security and a state that must guarantee it, that's one

thing. But when bowlers or batsmen, responsible for an activity essentially artistic and therefore individual, are dominated by the same principles, then the result is what we have. (211)

Chapter 15 is easily the gloomiest chapter of the book. James had not been around to witness the fantastic flowering of Weekes in India in 1948–1949, nor the 1950 West Indies tour to England. Nor did he at the time perceive the difference between the overseas professionals who played – as had Constantine – League cricket, and the typically conservative English professionals playing county cricket. Clyde Walcott, though, was awake to this crucial distinction. The leagues, he noted, kept the professional close to the grassroots of the game and resulted – in spite of poor standards – in the professional developing the same array of skills that James had observed flower in Constantine's game. The few professionals in county cricket, where standards were higher, had to play more attractively than their English counterparts, because their job was to draw crowds and inject vitality into a game that had become stodgy and unlovely.

Revival was taking place, though James at the time could see only decline. He reflects that this decline had started years earlier, perhaps since the ending of World War I. The body-line controversy James understood to be more than a simple brutal ploy to neutralize Don Bradman. It was "the violence and ferocity of our age expressing itself in cricket" (185). According to James, body-line had its political parallel in the "cultivated brutality" of totalitarian dictators and illustrated "the contemporary rejection of tradition, the contemporary disregard of means, the contemporary callousness". Body-line shattered the code by which the game used, and ought, to be played. James, who notes in his earlier chapters that George John for all his hostility never bowled bouncers, but aimed rather at the stumps, would not have approved of the short-pitched bowling that has been frequent in the contemporary era.

James laments the death of the Golden Age, the passage of the "sweet golden clime" of an era now seemingly forever lost. James' disillusion may not have been as extreme had he depicted the age of W. G. Grace in a less sentimental and more realistic light. W. G. Grace, as we have seen, was taken by James out of his Victorian context and presented as a pre-Victorian. While one realizes that James does not mean that Grace literally belonged to an earlier time, but that his cricket exuded the spirit of that pristine Romantic age, one cannot avoid the conclusion that James in his depiction of the Golden Age is engaged in a highly idealized verbal reconstruction of an ethos that he had never actually experienced, but which was part of the nostalgically recalled and abstract world of books in which as a child he had lived.

The real age of W. G. Grace foreshadowed the fourth decade of the twentieth century in several significant ways. It had an expanded factory system which generated enormous industrial waste, as the 'dark' novels of mid century Dickens, *Hard Times* and *Our Mutual Friend*, constantly remind us. It was the age of the Crimean War, the global reach of British and other imperialisms and the recurrent atrocities of conquest in India, Africa and the near East. The age of Grace could well be termed the age of disgrace, if we factor in all the social and political currents that James deliberately excludes from his rosy picture. The Boer War, Cecil Rhodes and his philosophy of 'philanthropy plus ten percent', the rape of the Congo, were only a few of the atrocities current as the age of Grace drew to its close. The most representative fiction of that *fin de siècle* era was Conrad's *Heart of Darkness*, which symbolically begins in the rosy haze of a post-romantic twilight, but ends in the "heart of an immense darkness".

The world did not suddenly grow more brutal after 1913. World War I and its aftermath were the culmination of all the latent and open dehumanization of history that had been taking place, often through the instigation of the very ruling classes who had been trained in institutions such as Thomas Arnold's public school. James, in his idyllic portrayal of the Golden Age, misses its major irony, which is that the same classes responsible for the brutalities of exploitation at home and in the colonies were the ones who swore by the moral codes of public school, playing field and puritanical pulpit.

What happened with body-line, then, is not just that the world had grown more brutal, but that social reality, so long locked out of cricket's enclaved universe, had found its way into the country club. It may well be that cricket had long been expressing grim social reality. For if the Jamesian thesis is at all sound, what needs explanation is how the real social tensions of W. G. Grace's age, everywhere evident in the literary discourse of the period, did not find expression in the grand nineteenth century game.

With Jardine and body-line, the game unmasked itself. By 1953 when James returned, bourgeois university-trained captains such as Hutton, May and later Cowdrey, men of the code and the old school tie, thought nothing of appropriating the aggressive Caliban spirit of proletarian fast bowlers such as Trueman, who, like C. L. R.'s W. G. Grace, was a sledger on the field and a true blue John Bull folk hero in England. Clyde Walcott's frank account of the 1953–1954 MCC tour to the West Indies discloses that there were several disputed umpiring decisions against which MCC players openly displayed their annoyance. There was also considerable violence of the tongue directed mainly at West Indian players, but sometimes even at umpires. Walcott writes that:

> Some of the fiercest characters in the side frequently offended, one against the letter, others against the spirit of the Laws. Further, some of the language used on the field and directed against West Indian players was revolting. There is no other word for it. (Walcott 1958, chap. 7)

The game was being played without compromise. Forty-five year old Headley was greeted by Trueman with a shower of bouncers, which told him as surely as anything else that his day and age were long gone. Bill Fergusson, Trinidad's loveable spinner and tail-end batsman, was flattened by a Trueman bouncer. Walcott notes that there was no visible attempt by Hutton to temper Caliban unbound.

Yet Hutton smoothly supported the plantation owners who controlled West Indies cricket, in expressing the fear that black players, who had begun to constitute the majority of the West Indies team, might not be able to maintain the codes, courtesies and traditions of the game. Hutton advocated that:

> White people should play the major part in the running of West Indies cricket. Hutton suggests that the cricket activity of our land is being more and more dominated by coloured people, and he goes on to say that 'the gradual exclusion of white folk is a bad thing for the future of West Indies cricket'. (Walcott 1958, 95–96)

Walcott rebutted:

> The work 'exclusion' implies something positive and deliberate, and no such thing is in fact taking place. As for the underlying feeling that contained the remark, does Hutton think that coloured people, on grounds of education or intelligence, are incapable of looking after the traditions and standards of the game? It is surely significant that West Indies sides are generally about 75% coloured and 25% white, yet I think it is true to say that we have a reputation for being cheerful tourists and good sportsmen in victory or in defeat. The MCC team which Hutton brought to our islands, was, of course, all white, but the most impartial judges would have no difficulty in deciding whose conduct did more harm to the game – theirs or ours. (Walcott 1958, 96)

Modern West Indian cricket, then, came of age in an era of relentlessness in which, honest at last, the English ruling classes unmasked their faces, laying aside what James terms "the chivalry that was always a part of the game" (James 1963, 189). Douglas Jardine, son of a Scottish lawyer, was educated at "one of the most exclusive schools in the country, Winchester" and later at Oxford University. Harold Larwood "began his working life as a miner in the Nottinghamshire mining village, Nuncargate" (Derriman 1986, 183).

> Some of the Australians used to call him the Little Miner. He was quiet, almost diffident in manner, but on the field with the ball in his hand he was extremely aggressive. Some of the Australians believed there was a real element of spite in Larwood's bowling in 1932-1933. He was avenging

himself for past indignities, and he seemed to take pleasure in doing it. (Derriman, 184)

Bill Voce, Larwood's left-handed body-line bowling partner, also started his working life as a Nottinghamshire miner. Body-line, then, was the result of British ruling class appropriation of proletarian terrorism, which was then not only diverted from its natural target, the ruling classes themselves, but advantageously redirected towards the 'enemy'. In this case, the enemy was the exploding batsmanship from the colonial periphery; the batsmanship of Bradman, Woodfull, Pondsford and McCabe. Two decades later, when Hutton unleashed Trueman, the 'enemy' was the collective magnificence of Worrell, Weekes, Walcott and Rae who had in 1950 done what the Australians had done in 1930: beaten England in England 2–1 in the case of Australia and 3–1 in the case of the West Indies: and this in a four-test series. The centre could not bear to be humiliated by the periphery.

C. L. R. James is perceptive in his analysis of the response of Bradman to Jardine's ruthlessness. Bradman met relentlessness with a tense, disciplined efficiency from which the quality of joyful elation, so highly valued by James in the Age of Grace, was totally absent. The relentlessness of the 1930s eventually emerged as the new tradition, bequeathing its legacy of grim and absolute encounter to the spirit of the contemporary game. Clyde Walcott, analysing the failure of the West Indies team in England in 1957, noted the tendency of West Indies batsmen – the youthful ones in particular – to let the bowlers out-think them, and to show a preference for "the gay life – and, thus, the short one". This he saw as the wrong attitude in a world where:

> the atmosphere of Test cricket is becoming ever more intense and hard. In my bitter moments I sometimes think that there is hardly a place left for the real old-fashioned player of strokes – the man who batted for his own enjoyment (not for national prestige) and hence for the enjoyment of the crowd as well. (Walcott 1958, 135)

C. L. R. James, observing the same intensity and hardness take over a game that he had loved, laments the terrible ugliness of the new age:

> Scarcely a tour but hits the headlines for some grave breach of propriety on and off the cricket field. The strategy of Test matches is the strategy of stalking the prey: you come out in the open to attack only when the victim is wounded. No holds are barred. Captains encourage their bowlers to waste time. Bowlers throw and drag. Wickets are shamelessly doctored. Series are lost or believed to be lost by doubtful decisions and immoral practices and the victims nurse their wrath and return in kind. (James 1963, 198)

Cricket as *real politik* has produced other horrors: ball-tampering, charges of bribery, crowd hostility, to the point where missiles have been hurled at players from the opposing side fielding close to the boundary. Similar things, of course, have long been happening in other sports. C. L. R. James' comments on what had by the early 1960s begun to happen in cricket as well, were uncharacteristically pessimistic. Society itself had fallen and nothing, no direct human effort, could restore it to the state of Grace. Mere legislation restricting bouncers would not curb the employment of terror, which Jardine had introduced to the game, nor would laws against negative field placing engender a spirit of adventure and affirmation in a game that had for him lost its point and savour. Only "if and when society regenerates itself, cricket will do the same" (190).

James lightens the gloom of this conclusion with a humanist optimism that is more characteristic of him when he writes:

> The values of cricket, like much that is now in eclipse, will go into the foundation of new moral and educational structures. (190)

He is not clear how this will happen, but he believes that only a return to the old style, the old days and ways, when the code was resolutely taught, can save the present age from the "night impenetrable" that he sees enveloping it. This conclusion is that of conservatism under threat. One recalls the gloom of the Tory satirists Swift and Pope: the pessimistic madness into which Gulliver descends, or the "universal darkness" which at the end of Pope's *Dunciad* covers everything. James' conclusion at the end of Chapter 15, is that of one who, having lived through six decades of traumatic change, longs for what he now sees as the coherence of a nostalgically evoked earlier time when giants used to roam the land.

It has been the argument of this essay that such an earlier time is as much a fictional construct as it may in part have been a historical reality. Stripped first of his Trotskyite ideology theme, after having painfully reconciled himself to Marxism, experiencing the difficulty of translating abstract theory into meaningful practice amidst the vagaries of the exasperating intransigence of the politics of pre-Independence Trinidad, an older, sadder James longs for what Derek Walcott terms "the amber twilight of another life", that idealized time within which his own mind and sensibility were shaped. In the early chapters of *Beyond a Boundary*, this time is lovingly recalled and endowed with an amber light that suffuses both his lived and vicarious experiences. All writers ultimately write their age, their peculiar nostalgia; but the world goes on, better in some of its aspects, worse in others. Cricket, reflecting and adjusting to the reality of each historical circumstance, has bred, as it continues to breed, giants and dwarfs appropriate to each era.

Writing the Renaissance

By the end of Chapter 17 it seems that James has recovered from the impending "night impenetrable" on which Chapter 15 closed. He now expectantly awaits the rebirth of the Hero, whom he characterizes as "some young Romantic [who] will extend the boundaries of cricket technique with classical perfection" (216). This deliverer "will be doing what W. G. Grace did – so reshaping the medium that it can give new satisfactions to new people" (216). These "satisfactions", James argues in Chapter 16, are essentially aesthetic ones: the satisfactions of dramatic encounter and of living kinetic visual art in which the spectator's delight is evoked by the player's style, elegance, grace, timing, physical coordination, and harmonious action (194–203). If the visual delight of the game involves the repeated performances of a range of actions by individual players, the dramatic appeal involves the encounter of two teams with different areas of strength, in the context of a specific time-frame which can, however, become alterable through variations in weather and over the process of time. In test cricket, because teams represent rival nations, their encounter can generate intense passion in the spectator, including the excitement that occurs when teams are evenly matched and the result promises to be a close one.

The renaissance of West Indian excellence under Frank Worrell provided James with the dual delight of exceptional individual performances and collective dramatic enactment. For drama, the tied test in Brisbane was hard to beat, though twice again in the series in the drawn fourth test at Adelaide, as well as in the fifth test at Melbourne, which Australia won by two wickets, there were close nail-biting finishes. The series itself was not determined until the fifth test. For individual genius, James would later say that he had seen no innings in his lifetime to surpass Sobers' century at Brisbane: "the most beautiful batting I have ever seen". For bowling, there was Gibbs' hat trick in the fourth test and three wickets in four balls in the third test, feats performed on firm, true pitches, and which undermined the Australian middle order when they least expected it. All of this was taking place under the astute and unruffled generalship of Frank Worrell, for which James had campaigned. According to James: "Worrell and his team in Australia had added a new dimension to cricket history" (248). Of Worrell's leadership he perceptively observes:

> He did not instil into but drew out of his players. What they discovered in themselves must have been a revelation to few more than to the Players themselves. (248)

One remarkable aspect of the Brisbane 'apotheosis' noted by James, was the enthusiasm that the team's performance generated in the Australian public, who lined the streets in hundreds of thousands, some cheering and a few even weeping to see the West Indies players depart. This was in every respect the opposite to the emotions evoked in 1932 by Douglas Jardine's remorseless warfare. The West Indies had narrowly – some still say, unfairly – lost the series, but had won overwhelmingly the moral victory.

The 'new dimension' that the West Indies had added to their own game was that for the first time since the 1948 to 1954 era, and more than during that era, the team as a *collective* of brilliant or competent individuals had through their harmonious interaction on the field of performance, become the Hero. Just months earlier E. W. Swanton had described the 1960 West Indies team as "unorganized and uncoordinated in several respects as compared with England's" (Swanton 1960, 268). Under Worrell, the team had gone beyond the boundary, not only of C. L. R. James' expectations, but of his tendency to perceive the game in terms of the soul-enthralling genius of the gigantic individual, rather than, or over and above, the total team effort in the game's three departments, batting, bowling and fielding. This is not to say that James was unaware of the necessity for team spirit. Far from it. He recognized the truth of Constantine's observation that "no one man can consistently beat eleven others at cricket" (136), and stressed the old Shannon virtues of self-sacrifice and cohesiveness as a model for future West Indies teams. Yet his emphasis throughout *Beyond a Boundary* was on the culture-hero, the representative man; the vitalizer of a flagging flag.

Analysts of the post 1980 period of West Indian dominance of test cricket have had perforce to recognize the wisdom of Constantine's remark and to focus on all the qualities that have together operated to create the West Indian game. They have had, that is, to move beyond the biases and idiosyncrasies of the Jamesian approach, while learning from and building on James' remarkable range of insights. It would, for example, be of little use to anyone to become buried in James' nostalgic dream for an era which no one alive has seen. Thus, while *Beyond a Boundary* needs to be reclaimed as a great classic, one must move beyond some of its limitations of vision.

There are several signs that the society has begun to do this. The clearest of these signs is the obvious impact that *Beyond a Boundary* has had on popular consciousness, via the medium of calypso. MBA (Maestro Born Again) offers a great homily to the Caribbean people about their responsibility to support and 'hang on to' their 'dream team', entitled "Beyond the Boundary". "Kerry Packer", composed by Winsford Devine and sung by Sparrow, reopened the discourse against the directorate of Queen's Park Oval begun in 1960 with C. L. R. James' campaign for Worrell as captain and for making the administrators of cricket aware of public sentiment. Rudder's "Rally Round the West

Indies", like C. L. R.'s *Beyond a Boundary,* to which it makes direct allusion, explores West Indies cricket as a metaphor of the capacity of West Indian peoples for self-assertion and sovereignty. It recognizes signs of faltering and weakness in an era of transition between cricketing generations and calls for regional solidarity in more than cricket.

Rudder's "Here Come the West Indies" (1994) is a boasting song: a statement of confidence in the ability of "dem rude bwoy" to bring all opponents to their knees. By characterizing the team, which had recently defeated Australia for the nth time since 1976, as "rude bwoys", Rudder acknowledges and confidently celebrates the Caliban element in their cricket; its proletarian, affirmative, explosive and even rebellious quality, evident since Stingo, George John, Herman Griffith, Martindale, John Trim, Roy Gilchrist and Charlie Griffith; its defiance of strictures loud in the arrogance of Richards, the Constantines, Sobers, Kanhai, the three Ws, Lara; its capacity to move beyond the boundaries of convention. The vigorous Jamaican-flavoured Puk-kumina, Zion Revival or Shouter-Baptist rhythm of this song is Rudder's way of suggesting the subterranean Orisha source of the team's strength.

"Legacy"(1995) comes in a year when calypsonians great and small have been hailing Lara's achievement of world record scores in test (375) and first-class cricket (501). The best of these songs have been Watchman's "Lara, Prince of Plunder", De Fosto's "Four, Lara, Four" and Superblue's overwhelming Road March winner "Signal to Lara". These all focus on what C. L. R. James too might have highlighted: the hero as a supremely masterful individual; the advent of the man of "dazzling personality, creative, daring, original" (James 1963, 209), the rebirth of the young Romantic whose batting "will extend the boundaries of cricket technique with a classical perfection" (James 1964, 216).

Rudder's "Legacy", however, comes closest to C. L. R. James' way of perceiving the great individual as being simultaneously individual and a product of tradition. This great naming song of praise and thanks and calm exultation says:

> I have never seen Headley and the three W's, but oh! I know them so well
> 'Cause I have seen Sobers and the beautiful line that walked through his passage
> Fredericks and Lloyd and Kanhai and Kalli, Dujon and the man we call 'The Bull'
> Haynes, Rowe and Greenidge. Oh, Collie Smith, Brother they got your 'message'
> And now is this Richardson era the Prince who promised so much is now the monarch of all he surveys
> And young lions are roaring from Jamaica's to Guyana's shores
> Look, the West Indies coming through! You better clear the way

David Rudder receiving an award from the University of the West Indies for outstanding contribution to cricket and popular culture.

Chorus
> What's the word?
> Legacy, legacy . . . Tell them again
> Legacy, legacy . . . Come on children, pound it in their brain
> Legacy, legacy . . . We are fuelled by an inward hunger
> Legacy, legacy . . . That is why the Caribbean man younger and stronger

Gilchrist and Gibbs and Valentine, Ramadhin
The great Constantine, Martindale, Griffith and Hall
Garner and Croft and Roberts and Walsh, Whispering Michael,
Marshall and Ambrose: just a few who have us standing tall
And even as I speak a young man walks through our islands
With a fire in his eyes and the cool, the cool of a champion's swagger
A frightening thought to those knights who stand on the way of our destiny
Today they think it's hard; but tomorrow is harder

Chorus
> What's the word?
> Legacy, legacy . . . Tell them again
> Legacy, legacy . . . Children pound it in their brain
> Legacy, legacy . . . Oh oh, Caribbean take over
> Legacy, legacy . . . West Indies rule forever.

The great individual, by this reading, does not become great only by his own effort, but is the product of a tradition of excellence from which he draws strength and to which he contributes his own individual achievement. This is remarkably similar to T. S. Eliot's belief that the individual talent in literature is always the product of an entire tradition of greatness which precedes him. It is C. L. R. James' position as well when he argues that the new and original players who arise to redeem the game whenever it is on the verge of death, will simply be rediscovering heights of greatness already conquered by their Golden Age ancestors.

While the chauvinism of "Legacy" might not have met with C. L. R. James' approval, no more than Richards' Rastafarian tendencies, it would have pleased him to see the extent to which his fervent faith in the capacity of the West Indian people and his sense of the legacy which the founding fathers of our game passed on to future generations, have permeated popular consciousness. It is the achievement of *Beyond a Boundary* to have defined for posterity the lineaments of this legacy: in George John and Old Cons, Caliban's natural rebelliousness, pride, dignity and independence of spirit; in Learie Constantine, disciplined control of spontaneity, inventive deployment of energy; in Frank Worrell, intelligence, grace, craftsmanship, leadership;

and in the Shannon cricket team, cohesion, seriousness, the will to win and a recognition that the team represents the aspirations of an entire people.

COMMENTARIES

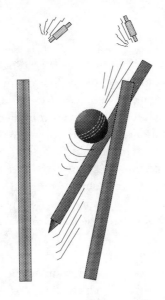

Viv's Example

Chris Searle

At the Headingley test match during the frigid English June of 1991, I was watching the progress of the West Indies first innings. It was late afternoon, and by that time much drinking had been done around the ground. It was a cold, cold Saturday, which had been warmed by two inspirational pieces of cricket from the young Ramprakash, a newcomer to the England team whose family roots were planted first in India and then in the coastal lowlands of Guyana. He had first launched himself sideways to take one brilliant catch, then minutes after thrown down the stumps from mid wicket after a lightning pick-up to create another wicket from nowhere. Those two electric acts had sparked the cutting atmosphere of the iciest cricket-watching day that I can ever remember.

At about 4:30 in the afternoon, however, it was the time of Viv Richards. As he strode out to the wicket with his implacable gait, unhelmeted and unperturbed by climate, crowd, match conditions or apparently anything else around him, a lone and dreadlocked West Indies supporter standing near the players' steps let out a loud cheer and Caribbean words of brotherhood and encouragement. The bond and magnetism of his cry was urgent and powerful. A group of white spectators standing near him, carrying their lager cans, slurring their words and grimacing their aggression, turned on him and Richards too with curses, racist insults and crude, provocative gestures. He stood his ground, as Viv always did, giving back everything piled upon him until other spectators intervened and warned off the insulters.

Now Headingley is certainly not the most friendly or hospitable ground in England for black cricketers and their supporters. Yorkshire cricket, its administrators, and followers have often been as cold as this June Saturday in receiving and recognizing the talents of black cricketers. The 'no foreigners' approach to Yorkshire cricket, and its century-long refusal to allow anyone not born in Yorkshire to play for the county before it opened its doors for prestige overseas players like Sachin Tendulkar and Richie Richardson, has meant that still not one single cricketer from the squads of excellent black cricketers playing every weekend in the leagues and inner cities of Yorkshire has been selected. Many of these, disrespected, excluded and ignored, have gone to form their own teams and leagues to play against each other, and have thus been forced into a Jim Crow cricket arrangement in the cities and old mill towns of northern England.

So when these drunken Headingley spectators spat out their invective at Viv Richards and his countryman, they were the worst of the cricket world insulting and trying to humiliate the best. The dreadlocked watcher was brave and full of resistance and had no doubt had to confront similar menaces before on the streets of Leeds or other places in England. Viv too, of course, was no stranger to such hostility, and in his career took on the gibes of taunting spectators, British journalists and their press campaigns, and the violence of Australian attitudes during the 1975 tour.[1] As he wrote in *Hitting Across the Line*:[2] "We came up against extreme savagery in that series, what many people would call extreme racism. Now what is a West Indian bouncer compared to that?" There is a perennial image of Viv Richards in my head, and it is of him walking to the wicket. The pride, the matchless inner confidence that shines out, the assuredness of movement, the purple cap as if an integral part of the scalp. Here was a whole people going out to bat and to combat, a ray of Caribbean nationhood and the proud individual citizen of that nation, from a small island yet knowing no smallness, only power and readiness. That is why that lone, proudly locked black man could resist and feel no sense of impending defeat from a group of cowardly and pathetic racists. There was a rock-like compatriot before him, striding towards the struggle of his people's cricket – and no bitter or envious postcolonial word-lash or threat was going to turn him around. In his autobiography Richards writes of the "deep, deep love" that binds cricketers and cricketer lovers of the Caribbean, a love and solidarity which beamed out from his own cricket.[3] Who was ever going to make Viv Richards or his Headingley brother 'grovel'? He was a great innovator of Caribbean cricket insurgency, but he also inherited the insights and understanding of pioneering forebears like Learie Constantine of Trinidad who, like him, knew of the aggression that surrounded the cricket world in which he played, with its "failing intelligence . . . clinging to its wars and inequalities, its racial barriers and shibboleths".[4]

I believe that this incident at Headingley crystallizes the effect of Viv Richards on his region's cricket, but also on his people. There is a parallel too with the deeds and words of Maurice Bishop. Viv was a symbol for the Grenada Revolution and those who led it on their small, struggling island. They saw him, as C. L. R. James would have expressed it, 'as their man', but also the whole Caribbean's man, their living emblem and inspiration too: the anti-imperial cricketer, the free West Indian of the crease. As Bishop had a dream of 'One Caribbean!' so Richards too manifested the region's essential unity: "Our pride in the West Indies binds us all together. If only we could work together. Perhaps sport should be the model for all life." And as Bishop's words and Grenada's achievement sought to repel the new imperialism, the Reaganism of the north to "Leave Grenada alone! Leave the Caribbean people alone! Leave the Revo alone",[5] so Richards declares in *Hitting Across the Line* :"I want to warn people to stop their racism. I want them to leave West Indies cricket alone!"[6] For there has never been a cricketer so proud and combative as Viv Richards. Before him Constantine, Weekes, Walcott, Gilchrist, Hall, Griffith and Lloyd had brought a concentrated power; Headley, Worrell, Sobers and Gibbs a certain grace, fluency and phenomenal talent; and Ramadhin, Valentine, Collie Smith and Kanhai a unique ingenuity and creative genius. But Richards brought all these with a sense of assertive dignity, self-confidence and outright challenge that made the racists boil and his own people come out with all their strength and defiance of oppression. He was a product of the Caribbean cricketing achievement that came before, but provoked its emulation in others through the Caribbean and across the diaspora. The greatest prize for its upholders, along with Richards himself, was Ian Botham. But he could not look into his friend's eye had he gone to South Africa, so thus he stayed away. As the contemporary of Marley, of Bishop, of Walter Rodney, of Caribbean women such as Jacqueline Creft or Merle Hodge as well as of Holding, Marshall, Roberts, Garner and Greenidge, he played for a generation of courage and creation too, across the many currents and depths of culture through the Caribbean.

It did not occur to me, on that Headingley Saturday, that it would be Richards' countryman and successor to the captaincy, Richie Richardson, truly the metaphorical son of the father, who would do much to help break down the racism in Yorkshire cricket. For that is what he did when he became the county's second overseas player during the 1994 season. He is absolutely his own man and his own brilliant cricketer, but perhaps Richards' huge and empowering courage also moved him. So our young black cricketers here at school, rushing to their lunch hour practices and squeezing in some five-a-side between the end of afternoon school and the beginning of mosque, chalking up stumps anywhere there is a street space or a brick wall, and listening closely to the cricketing experience of their Jamaican coach – perhaps they too, in the heart of a Yorkshire inner city, owe a debt of emulation to Viv Richards, as we all do.

In his vibrant and beautifully presented coaching manual, *Cricket Masterclass* – a gift of a cricketing experience to any young enthusiast – Richards declares: "Work at the basics but never be afraid to do something different. My fundamental wish for every cricketer is to keep his panache while observing the basic principles."[7] Sound rules for life itself, and a grounding for Caribbean cricket also voiced by Constantine. "Try to contribute something new," he advised, "and carry the spirit of your cricket into your life."[8] It is that very sense of difference, a different intrepidity to challenge and overcome domination, racial arrogance and injustice, that we take from Viv Richards into our own lives with the memories of the wristband of African colours swinging with the arm-whirls of the bat and the uncompromising step, forward ever, towards the contest in the middle. That was Viv Richards at his cricket and for millions his example can never fade.

Notes

1 See Chris Searle, "The mirror of racism", in *Race and Class* 34, no. 3 (1993).
2 Viv Richards, *Hitting Across the Line* (London: Headline, 1991).
3 Richards, *Hitting Across the Line*.
4 Learie Constantine, *Cricketers' Cricket* (London: Eyre and Spottiswood, 1949).
5 Chris Searle, ed, *In Nobody's Backyard: Maurice Bishop's Speeches, 1979–1983* (London: Zed Books, 1984).
6 Richards, *Hitting Across the Line*.
7 Viv Richards, *Cricket Masterclass* (London: Macdonald Queen Anne Press, 1988).
8 Constantine, *Cricketers' Cricket*.

'The Conquering Lion'
The Media Cage and
Viv Richards

Vaneisa Baksh

West Indians are acutely aware that cricket, as intellectual contest and politicized social discourse within and between places once known as 'The Empire', constitutes a most public space for the exorcism of old nightmares and the realization of new dreams. It is a theatre in which conflicts are ritualized and heroes constructed. For more than a century they have embraced the game and taken to its moral culture with a zeal that surprises those who do not know of the region's journey from empire. Along the trail, small places that once created rich men now produce great cricketers. Such men are celebrated as heroes and liberators, and more often than not betrayed in short time; it is part of a process, but cricket, as metaphor for the condition of the Indies, remains a fertile womb for the creation and nourishment of an irrepressible, antisystemic mentality.

There are many precise questions and fewer clear answers. How does a child coming from a small island named Antigua, believing himself no different from all the other little boys growing up around him, negotiate a space for himself as he enters manhood and finds it has thrust upon him a chalice brimming with his people's struggles and dreams? How does a young man from this former plantation place enter the global dominion of his dreams to find it rich in fantasy and nightmare, and still wake up with the chalice's contents intact? How does a West Indian retrace the voyage of the *Santa Maria*, having been declared a hero, only to find that discovery has a high social price? Can he return, must he go forward? How does he negotiate terms of endearment and find a space for himself? Does he draw a line between the public enterprise and private journey?

On coming of age Vivian Richards realized that his dream was to play cricket for the West Indies. It was a common sort of desire that did not set him apart. What pulled him onto the margins of reality, however, was a determination of extraordinary intensity, and the special gift of inherited capability. His father, Malcolm, had played good cricket and his brothers, Mervyn and Donald, did too. The Richards boys grew up under the fairly rural circumstances common to the islands; but their father's job as a superintendent in the prison (located near the St John's Recreational Ground) brought home a strong, almost military sense of discipline. Vivian, for most of his teachers, was not an outstanding scholar, but for his sports master he possessed an intense intellect that expressed itself in creative, innovative and radical ways. Like other boys, he recognized the excellence of cricket stars, and his dreams of stardom resided within an understanding of this condition. But as he wrote in his autobiography, *Hitting Across the Line*, "Nobody expected this little island to produce sportsmen of international standard." He was highly motivated, but wondered whether his dreams were no more than private ambitions.

The tensions that exist between desire and reality are oftentimes socially destructive. Cricketers know this space well, as their journey to excellence is often punctuated with violations of social expectations. Richards' case was traumatic. He was 17 years of age when he first encountered a public incursion. It was at a Leeward Islands Tournament in a match against St Kitts when he reacted badly to an umpire's decision. As he walked from the wicket, the crowd protested and soon placards were threatening "No Viv, No Match". In his inexperience, he says, he went back to bat at the officials' request; he was banned subsequently for two years, labelled a bad sportsman, and tasted the acidity of a crowd gone sour. "I went under for a while and refused to go out," he wrote, but it improved his approach to the game, tempered his reckless determination, and focused his growing self-confidence. At the end of the two years, Antiguans banded together to raise funds to help him and Andy Roberts to go to the Alf Gover coaching school in England, a community's investment in its emissaries.

When he delivered the inaugural Sir Frank Worrell Memorial Lecture at UWI, Michael Manley said, "West Indians crowding to tests bring with them the whole past history and future hopes for the islands." Richards was beginning to understand cricket's hold on the West Indian psyche. He was yet to grasp what it would mean for him personally. Coming to terms with the cultural shocks England offered would have been significant in helping to locate Richards in his West Indian context. Things began to happen once he had settled down to his game. Consider his career briefly: playing with Lansdowne Cricket Club, then a two-year contract with Somerset, where he quickly made his presence felt; then the call to join the West Indies team on its way to India in 1974.

It was the start of a test career involving 36 matches against England, 34 against Australia, 7 against New Zealand, 28 against India, and 16 against Pakistan. At the end of it, he had played in 121 tests, had accumulated 8,540 runs with an average of 50.23, and had hit 24 centuries. (His highest score was 291 against England at the Oval in 1976; and his fastest century was a record in 56 balls at the first test in Antigua in 1986.) In 1976 alone, in 11 test matches he scored 1,710 runs at an average of 90. When Clive Lloyd retired, he was made captain of the West Indies team – a position few would have thought him unqualified for – although he felt that the WICBC was reluctant to make the appointment. In his autobiography he says he believed that "at one time there was a conspiracy of sorts to prevent me from taking over the leadership of the squad". They wanted, he said, a "blue-eyed boy", rather than an uncaged lion. Of course, the media had been tuned in to him from early. He had been bestowed with the titles of Master Blaster, Smokin' Joe, and had become known as a hard, aggressive, supremely confident player. He would find his every word and action reported in and out of context. His captaincy, though statistically the best in West Indies cricket, was compared with Clive Lloyd's and critiqued, often too harshly, he complained. And he discovered the predatorial nature of the international press. His friendships, his lifestyle, everything was up for scrutiny in a media free-for-all.

Public figures have always had ambivalent relationships with the press. Cricketers especially have difficulty coming to terms with the fickleness of a relationship that seems based on a darling- today-demon-tomorrow principle. Journalists are frequently accused of telling only one side of a story. Unfortunately, that accusation too is often only one side of the story. Constraints of time and space, and even poor editing, may be contributing factors. Editors seem to prefer stories that titillate and offer scandal, leaning towards what is perceived to be a public demand for private details. Sophisticated communications technology has imposed the facet of immediacy on the transfer of news. The scramble is not necessarily now for who can produce the best news, but who can get it out fastest. For the larger media houses, particularly in the larger societies, where there is a high degree of specialization in terms of journalism, the beat reporter has to come up with a story, sometimes daily, even when the news is not apparent. The cricket 'hero' is expected to represent all the ideas, ideals and nationalist project of the people, particularly as elected representatives have lost much of the public confidence. The obsession of press and public intensifies as social confidence decreases; balanced judgements do not thrive under these circumstances.

For those with a flaccid sense of integrity, it would not be out of line to manu-facture a story or a headline; and that is when the punches roll off the press.

Viv Richards was not particularly comfortable with the constant surveillance. He seemed to be always conscious of how the press viewed him, and he often reacted to the comments. "They don't know the real Viv Richards", he would repeatedly complain, meaning that the 'real' Viv Richards was a multifaceted person. He was not only the West Indian hero, not only the black champion, not only the hard hitter, not only the ladies' man, not only the anti-apartheid campaigner, not only the conquering lion; he was all of those things, and more. Could he convince the world of his complexity? He tried to do so.

In an interview with the author in March 1996, Richards spoke about his bouts of shyness and how he regards the feeling that he is a public commodity, whose time and energy are open for the taking. "A lot of people have always looked upon me and think that I am a brash person," he said,

> but that's when I used to say to people, a lot of people do not know Viv Richards. A lot of people do not know what's in your heart. They see sometimes, maybe in public that reaction of that individual and they think: that's the animal. But a lot of people, deep down, do not really know how you feel and your sentiments and things like that. They do not think that you have a soft spot, but certainly there's quite a lot of that.

He admitted that the attention can sometimes be too much, but,

> It's a good and it's a bad thing, because you do not have the negative without the positive, and I think with both you get things working. I'm pleased I'm pretty open because this is what I represented. I think I represented the people. I represented the spirit of the Caribbean-ness, whatever that is. So I feel that I am open to the people. In a way, I myself may have brought this upon myself because of how expressive I am about the body and the people I represent. So I think I invite this feeling where people think I'm approachable. So I have no hiccup about that. If that's the way I can represent the people, I'm happy with that.

His Caribbean people, while they have admired him, have had varying relationships with him. In Antigua, it is nothing short of hero worship. Here is the man who has risen, taking his island into prominence on the cricket landscape. Here is the brother, black and proud, always accessible to the masses. Antiguan calypsonian, Short Shirt, sang about the hero, "Vivian Richards",

> Vivi is the name
> Cricket is the game
> Brother I don't know
> How he could play cricket so
> But his batting, bowling, fielding, catching is
> breathtaking

Sometimes I does wonder if he's a next Sobers
in the making . . .

and Trinidadian poet, Faustin Charles describes "Viv" thus:

Like the sun rising and setting
Like the thunderous roar of a bull-rhino
Like the sleek, quick grace of a gazelle,
The player springs into the eye
And lights the world with fires
Of a million dreams, a million aspirations
The batsman-hero climbs the skies
Strikes the earth-ball for six
And the landscape rolls with the ecstasy
of the magic play . . .

For in the West Indies, he has been more than a cricketing icon. He himself
noted that the very playing of the game of cricket was a political action, and
when he refused a million Eastern Caribbean dollars to play in apartheid South
Africa, he was putting his mouth where his money could have been. The
decision to refuse these offers, he says, was an easy one.

They all carried a political burden and in each case it was a very simple
decision for me. I just could not go. As long as the black majority in South
Africa remains suppressed by the apartheid system, I could never come to
terms with playing cricket there.

He had resisted efforts to cut off his Rastafarian friendships because they were
perceived to be bad for his image. His image as a champion for the black cause
was not unfounded. "It was perfectly natural for me to identify, for example,
with the Black Power movement in America, and to a certain extent with
Rastafarians." But he sought perhaps, through his close friendship with Ian
Botham, to show the world that hey, I might be black and proud, but I'm not
anti-white. He sees his struggle as one for social justice and is critical of all
forms of racial arrogance. In Trinidad and Guyana where the Indian populations are large, while he remains a hero, there was an uproar when he described
the West Indies team as a 'black' one. He was asked to apologize. He had used
the term 'black' collectively, as is the case in England. In this he included all
West Indians. The Indian community objected to the categorization.

In all the other islands, his career has been followed with deep interest and
reverence. You can go to any Caribbean island and find in some cricket lover's
home a poster of Vivian Richards. Whenever he lands in one of the territories,
the media are on to him immediately. Even five years after his retirement, he

is still hounded by the press. And generally, he has negotiated the Caribbean media well. His complaints of press harassment usually arise out of English coverage. In the 1990 test against England, both he and Desmond Haynes came in for criticism. He for the 'ceremonial jig' he did while advancing toward the umpire, after he took a catch, which caused a comment from Christopher Martin-Jenkins about both teams cheating and having a win-at-all-costs attitude. In his autobiography, he says that although a lot of the press coverage was critical, but fair, a substantial amount had been personal and abusive. This he felt was because of the great press interest in the test series; by his estimation there were about 80 journalists following the tour, and they were all vying for exclusives; what they could not find, he said, they invented.

He cited the incident with James Lawton of the *Daily Express* as an example of irresponsible journalistic behaviour. Lawton had questioned him about a signal he had mistakenly thought Richards had made to Allan Lamb. This annoyed Richards and Lawton's persistent questioning only aggravated him. He was verbally aggressive to Lawton who responded that he would publish the words. Richards, losing what journalists would call his famous temper, let him know that if he did, he would come looking for him in the press box. He did go looking for Lawton the next day, but it made him late on the field and he had to apologize to the WICBC and the rest of the team. "But I really felt that the limits of good reporting had been pushed too far," he wrote, "and I wanted to make a stand against such journalism." Another journalist wrote a piece suggesting that he should be banned from playing in England and his contract with Glamorgan terminated. When he returned to England, it was to a hostile environment, and he received a police escort through Heathrow Airport. He also received several "offensive, racist letters". It upset him deeply.

Whatever his own feelings towards these kinds of intrusions, Richards has never been one to mince words on matters he considers important. He has taken strong positions on racism, on women in cricket, on better payments for cricketers. During his captaincy, he marshalled his team without kid gloves and received heavy criticism for it. He has dealt with press speculation about his private life, and although he has lost his cool many times, he seems to have finally resigned himself to an acceptance that once you are a public figure, you are an open target. It is why, perhaps, he feels that he can commiserate with Brian Lara's plaintive cry that "Cricket is ruining my life!" Lara, as West Indies cricket's latest star, has been hounded unmercifully by the media. Frequently, he has not borne the scrutiny with good grace; frequently his conduct has been greeted with outrage and incomprehension. When Lara says that cricket is ruining his life, he is perhaps now encountering the multiple incursions that fame and stardom bring.

Richards has been there, and perhaps because he is at a stage in his life where the past, the present, and the future stretch out like a vast savannah, his vision has more clarity. He feels a great deal of sympathy for Lara because he sees him on the threshold of a whole new era for cricket.

> A lot of what we have to realize is that he is one of the first in our region who has had so many things coming his way, often in terms of commitments, appearances, lucrative contracts and everything. I think he is the first cricketer in the world who has been involved in all of this. And I think we have to have a little forgiveness in our hearts for him, because it can be too much sometimes.

Here, Richards reveals the depth of his empathy for Lara as he unconsciously links them with his choice of the first person plural.

> I think sometimes, for the young individual, and certainly from the environment we're in, and having all of this thrust upon us, we feel it can be a burden and there are times when we go a little overboard, and where pressures take over, and you may not handle it the way you would like to, or other people would like you to.

It can be too much, he says, speaking obviously from his personal experience. And he wants the young cricket star to know that there are people who can help put things in perspective; just as there are those who can easily make a 'martyr' of him.

The perspective Richards seems to have adopted is that, in the long run, you go out into the public space, you become their hero while you fulfil your private dreams, and in return you give them the greater part of yourself. David Rudder sang in the cricket anthem, *Rally Round the West Indies,*

> In these tiny theatres of conflict and confusion
> Better known as the isles of the West Indies
> We already know who brought us here
> And who created this confusion . . .

Richards is saying that as we struggle to forge our sense of West Indianhood, we must recognize that "we need heroes we can look upon". We need, he says, "people who we look up to, and we can shout about, and we can put up on our walls, and things like that. It's important". And while he may be right and they do not know 'the real Viv Richards', they know the one he has shown them: the conquering lion, uncaged still, carrying a chalice brimming with hopes and dreams.

Viv's View

Interview with
Isaac Vivian Alexander Richards

Vaneisa Baksh

Comments on West Indies' performance in the recently concluded World Cup . . .

Well, I felt we started very badly in terms of losing against India, losing against Kenya and I think maybe at one stage it did look like it was a dismal performance – when we played against Kenya – that was all lost. But I thought after that performance that we came back well. We came back and we've shown, I think, after being beaten by Kenya, that regardless of whatever changes we might be going through right now, we can still compete with the best. With wins against Australia in the preliminary round, and beating, in my mind, what was the best team in the competition, South Africa. We find that we're competing with the very best. So it is just a matter I think, because of the start we had and the indifferent sort of finish towards the end, I just felt that there is something there that I believe we can work with and there's more positive out of the last World Cup than the negative.

How would you improve the current team?

I would not get into that argument in terms of who they should pick.

In terms of one-days for example, should the team be composed differently? More batsmen . . . bowlers . . .

Well, I think maybe you gotta pick horses for racecourses; and if we haven't been doing that, I'm quite positive that there's going to be a case where they will look at the modern day style of cricket which changes the nature of the game. There's quite a lot to learn and it's not maybe the fancy teams over the years, like maybe the Englands and the Australias we can look to learn everything from. But at least maybe the team which won the other day, Sri Lanka, and some of the lesser teams, because obviously in anything that is negative, in order for it to work there must be a positive.

On the Sri Lankan team's last performance . . .

I think it was a great performance because it's a team over the years who've basically been walkovers, and so seeing them now in this capacity, and to see them the way their confidence . . . I think they've always lacked maybe self-belief: believing that certain things can be achieved, having that mental confidence. I think that's what we're seeing now. I think they've done their lessons and learnt them well.

On the shift in the West Indies team towards individualism and professionalism . . .

I'm not disturbed about individuals as sportsmen and women, whatever they get in terms of monetary returns, because I think that maybe it's long overdue for some of them in the region . . . that we haven't had our full share of what's been passing. I feel that it's good for the sport. But I also feel that players thinking of it shouldn't be carried away with the fact that, because there are so many lucrative things in the sport today, that they neglect what got them that lucrative contract. You've got to remember at all times that I hope that it doesn't get to an individual's head, that all of a sudden they believe that you've become bigger than the game, because that's the sport that gave you the so-called revenue or the avenue for you to negotiate and for you to get lucrative things done. So I hope that we don't lose focus and we continue to believe as well that there are so many millions of people in this region who we owe our performances to and to whom we owe playing in that sense because of the satisfaction we can generate from the West Indies doing well.

I think over the years I've always looked upon myself as being someone who represented not just myself. I set myself high standards but I know there are people out there who were hoping and believing we'd deliver the goods and thinking about that made you a little bit more conscious.

You only have to look at when cricket's being played when something happens, the call-in programmes, the media, everybody gets involved. So it is a sign that it is very much in our blood and that cannot go away. I think that we are representative of these people and we've got to take them seriously into consideration.

What direction for West Indian cricket?

Well, I hear there may be some changes at the top, at board level. Maybe if the talk is correct in terms of some of the individuals who they've got earmarked for the big positions, some of these people . . . There are people who, over the years, I've got an enormous sense of respect for and people who I think judging from the work they have done in the past, they have only got their best judgment to give to West Indies cricket. I hope that with these people in place it may open the avenue to improve the relationship between board and players, and overall West Indian cricket and the future and how it's going to be run. I've got confidence that people are going to be in place to handle these.

Will you identify these people?

Well, I don't want to jump the gun.

Who do you think would be good people to run things then?

Well, I'm thinking of the Rousseaus and the Julian Huntes and people like that. To me, over the years they've always had West Indies cricket at heart. And I just wish they could find various avenues that they could let some of that energy go to work.

Talk of the team's low morale . . .

What do you think can be done to pull the team back together?

I believe that there were some positive signs towards the end of the World Cup. It's a pity we had to end up losing that match. And I think that is the positive we can work with and look to improve on. And now with a new captain in place, I'm quite certain he will have new things that he'd like to introduce. So it will be some time before we really see exactly what changes there should be. I think we are in our trying-out stages now. Because certainly there are going to be changes in the team. And one's got to wait and see what sort of team we have and select for the games coming up against New Zealand. And then I think that we won't be just trying out just one or two, we will be looking at the wider issues in terms of touring and people who can fit into a team and who look good for the future. I think that it's a cat and mouse game at this stage and it's going to be so hard in any structure where you are going to be seen to be rebuilding. It's going to be difficult, but I'd like to think that the positive side in this massive undertaking is in the board aspect, that we can channel that into our cricket so that everyone, notably board and players, everyone in that vicinity is representing one body, that is West Indies cricket.

I'd like to think that if the fellas can observe in the team that they can be better individuals, we can see a better commitment in the team in terms of mind and body.

Periods of cricket have been defined by captaincy. How would Richardson's era be defined?

Well, I would like to think that he's done it his way, and I've always felt I've looked up to people who I believe started that era in terms of our success period. And the person I look up to is Clive Lloyd for starting that era. I certainly, when I took over, started to try and do things and to follow the patterns which had made us and which had become successful over the years. So I would say that because of that, I'd like to think that maybe because Richardson is in the position, knowing he played under myself, he played under Clive Lloyd as well, that this was the pattern he followed. Everyone, even though you may have certain patterns, you think differently. It's not for me to say, but I think judging from, ah, maybe in his mind he was satisfied to run West Indies the way he did. There are times when you finish and you feel a little down that you think that you didn't do things the way you'd like. But I would like to think that he was satisfied with the way he played. And I have criticism publicly in what way he chose; whether to say he should run it this way or that way. But what I can say is I did look upon someone whom I tried to emulate and I think you'll have to see someone like maybe Richie to find out who he emulated.

What were his strengths as a leader?

He believed a hell of a lot in what he was doing and this is what I think it is all about. Regardless of whether things go wrong or right – believing that is the decision you've taken – and I think that is a leadership quality.

Did you have that kind of self-confidence when you were captain?

I felt that it was needed. I felt I thought I did what I believed in. I wanted to be perfect. Too many times you get people who are on the outside who tell you how you should do things, and you're being moved in so many different directions. I tried my best to do what I think makes my mind click and what I think may work at that time. I think you've got to go with your instincts as well, and some of the supporters of the team and people whom you've had an enormous amount of respect for over the years, with their help as well too.

What would you say were Richardson's weak points, his shortcomings?

Again, I cannot judge from the outside. One would have to find that out from people who have been involved because when you are living with an individual for a number of years, you can stay from the outside and see things differently. But maybe because I've been in that capacity before it would be harsh of me to say and, how would I like someone to assess me from the outside and not being on the inside? So I think that would be a hard one for me to tap.

Thoughts on the proposed cricket academy?

I haven't heard anything officially, but I do hear from various conversations around that this is the plan and certainly I started advertising that we need a cricket academy. I haven't heard anything yet on the academy.

How do you feel such an academy should be structured?

I think some past and present West Indies players can have an input. And one of the first categories that I think: We've been working our cricket off the English coaching manual and I believe that cricket has been proved to have taken another step. So I believe we've got players and enough people here in position, knowing some of our great fast bowlers, some of our great batsmen, who I feel we can put a coaching manual together and play cricket the West Indian way; and not maybe the Colin Cowdrey of England way. You know, I believe we've got enough players and we've made enough inroads in the cricketing fraternity for us to be in that position to start working on a book.

Would you be willing to contribute?

Most certainly. I believe it would be wonderful for us as a region because I believe that the cricket manual out of England is outdated at this stage, what with modern day life and the way we are. We need to adjust things, improve things. We've got to look at the modern way of doing things and I believe that this is one way we can benefit.

Schedule since retiring . . .

Well, I spend a lot of time these days in a place called Brunei, assigned to some members of a family, a very prestigious family in that sense. And I am coach to their sons. So I spend 14 days in each month in that part of the world. I spend some time there, and whatever other little time I may have to go to whatever I'm invited to, and we have after-dinner cricket talks. It's quite a lot. I never really expected that I'd be this busy when I packed up playing. I thought that maybe I'd cut everything off then – and I swore I'd be spending a lot of time on the beach in Antigua. But I found that ever since my retirement, I've been doing more travel than when I actually played.

I also work for Club International, a chain of hotels which I represent. I never thought I'd be this busy and that I'd be still in demand because when you pack up and you've been doing something like my cricket for a number of years, you contemplate what you're going to do next, and whether you're going to find the same level of enjoyment as when you played.

All that can be put to rest now because I'm reasonably happy and I'm spending a lot of time in new parts of the world. I'm extremely happy with the course my life has taken.

How often do you actually play cricket now?

About four meetings a year. The last time that I played was in Sharjah in the Middle East. We were involved in a small tournament with England, Pakistan and India. So on that basis we meet other members of the West Indies team. People who have formed a unit over a number of years and we are just very happy to see each other at this stage in our lives, to see some very fit, and some a little unfit. So it's been good fun and these are the things which keep me my 365 days.

Are you involved officially in cricket in Antigua?

I've always been a little bit reluctant to [get involved] mainly because I don't spend enough time. And you do need to be invited into these things. Everyone thinks that you are in a position and their position is threatened because they think that maybe Viv Richards played and he's gonna come and have an input. So I think that if that's people's baby and if that's what makes them famous or makes them feel important in some way, well, I'm not going to get down to their hatch, because quite a lot of these things go on in our society, where we have made contributions and people who haven't made contributions try and take all the contributions. So I'm a little bit reluctant too at this stage because people are not all that forthcoming in terms of how they feel about you and how much they'd like you to do.

So you keep a low profile in Antigua then?

I still go and watch as much cricket as I can at home, because I think it gave me a chance to get involved in something else apart from Caribbean cricket. It gives me a chance to get away for a while.

What direction for Viv Richards?

I'd like to think that notably all my cricketing knowledge – I'm a little bit, as I said, restrained in so many different areas where people who have made a contribution have been placed in positions. When we do these things in our region, everyone looks upon you as being intimidating. You are gaining too much power, and things like that. I'd like to think that there's still a lot of time when we need people who have a conscious vein, we can hopefully have these people in positions and then I'll be up and working hopefully in position.

So do you see for yourself a more active role in West Indies cricket?

I think so. I know so, because having made a contribution at a healthy time, at a period when we were doing well, I believe that certainly I would like to see someone who hasn't made any contributions and who are in positions – just to try to look like they're making a contribution – I would like to be in that position – but because of the input which one made to West Indies cricket – yes, I do have a lot to offer in terms of advising, which some people see as threatening.

Cricket is full of political intrigue . . .

It is. It is like that. Which is why I am so reluctant to make a move at this moment because I'd like to know, if I'm going to do it, we can do it on a most genuine basis, rather than for what I can make out of it and for what prestige and who I can have a drink with later and . . . no, I'm not into it for that. I'm in for just the basic results of the betterment and the future of West Indies cricket.

Would you say that you are a shy person?

I think I've had bouts of shyness. A lot of people have always looked upon me and think that I am a brash person, but that's when I used to say to people a lot of people do not know Viv Richards. A lot of people do not know what's in your heart. They see sometimes, maybe in public, that reaction of that individual and they think: that's the animal. But a lot of people, deep down do not really know how you feel and your sentiments and things like that, and they do not think that you have a soft spot, but certainly there's quite a lot of that.

How do you cope with this public feeling that you belong to them? People see you as Viv Richards, Master Blaster, world famous cricketer whose time and energy are just open and available for the public taking . . .

It's a good and it's a bad thing because you do not have the negative without the positive and I think with both you get things working. So it has its advantages and disadvantages. I'm pleased I'm pretty open because this is what I represented. I think I represented the people. I represented that spirit of Caribbean-ness, whatever that is. So I feel that I'm open to the people. In a way, I myself maybe have this upon myself because of how expressive I am about the body and the people I represent. So I think I invite this feeling where people think I'm approachable. So I have no hiccup about that, if that's the way I can represent the people I'm happy with that.

Do you feel there is still alive that spirit of the Caribbean you talked about?

I hope so. I feel sometimes that I see a little bit of how our values go. We've got to have things that we can turn back on and say this is a little bit like the Caribbean or this is a little bit like the country we live in. Maybe in living abroad people see different standards of living and want to be like that, but I'd like to believe that what you see painted on me, this is what you get.

I'm into my country. I love my country. I don't think I can say I love another country more than my country and whatever region in the Caribbean – because I don't just mean Antigua. I look upon all the regions in the Caribbean, because having represented these people in the past, and people saying things about you and so I have a deep affection for this region. I would never leave that aspect of life at all.

On Brian Lara . . .

A lot of what we have to realize is that he is one of the first in our region who has had so many things that have been coming his way often in terms of commitments, appearances, lucrative contracts and everything. But, I think he is the first cricketer in the world who has been involved in all this. And I think that we have to have a little forgiveness in our hearts for him, because it can be too much sometimes. I think sometimes for the young individual and certainly from the environment we're in, and having all of this thrust upon us, we feel it can be a burden and there are times when we go a little bit overboard and where pressures take over and you may not handle it the way you would like to or other people would like to.

I do believe that Brian Lara may realize it as well. He's got a little frustrated, but there's a whole lot of persons I believe he can speak with. People who have been in similar positions and who can guide him and just basically let him know that he's got a lot on his shoulders in terms of making a positive whatever for himself and also for him to learn that the people who depend on him that he can be a martyr.

We need the Brian Laras, so for that sake . . . we need heroes that we can look upon, because the real heroes are not the ones that sometimes you put an 'X' on. I hope for his sake and for West Indies cricket's sake, that he may find a solution, and he may come to peace if he's not happy at this stage and do the things that he does best.

Would you be willing and available to him?

Oh yes. I've always talked to him. I hope that he's not being misguided along the way, but he's got a great opportunity which only comes once. He's in a position to make it and to make a wonderful name for himself and to be up there with the all-time greats of the sport. And I say it many times, he's a guy that I got a deep affection for and I see that he's the one who can carry on that role and keep our people happy the way we're accustomed to. I think that we need to offer our help and not to run him down because of our hopes – you take away Brian Lara now from West Indies cricket and what do we have? Apart from the Ambrose and the Walsh and things like that, we'd be struggling for personalities ... people who we look up to and we can shout about and we can put up on our walls and things like that. It's important.

How do you feel about tomorrow's game?

I am just very pleased to be involved and to be playing with some of the younger folk. I'm just very happy and pleased that at least I got an invite and I made myself available – because I still love my cricket and I'm still very much into my West Indian Cause – and for this particular cause too, involving the University and helping to raise funds, the trip could not have been more worthwhile at this stage.

Thank you. Have a good game tomorrow.

Bibliography

African National Congress. 1994. *The Reconstruction and Devleopment Programme*. Johannesburg.

Archer, Robert, and Antoine Bouillon. 1982. *The South African Game: Sport and Racism*. London.

Bailey, Philip, Philip Thorn, and Peter Wynne-Thomas. 1984. *Who's Who of Cricketers*. London.

Blofeld, Henry. 1978. *The Packer Affair*. London.

Carnegie, James. 1995. "Dancing down the wicket: notes on cricket and the dance". Prepared for Rex Nettleford. Mimeograph.

Cashman, Richard. 1980. *Patrons, Players and the Crowd: the Phenomenon of Indian Cricket*. New Delhi.

Cobley, Alan. 1994. "A political history of playing fields: the provision of sporting facilities for Africans in the Johannesburg area to 1948". *International Journal of the History of Sport* 11, no. 2 (August).

Constantine, Learie. 1933. *Cricket and I*. London.

Constantine, Learie. 1949. *Cricketers' Cricket*. London.

Constantine, Learie. 1954. *Colour Bar*. London.

Constantine, Learie. N.d. *Cricket in the Sun*. London.

Cotter, Gerry. 1991. *England versus the West Indies*. London.

Cozier, Tony. 1978. *The West Indies: Fifty Years of Test Cricket*. London.

Crowley, Brian. 1983. *Cricket Exiles: the Saga of South African Cricket*. London.

Couzens, Tim. 1983. "An introduction to the history of football in South Africa". In *Town and Countryside in the Transvaal: Capitalist Penetration and Popular Response*, edited by Belinda Bozzoli. Johannesburg.

Dale, Harold. 1953. *Cricket Crusaders*. London.

Derriman, Philip. 1986. *Body-line: the Cricket 'War' between England and Australia*. London.

DuBois, W.E.B. 1985. *Black Reconstruction*. New York.

Duffus, Michael Owen-Smith, and André Odendaal. 1986. "South Africa". In *Barclays World of Cricket*, edited by E. W. Swanton. London.

Fanon, Frantz. 1967. *Wretched of the Earth*. London.

Gibb, James. 1979. *Test Records from 1877*. London.

Green, Benny, ed. 1986. *The Wisden Book of Obituaries*. London.

Hamilton, Bruce. 1947. *Cricket in Barbados*. Bridgetown.

Harte, Chris. 1993. *A History of Australian Cricket*. London.

Holding, Michael. 1993. *Whispering Death*. Kingston, Jamaica.

Hobsbawn, E. B. 1994. *The Age of Extremes 1914–1991*. London.

James, C. L. R. 1933. *The Case of West Indian Self-Government*. London.

James, C. L. R. 1937. *World Revolution*. London.

James, C. L. R. 1963. *Beyond a Boundary*. London.

James, C. L. R. 1969. *A History of Pan-African Revolt*. Washington.

James, C. L. R. 1986. *Cricket*, edited by Anna Grimshaw. London.

James, C. L. R. 1995. "The proof of the pudding". In *Liberation Cricket: West Indies Cricket Culture*, edited by Hilary Beckles and Brian Stoddart. Kingston, Jamaica.

Jokl, E. 1949. "Physical education, sport and recreation". In *Handbook on Race Relations in South Africa*, edited by E. Hellman. Johannesburg.

Kazantzakis, N. 1961. *Zorba the Greek*. London.

Kraus, Richard, et al. 1991. *History of the Dance in Art and Education*. New Jersey.

Lange, Roderyck. 1975. *The Nature of Dance: the Anthropological Perspective*. London.

Lemmon, David. 1982. *'Tich' Freeman and the Decline of the Leg-Break Bowler*. London.

Lloyd, Clive. 1988. "Introduction". In *A History of West Indies Cricket* by Michael Manley. London.

Manley, Michael. 1988. *A History of West Indies Cricket*. London.

Marqusee, Mike. 1994. *Anyone but England, Cricket and the National Malaise*. London.

Marshall, Trevor. 1994. "Ethnicity, class and the democratization of West Indies Cricket", in *An Area of Conquest*, edited by Hilary McD. Beckles. Kingston, Jamaica.

McLean, T. P. 1986. "New Zealand". In *Barclays World of Cricket*, edited by E. W. Swanton. London.

Metcalfe, Alan. 1987. *Canada Learns to Play: the Emergence of Organized Sport 1807–1914*. Toronto.

Miner, H. 1965. "Body ritual among the Nacirema". *American Anthropologist* 58, no. 13.

Mullins, Pat, and Philip Derriman. 1984. *Bat and Pad: Writings on Australian Cricket 1804–1984*. Oxford.

Nettleford, Rex. 1985. *Dance Jamaica: Cultural Definition and Artistic Discovery – The National Dance Theatre Company of Jamaica 1962–1983*. New York.

Nettleford, Rex. 1990. "Afro-Caribbean dance". *Dancing Times*. Dance Study Supplement, Part 8 (May). London.

Nicole, Christopher. 1957. *West Indian Cricket*. London.

Odendaal, André. 1988. "South Africa's black Victorians: sport and society in South Africa in the nineteenth century". In *Pleasure, Profit, Proselytism: British Culture and Sport at Home and Abroad 1700–1914*. London.

Playfair Cricket Annual 1949.

Polhemus, Ted. 1975. "Social bodies". In *The Body as a Medium of Expression*, edited by J. Benthall and T. Polhemus. New York.

Richards, Vivian. 1988. *Cricket Masterclass*. London.

Richards, Vivian. 1992. *Hitting Across the Line*. London.

Roberts, R. A., and D. J. Rutnagur. 1974. "India". In *Barclays World of Cricket*, edited by E. W. Swanton. London.

Rehm, Rush. 1994. *Greek Tragic Theatre*. London.

Report of the National European-Bantu Conference, Cape Town, February 6-9. 1929. Lovedale.

Russo, Carlo Ferdinando. 1994. *Aristophanes: an Author for the Stage*. London.

Sandiford, Keith A. P. 1983. "Amateurs and professionals in Victorian County Cricket". *Albion* 15 (Spring): 32–51.

Sandiford, Keith A. P. 1994. *Cricket and the Victorians*. Aldershot.

Sanyal, Saradindu. 1974. *Forty Years of Test Cricket: India vs England*. Delhi.

Searle, Chris. 1984. *In Nobody's Backyard: Maurice Bishop's Speeches 1979–1983*. London.

Searle, Chris. 1993. "Cricket and the mirror of racism". *Race and Class* 34, no. 3.

Short, Peter D. B. 1972. "A brief history of the formation of the West Indies Cricket Board of Control". Mimeo.

Steen, Rob. 1993. *Desmond Haynes: Lion of Barbados*. London.

Surin, Kenneth. 1995. "C. L. R. James' materialist aesthetic of cricket". In *Liberation Cricket: West Indies Cricket Culture*, edited by Hilary Beckles and Brian Stoddart. Kingston, Jamaica.

Swanton, E. W. 1960. *West Indies Revisited: the MCC Tour of 1959/60*. London.

Thorn, Philip. 1991. *Barbados Cricketers 1865–1990*. Nottingham.

Vundla, Kathleen. 1973. *P. Q. The Story of Philip Vundla of South Africa*. Johannesburg.

Walcott, Clyde. 1958. *Island Cricketers*. London.

Walcott, Derek. 1965. "Air". In *The Gulf: Poems by Derek Walcott*. New York.

Walcott, Derek. 1992. *The Antilles: Fragments of Epic Memory*. The Nobel Lecture. New York.

Webber, Roy. 1953. *The Australians in England*. London.
West Indies Cricket Annual 1980. 1980. Bridgetown.
Wilde, Simon. 1994. *Letting Rip: the Fast-Bowling Threat from Lillie to Waqar*. London.
Wisden Cricketers' Almanack, 1953. London.
Wrigley, Arthur. 1965. *The Book of Test Cricket*. London.
Wynne-Thomas, Peter. 1982. *England on Tour*. London.